Edmund William Forrest

Ned Fortesque

Roughing it Through Life. A Story Founded on Fact

Edmund William Forrest

Ned Fortesque
Roughing it Through Life. A Story Founded on Fact

ISBN/EAN: 9783744744409

Printed in Europe, USA, Canada, Australia, Japan

Cover: Foto ©Thomas Meinert / pixelio.de

More available books at **www.hansebooks.com**

NED FORTESCUE.

NED FORTESCUE:

OR,

ROUGHING IT THROUGH LIFE.

A STORY FOUNDED ON FACT.

BY E. W. FORREST,

LATE HER MAJESTY'S INDIAN ARMY.

Ottawa and Toronto:

HUNTER, ROSE & COMPANY.

1869.

OTTAWA:
PRINTED BY HUNTER, ROSE & CO.

PREFACE.

—

In the following pages I have endeavored to portray a phase of life upon which many romances have been founded, and it has been my object to give the reader, who may be unacquainted with the *Vie Bohemienne* of the army, a true idea of the feelings and circumstances as felt and seen by a soldier in the "ranks," who gradually wins his way from the first step of the ladder to that position from whence most other story-tellers start when they adopt a military hero.

Many chapters in this book relate to what is now matter of history, and the whole are the experience of a life of active soldiering, with the uninteresting and dry details of General Orders left out. The guard-tent and barrack, instead of the mess-table and ante-room, has supplied me with material for many of my scenes. In this I have deviated from the beaten track, and hope the reader may find that in so doing I have not injured the interest of the narrative.

THE AUTHOR.

NED FORTESCUE;

ROUGHING IT THROUGH LIFE.

CHAPTER I.

"Omne beni sine pœnâ
Tempus est ludendi ;
Venit hora absque morâ,
Libros deponendi."

BURST joyfully from the throats of at least a dozen youths of
various ages, from eight to eighteen, who crowded the in and
out sides of the smart stage coach, with its splendid four grey
horses, on the morning before Christmas. Among this happy
group, figured conspicuously my brother and your humble servant, comfortably located in the rumble, which afforded us an
excellent view of the surrounding country as we bowled along
the turnpike road to London. As we turned out of the little
village of Pinner, through an opening in the now leafless trees, we
caught sight of the numerous gables and quaint old chimneys of
the Manor House, where, for the past six months, our preceptor,
the learned Dr. Bogue, had endeavored to inculcate in our minds
the beauties of Johnson, Lindley Murray, vulgar fractions, and
scraps of classic lore. The glimpse was but a short one ; and, as the
scene faded away in the distance, it passed from my memory—
my thoughts being turned to the coming festivities, the panto-
mimes, and the sights that we were usually indulged in during
the vacation, at this season of the year.

On reaching the metropolis, we were met by my father, and

conveyed home; not to the one we had left in the summer, but to one of more moderate pretensions in Chelsea. The reason of this change was not explained to us, nor did I think of enquiring, being engrossed in my own anticipations of coming pleasures during the holidays; the greater portion of which I was to spend with my grandfather and uncle, who were merchants, and had their establishment at the West End of London. At the termination of the holidays it turned out that we were not to return to school. Some financial difficulties having arisen—some speculation in which my father was engaged, by which he was a considerable loser; so much so, that his affairs became somewhat embarrassed—and he came to the determination of quitting England, in hopes of rebuilding his fortune in one of the colonies. After several pros and cons it was decided that the family should proceed to Canada, early in the summer. This being the case, it was not deemed expedient or necessary that we should return to school; and I was permitted, much to my delight, to remain at my grandfather's. A few days prior to the departure of the family for the colonies, an arrangement had been entered into by my relatives for my remaining in England. This suited me exactly. The pleasures of a London life had more attractions for me then than a trip to the New World, and so I remained behind. My uncle was of a cheerful turn of mind, and fond of public amusements and exhibitions generally. When visiting these places I was usually his companion; consequently I soon acquired a taste for such things (so natural in youth). My grandfather was one of the old school, plodding, methodical, and punctual in his business, to which he devoted all his energies, seldom relaxing on the score of pleasure; a man of strict integrity, an exemplary father, and a thorough good man every way. On Sunday mornings he regularly attended Divine Service; then, after dinner, his custom was to stroll out of town to Hornsey, Highgate, Hampstead, Battersea, Kew, or some other of the suburban localities, and in some quiet little hostelry, snugly ensconced in a shady nook or bower, he would enjoy his glass of ale, and smoke his long clay pipe, as was customary among men of his class some thirty years ago. I always attended him on those peregrinations, and thus I acquired a thorough knowledge of the environs of London. For the first two or three years I enjoyed this sort of life exceedingly. At my grandfather's, being of an enquiring disposition, I was continually in the manufactory, asking questions of the *employés* concerning the manufacturing of the different articles they were preparing for shipment to foreign ports—in fact I obtained a considerable insight into the business. But I was advancing towards manhood, and I began to think what my future lot in life must be. I had always had a strong dislike to trade or commercial speculations of any kind. The Church was out of the question, and the study of law I had a strong aversion to ; as for medicine or anatomy, I turned from them with almost loathing. While revolving these matters in my own mind—to decide what I was most fitted for— an actor appeared upon the scene that settled this point, at least for a time. My brother, some eighteen months older than myself, and who had chosen for his profession the service of the Merchant Marine, arrived with his vessel in the London Docks. This was a source of much pleasure to me, as the vessel had to remain in dock all the winter. Of course my brother was anxious to hear and see all that could be seen of London life during his stay, having been at school nearly all the time prior to the family's departure from England, not having enjoyed the same facilities that I had for witnessing the gaieties of that very gay city ; so I became his *chaperon*, and a right jolly time we had of it. Frequently, when his duties compelled him to remain on board by night as well as by day, I would keep him company ; and in the comfortable cabin, with a cigar and some wine, would I listen to his funny yarns about Canada and the Canadians. His description of different ports he had visited highly interested me, and I began to ask myself whether it would not be much

pleasanter to go to those places and see for myself, than to loiter
uselessly about a manufactory from day to day, whence no possible future good could be derived by me.   But how could this be
managed ; to travel requires cash, and although my grandfather
and uncle supplied me with a liberal allowance for pocket
money, I knew well that they would not spare me a sufficient
sum to carry out my wishes.   I mentioned this difficulty to my
brother.   " Why," said he, " the thing is easy enough ; why not go
home to Quebec ?   They will all be happy to see you.   You can
then decide what step you will next take.   I know that the
agreement with our grandfather was, that if you wished at any
time to rejoin the family in Canada, he was to provide you with
a passage out.   Of course you cannot sail until the spring ; and, if
you take my advice, you will acquire as much knowledge as
practicable of the working of a ship, and the various duties
required of its officers and men, while on your passage across
the Western Ocean ; it may stand your friend some day, if
you have a roving turn of mind.   I will teach you how to
pull and steer a boat, during our stay in the docks."   And
he kept his word.   We went out in the ship's jolly boat,
but I very nearly came to grief at the outset.   The boat was
alongside, with a quantity of water in it, and my brother
requested me to bail it out.   I set to work with a good will, and
while so doing, I struck my hand against a wooden plug, driven
into a hole in the bottom of the boat, to drain her when on deck.
Now, as I always had an aversion to more hard work than was
actually necessary, a bright thought struck me ; why not pull
out the plug and let the water run out, as I had seen it done
on board.   In a moment out it came, but instead of running out,
to my surprise and consternation, the water rushed in and the
boat filled and sank.   Fortunately, I had learned to swim while
at school, or I should have paid pretty dear for my stupidity.
Striking out for the first boat, I got in, and from thence on board,
where I took off my clothes and had them dried—using a suit of

my brother's, for the time being. However, nothing daunted, into the boat we got, and pulled about for several days at different times, until I could manage the oars and use the yoke lines. We then went on to the Thames, and had many a good row to Battersea or Richmond.

Early in the spring I broached the subject of departure to my relatives; they at first objected, but seeing my mind was made up, they consented, and procured me a passage on the fine clipper barque "James Holmes," and bidding farewell to relations and friends, also paying a last visit to my favorite haunts— for it might be many years before I again returned to that part of the world—I went on board, on a chilly morning in April. About 11 a.m., the tide served, and as the flood-gates of the dock opened, out we floated into the Thames—down the pool, winding our way in and out between the various craft with which that famous river is at all times studded, and dear old London was soon lost in the distance. The day being raw and blustering, I did not remain long on deck, but took refuge in my snug little state-room, and busied myself in arranging my books, writing materials, etc., until the steward came and announced dinner. I had a good appetite and enjoyed it very much, but it was the last meal I could eat for many days. The weather was squally, with a fair wind, and we made good running all that night. The next morning I began to experience that great drawback to ocean travelling, "sea sickness." I suffered very severely for several days, and we were far from land before I could leave my berth and go on deck. Being the only passenger, I received all the attention from the officers and crew that I required, and I had not been more than a month on board before I knew the name of every rope and sail, and the purposes for which they were intended. I had also been several times up aloft in fine weather. I had acted on my brother's suggestion, and brought on board several pounds of tobacco, and by judiciously distributing it, I acquired a great deal of useful informa-

tion on nautical matters. From the chief officer, I learned to
"box the compass," heave the lead, and keep the daily log of the
ship's progress. I was also permitted to take the wheel and
steer the ship—of course, under the supervision of the helmsman,
or one of the officers. I do not remember much of the voyage
until we arrived at the banks of Newfoundland, where we had
to keep the ship's bell constantly going, as a warning to the fleet
of small vessels engaged in fishing in that region. We heard the
bells of several ships, but so dark was the atmosphere, that
they were generally invisible. It was with great satisfaction
that, one fine evening, I received from the captain the cheering
intelligence that by daylight, the following morning, we should
reach Grosse Isle, distant only thirty miles from Quebec. This
turned out to be the case, and at an early hour, we were
boarded by the medical officer, whose duty it was to inspect the
passengers and crew, to ascertain if there was any sickness or
epidemic amongst them. Having a clean Bill of Health we were
allowed to proceed up the river.

On arriving at Quebec I landed at the Cul de Sac. I directed
my steps towards my father's office, the whereabouts of which I
had been made acquainted with previous to quitting England. On
crossing the end of Mountain street I observed my father coming
towards me. He recognized me at once, and calling a *calèche*, we
drove home to a neat little cottage in St. John's suburb. My unexpected arrival created quite a sensation in the family circle for
some days. My eldest sister, a beautiful and interesting girl,
some three years younger than myself, hailed my appearance
with delight, and many a time and oft did we ramble together
through the beautiful and romantic spots for which Quebec is so
celebrated. During that summer, except when on a visit to
Montreal, I spent most of my time in shooting and fishing, and frequently supplied our table with fresh fish from River St. Charles
or Lake Beauport, which were my favorite haunts for capturing
the finny tribe. But the appearance of hoary winter put an end

that sort of thing. The snow fell thick and fast, and all nature was shrouded with a white mantle—all verdure disappearing from view for several months. I had never liked the winter season, even in England, and therefore felt that the severity of the climate was a death-blow to all pleasure—for Quebec, at that season of the year, is completely ice-bound. Of course, to those born in the country, the ice and snow afford considerable amusement. Sleighing and toboganing parties are much enjoyed by the Canadians generally. I was fond of skating, and there was a great field for that healthy exercise, although not then entered into so generally, or with such spirit as at the present day. Few of the **fair** sex ever donned the skate—the weather on the St. Lawrence being so intensely cold—and covered rinks not having yet come into fashion. Since that day I have seen beautifully illuminated rinks, crowded with from fifteen hundred to two thousand persons, of all ages—emperors, mailed knights, queens, sultanas, Turks, fairies, demons, and every conceivable character, in gorgeous **and** grotesque apparel, gliding smoothly and gracefully about on the polished ice, in a seemingly confused mass, to the soul-inspiring strains of some two or three regimental bands,—the fair ladies waltzing, and the gentlemen tracing strange figures and devices. These carnivals certainly remind us of what we have read concerning "Fairy Land."

My education, for the past four years, had been somewhat neglected, so I made a virtue of necessity, and during the long winter evenings resumed my studies under the direction of my father, who was an excellent scholar, and whose penmanship was the best I have ever seen, before or since. At length this, to me, gloomy season passed; smiling Spring unfolded her generous presence of sunshine and tears; the snow disappeared, the floating ice was carried from the rivers by their rapid currents, to the far away north, and the harbour was soon alive with shipping. I had obtained an appointment in my father's office, but close confinement to a desk was ill-suited to a roving disposition like mine, and I longed for a change of scene.

Just about this time, troubles began to arise between the government and a certain portion of the population. Disaffection and disloyalty appeared, and soon openly avowed rebellion was seen throughout the land. Fresh troops were ordered out from England, the militia called out, and a draft made upon all males between the ages of sixteen and thirty-five, to quell the rising, and support the government and the Queen's authority. Not wishing to embroil myself in a political contest for a country whose climate I so much disliked, I determined to leave it on the first favorable opportunity that presented itself.

This I had not long to wait for. The nature of my occupation threw me a great deal among the captains of sea-going vessels. One day I mentioned casually, in course of conversation, with the captain of the brig "Isidore," bound for Scotland, and from thence to the West Indies, my desire to leave Quebec. He said, that he would be happy to forward my views, and that if I would accept the post of supercargo on his vessel, the appointment was at my service. Matters were soon arranged, and after an affectionate leave-taking of my family, I, on the 27th of August, reported myself for duty on board the "Isidore," outward bound, for the port of Troon, in Ayrshire, Scotland.

The hour of seven tolled upon the evening breeze from the bells of the different churches in the upper and lower towns, while the silver moon arose majestically, in all its splendor, from behind the forest-crowned heights of Pointe Lévis, shedding its refulgent light upon tower and steeple, showing forth with vivid brilliancy the tin roofs and cupolas, with which the old city abounded. I stood leaning over the taffrail of the vessel, watching the scene with deep interest, for a few minutes, until we were borne beyond its influence by the current, and the light breeze that filled our swelling sails and impelled us onward towards the gulf. The weather was delightful. We set our

studding sails when opposite Grosse Isle, and did not take
them in until we had crossed the broad Atlantic—which we
effected in the then remarkably short run of twenty days—sight-
ing the Skerry Rocks, off the Irish coast, on the evening of the
sixteenth of September. Ts the night closed in, the south-west
breeze died away to a dead calm. Dark, heavy, murky clouds
surged up from the horizon, passing fitfully across the young
moon, which soon disappeared, leaving all in pitchy darkness. A
thick drizzling rain continued to fall for some hours, when a
light breeze sprang up from the land, and continued to increase.
The sea rose with it. Our studding sails were taken in, the
royals stowed, the top-gallant sails clewed up, and the flying
jib lowered. We endeavored to beat up to windward, but the
wind increased with such violence that we found it necessary to
furl the top-gallant sails, and double reef the fore and main top
sail. The storm still increasing—it blowing a regular north-
easter—the storm trysail was set, and every halyard, clewline,
and preventive brace set and properly secured, but to no purpose. The sea, lashed into fury by the violence of the storm,
was now making clean breaches over us. The first sea of
any note, that we shipped came over our starboard bow, carrying away the galley; next our flying jib-boom snapped short
off at the cap. A little before daylight our maintopmast went by
the board, wrenching off the standing rigging. This caused the
vessel to keel over considerably, but a few blows from the boatswain's axe cut it clear away, and we righted, although for a short
time only. The next heavy sea struck our starboard quarter, un-
shipping the rudder; the ship became unmanageable; and there
was nothing left but to take to the long boat, as the brig was fast
settling down in the trough of the sea. We had shipped so
much water that it was impossible to get below to save our
effects. Fortunately for me, I had, the morning before, taken out
of my chest my best suit of blue, to brush and give it an
airing; after so doing I wrapped it up in a piece of old sail-

2

cloth, and stowed it away in the stern of the long boat, until I could have an opportunity of taking it below; and so accidentally saved it. After several ineffectual attempts we succeeded in launching the boat on our larboard quarter; it was well for us that we had thus succeeded, for we had hardly pulled out more than fifty yards when the brig pitched heavily forward, and went down head foremost. We were now in an open boat, in a heavy sea—no very pleasant position, truly—but the storm shortly after had exhausted its fury, and the sea went down, much to our relief. I very much doubt, however, if any of us could have reached the shore alive but for the timely arrival of a coasting lugger, that bore down upon us. By the exertions of their crew we got on board, when she immediately shaped her course for Dublin.

CHAPTER II.

It was with no small degree of satisfaction that I beheld—as we rounded Ireland's Eye—the Bay of Dublin, with the snug little harbor of Kingstown, the romantic view of old Dunleary, and the Hill of Howth, rising, as it were, out of the ocean; all looking so tranquil and picturesque on that fine clear autumn morning. The wind and tide being against us, we had to kedge our way up stream after the following fashion : the jolly boat, with a small kedge anchor in it, was sent some fifty yards in advance, and the anchor dropped; the hawser to which it was attached was then hauled upon by those on board, which brought the vessel up to the boat, the kedge was then weighed. Proceeding in this way, we at length reached the river Liffey, that runs through the city of Dublin, like the Thames through London. On the sands, by the Pigeon House, some troops were going through their rifle evolutions, which had a very pretty effect from the water. I noticed some remarkably fine quays, on which were situated the Custom House, Trinity House, the Four Courts, and other public edifices. The lower quays, on the south side, were used principally for colliers, while those on the north were crowded with merchantmen from all parts of the world. I was much pleased with my visit to Dublin ; the people seemed hospitable, good humoured, and pleasant, and during my stay I had an opportunity of seeing a great deal of the wit and humor which is the peculiar characteristic of the people. My stay at the Irish Capital on this occasion was of short duration, for Captain Millett succeeded within a fortnight in obtaining charge of a brig bound to the Port of Troon, in Ayrshire, some nine miles distant from Irvin, his native place. He requested that I should accompany him, stating that on his arrival at the latter place he could obtain the command of a fine vessel in the West India trade, in which he would give me employment in the tropics during the coming winter. To this I acceded, and sailed with him for Scotland. The weather being rough and unfavorable, it was several days before we made the port of Troon, a small coal depot in Ayrshire. It was scarcely daylight when we came to anchor, and everything was made snug before 7 o'clock, the rules of the port not permitting any fires on board the vessels in harbor. We had to go on shore for our meals; the captain took the crew with him to get their breakfast, leaving the chief officer and myself on board until they should return, which they did in about an hour. The mate and I then started in the direction of the house pointed to us by the captain; the knocking about at sea had worked our appetites to a keen pitch, and visions of beef-steaks, eggs, coffee, hot rolls, and buttered toast, rose to our hungry fancies, but there also we were doomed to disappointment, for a time at least. On entering a large room—clean, and the floor covered with white sand, all comfortable enough—we were followed by a short stout "red-headed" little lady, who announced herself as the landlady of the establishment. " Has Captain Millett, of the 'Rob Roy,' ordered breakfast for us," enquired I, bowing politely to the dame. "If so, I should like to see it." " Quite right," replied she, "and there it is, all ready for you," pointing, as she spoke, to a side table, where stood a large bowl of oatmeal porridge, into which were thrust two spoons ; and on each side of the said bowl was a small basin of milk, and a plate of "oat cake" known to the initiated as " snap and rattle " from its brittleness. The mate and I eyed the composition for a few seconds, then turning to the red-haired mistress of the house enquired whether she took us for a couple of sucking pigs—that were to be fattened on milk and meal, and fed out of one trough. The look of bewilderment that spread over her features assured us that she considered the repast prepared for us was all that any one could require.

Not fancying an outburst from woman's natural weapon, we 'bout ship and started on a fresh tack further into the town. After some difficulty we succeeded in obtaining an excellent breakfast of "Finnan haddies," fresh eggs and soft bread, good butter and some capital coffee—nor did we fail to try, on our host's recommendation, some of his real old "Glenlivat." Whether Captain Millett had over-rated his interest, or was in ill luck, I know not, but he did not succeed in getting the vessel he anticipated, or any other, so after a sojourn of two weeks in the "land o' cakes," I shipped on board a collier brig, the "Dundonald," bound for Dublin. A few hours after leaving port, the wind, which was right aft, increased to a hurricane, lashing the waves into fury, and driving us through the water at a terrific rate. While passing the Ailsa Craig, an immense rock that rises out of the sea, we recognized the schooner "James," of Workington, with her distress signal flying, and laboring heavily in the trough of the sea. We were at no great distance from the shore, and could distinctly see the people on the beach endeavoring to launch boats for her assistance; but no boat could live in such a sea—and we could render no aid, as we, ourselves, were in imminent danger of going under. The little schooner struggled bravely, but all to no avail, and in twenty minutes from the time we came in sight she foundered, and all on board perished. The last soul that was seen was the mate, high up in the main rigging, waving his hat for succour. Shortly after, the gale moderated, and in a few hours we made Dublin without the loss of a spar. I remained at the Irish Metropolis until my finances had sunk to a very low ebb. All that could be heard or seen gratis, I did not fail to avail myself of, and during my stay picked up many of the Irish peculiarities. Being unable to obtain a berth on board any vessel going to a foreign port, I determined to return to London. To accomplish this end, I shipped on board of a brig bound for Liverpool, and worked my passage to that port; signing articles for one shilling. Our trip was short and pleasant;

and thus, after an absence of nearly two years, I again found myself in England, though many miles from friends or relations, and a perfect stranger in Liverpool.

"Well, what are you going to do, youngster," was the enquiry of the captain, as I entered the cabin to receive the amount of my nominal wages. "I am going to London," was my reply. "Do you go by water, or take the stage?" "Neither; I intend to walk. This," said I, pointing to the shilling that still lay on the table, "is all I possess; so, as I cannot remain in Liverpool, or pay coach hire, I must, of course, tramp it up to London, for I have no intention of earning my bread through life upon the waters." He looked up with surprise, and said, "You have a tough journey before you, for I am told it is something over two hundred miles; the weather is cold, and the clouds look like snow. I am sorry it is not in my power to assist you to any great extent, but here is half a crown, and tell the steward to give you a good piece of boiled pork and some biscuits; that will help you along for a day or two." This was a real act of kindness, and I felt grateful to the rough sailor for his thoughtfulness.

I remained only a couple of hours in Liverpool. I sold a few small trinkets, which added a little to my very small capital; then set out at a brisk walk along the London road, and soon left that great shipping port far behind. I continued walking until about nine p.m., when observing a bright light a little distance from the road, near the entrance to a small hamlet, I went over and found it to be a kiln, in which bricks were burning, with only a lad near, whose duty it was to attend to the fire during the night. I sat down and warmed myself, then made a hearty supper of pork and biscuit, some of which I gave to the boy, who, in return told me there was plenty of clean dry straw in the shed, close by, where I might sleep if I chose. I did choose, being tired with my long walk, for I had accomplished twenty miles since leaving Liverpool, and was very glad of the bed, rough though it was, and soon fell fast asleep. The sun was shining brightly when I awoke. After making a **hasty toilet** I breakfasted, then started with a light heart, in hopes **of shortening** my journey by twenty-five miles before nightfall. I found the **people,** small farmers, and others, very hospitable, frequently when I stopped to rest, or ask for a drink of water, beer, cider, or milk, with bread and cheese, would be offered **me. My** dress and general appearance proved me to be no beggar, and on more than one occasion I was asked to take supper, and remain all night. The parties appeared to be well satisfied, and much interested with the account of my shipwreck, and the numerous anecdotes I related to them, which **I** had picked up during **my stay** in Scotland and Ireland. One family wished me to remain several days with them, but my object was to get to London before my brother's ship left for Canada, so I went on my way, sometimes getting a lift in a waggon, or market cart. I had arrived within a few miles of Coventry when a snow storm overtook me ; the day was bitterly cold, and the snow froze as it came down. I had only a pair of very thin-soled, long-quartered shoes on, and felt the cold exceedingly, but I trudged on until I came to a tavern in the outskirts of the city. Benumbed with cold and quite worn out, I entered, and ordered supper, and a bed About midnight I awoke with violent pains in my feet and legs ; by the morning they were so much swollen that I could hardly manage to hobble downstairs. Being severely frost-bitten, walking was quite out of the question, the landlady very kindly bandaged them for me, which gave considerable relief ; but what a position was I then placed in, without friends or acquaintances, unable to walk, and with only eightpence then in my pocket—barely sufficient for one day's subsistence. While cogitating on my rather forlorn condition, and endeavoring to shape out some course that would **steer** me through the present **difficulty, a** gentleman entered the parlor, covered with snow, for it **had** fallen fast since the former afternoon, and was much deeper than had **been** known for many years ; in **fact, it** was one

of the most severe winters ever known by that ancient individual, the oldest inhabitant. "Fearful weather," sir, said he,
addressing me, "did you ever see anything to beat it since you
were born." "Indeed, I have seen the snow laying six feet deep in
the principal streets, and frozen solid at that." "And where might
that be," said he, with surprise pictured on his now glowing
countenance, for he was standing before the fire, imbibing a stiff
bumper of steaming hot rum and water. "It was at Quebec, in
Lower Canada," was my reply. "At Quebec," said he, hastily
putting down his glass, "have you really been there ; tell me, did
you know a gentleman of that city named S——, he married my
only sister a few years ago, and for several months I have heard
nothing of them." Now it fortunately so happened that, although
not personally acquainted with the parties, I knew sufficiently of
them to give him all the information he required concerning
their whereabouts. He was delighted, and insisted on my joining
him in a bumper of his favourite beverage. Nothing loath, I
consented, and thinking this an opportunity not to be lost, I
candidly told him of my unfortunate position. "This is sad,
indeed," he replied, "I am sorry that business compels me to visit
a neighbouring town for several days, or I could have entertained
you at my bachelor establishment ; but," added he, after thinking
for a moment, "the best thing I can do for you under the circumstance is to drive you at once to the City Infirmary ; being an
alderman I can procure you immediate admittance, there you will
meet with all the assistance, medical and otherwise, that your case
demands, and as soon as you are convalescent call on me, and I
will see what can be done towards forwarding you to London."
This kind offer I cheerfully and thankfully accepted ; he immediately called the landlord, settled his bill, and mine likewise,
then, with the assistance of the ostler, I was seated in the gig, and
in less than an hour comfortably domiciled in the excellent institution mentioned by the worthy alderman, where I remained
until I was sufficiently recovered to be able to walk. One

morning, while looking over the *London Times*, I noticed that my brother's vessel was still lying in the London Dock. Without delay, I wrote and informed him of my situation. In a few days I received a letter from him, containing a bank note of sufficient amount, which enabled me to procure what few necessaries I required, and book my passage in the London stage. I called at the house of my friend, the alderman, but did not succeed in seeing him, he being engaged in his office in town. Having nothing further to do in that good city, the next morning I entered the coach, and soon was bowling along the turnpike road as fast as the four horses of Her Majesty's royal mail could carry us.

We entered London early on the night that the fine old structure on Corn Hill (the Royal Exchange) was destroyed by fire. I passed the spot just as the great tower fell in, the musical clock of which was at the time playing the old Scotch air, " There is no luck about the house, there is no luck at all." This I argued was a bad omen for my future success in the great city. As I wended my way westward along Cheapside, and down Ludgate Hill, through Fleet street, and up the Strand, I met thousands of people flocking towards the scene of the conflagration. I had been but a few days in London when my feet became so painful that I was compelled to enter St. George Hospital, near Hyde Park. I was nearly six weeks an inmate of that excellent institution before I was sufficiently recovered to admit of my applying for any employment. However, a few days after I became convalescent, I was fortunate enough to obtain a situation in the firm of Messrs. Fraser, Dunn, and Brooks, Italian warehousemen, who had an establishment near Hanover Square. This suited me at the time exactly ; the salary was not a very large one, certainly, but it was sufficient for my present wants, for I possessed the valuable tact of knowing how to live frugally, but well, and dress fashionably, if not elaborately, on a very limited income. There is no place in the world where

things can be obtained of first-rate quality for so trifling an
outlay, if you but have the knowledge where to procure them, as
in this great city. This knowledge I possessed, by what means
obtained it is not necessary here to say. The hours of business
suited me very well, being from 8 a.m. to 5 p.m.; thus I had the
whole of the evening, and the greater part of the night to spend
which way best suited my tastes and inclinations. I seldom
went to bed before 12 o'clock. The old adage that one hour's
sleep before midnight was worth three after it, I could never
believe in. Being now well fed and dressed, with all the care and
the greatest attention paid to "cut and fit," I began to look
around to see how I could obtain the greatest possible amount of
pleasure compatible with my small means. In this I was particularly fortunate. Two of my relations, on my father's side, held
the honorable position of yeomen of the Royal Guard, but were
of that select number who are only on duty when Her Majesty appears in State. On these occasions they always attended her.
To them I was indebted for admission to the ante-room leading
to the presence chamber in St. James' Palace, whenever there was
a levee or drawing room, from whence I could behold the Peers of
the realm in their robes, stars and garters, and marshals, generals,
admirals and ministers, from every court in Christendom, in
gorgeous uniforms, bearing on their breasts crosses, medals, orders
and ribbons, (honorable *souvenirs* of services performed in camp or
cabinet,) peeresses, noble dames, England's aristocratic daughters,
as they swept by in the pride of their resplendent beauty, blazing
with diamonds, and from beneath whose waving plumes the bright
gems of their coronets gleamed and flashed as they passed into the
presence of their sovereign. A sight the most brilliant that
can be conceived. My relations were likewise connected with
the Theatres Royal, Drury Lane and Adelphi, and had some
interest in the management of Vauxhall Gardens. To all these
places of amusement they presented me with free admissions,
whenever I requested them to do so, which was very frequently.

These orders entitled me to admission behind the scenes; I had thus an opportunity of becoming acquainted with many of the stage celebrities of the day—likewise those of lesser note. I found them, as a body, remarkably pleasant people, and I took a great fancy to acting and theatricals generally. About this time the Louther Rooms, on King William Street, were opened for select quadrille parties, which were just then all the rage. From one of the lady patronesses with whom I was acquainted—having met her brother in Quebec—I received a season ticket as a present. Being passionately fond of dancing, I never missed a night during the season. On one of these occasions a very pretty young lady appeared in white satin boots, with gold fringe round the tops—pretty, 'tis true, but this was an innovation—slippers only being recognized at the time in a ball room. While drinking with some young fellows in the *salle à manger*, I talked loudly in praise of the young lady and her boots, and got showed up for my foolishness in a newspaper called the *Town,* which noticed my infatuation in the following manner :—" We advise the young Canadian, residing not one hundred miles from Soho Square, not to talk soemphatically about Miss Robinson's white satin boots." This caused me in future to keep my mouth shut; so what with sights at the Palace, fire-work displays, the theatre, and dancing, I was having a good time of it. But I was not satisfied with this, my aim was to get on intimate terms with some good families, by which I could obtain the privilege of entering into the social circles of some of the country gentry, who come up to London for the season only, and have no time to enquire particularly into one's standing in society. Chance gained for me what I could not have otherwise obtained. After leaving St. George's Hospital, I took up my quarters at a quiet little coffee house, close to Soho Square—not far from the East India Company's recruiting depot, and Howard's Hotel, the head waiter of which was a brother of my landlady's, and a very good fellow to boot—after I entered Fraser & Co.'s employ, where I

boarded but did not sleep. I still retained my little attic room
for more reasons than the one of finance. Being constantly at the
different public places of amusement I became acquainted with
several young fellows of good standing, and frequently made
appointments with them to spend the evenings together who if
they had known of my occupation, or whereabouts, would never
have done so. I arranged with my friend Stephens, the "major-
domo" of Howard's, who, for a small consideration, consented
to receive messages and notes, and answer all inquiries, which
led visitors to imagine that I occupied rooms in the establishment.
Of course when any one called to see me, I had just gone out,
but might be expected in about an hour. Thus I had the name
of a first-class hotel without the expense attending it, and my
assumed position remained unquestioned. So much for management. One afternoon, while returning from the city, where I had
been sent on some business for the firm, and while in the act of
crossing Cockspur Street, a gentleman advancing from the
opposite side was knocked down by the horse of a hansom
cab driven furiously along, and would have been run over, and
in all probability much injured or killed, had I not sprung
forward and seized the head of the animal, and forced him with
a sudden jerk back upon his haunches. The person scrambled as
best he could from beneath the horses' feet. I then relinquished
my hold, and cabby, fearful of being called to account for his
furious driving, made himself scarce with all possible speed. I
then assisted the gentleman to rise, and offered him my arm,
which he gladly accepted. He was not much hurt, but a great
deal shaken by the fall. I accompanied him to his rooms close
by, in Spring Gardens, saw him safely up stairs, handed him
over to his valet or *factotum*, then turned to depart; but this he
would not hear of, and politely requested me to remain, that he
might have the opportunity of thanking me, and learning to
whom he was indebted for such an essential service. He directed
his man to shew me into the sitting room, then excused himself

for a few minutes while he repaired the damages to his toilet. I bowed an assent, and throwing myself carelessly into an easy chair, awaited his reappearance.

CHAPTER III.

As soon as the valet closed the door, I commenced a survey of
the region into which I had been thus unexpectedly thrown. It
was a handsomely furnished room, and the large bow window at
the end commanded a fine view of St. James' Park; to the right
could be seen the Duke of York's column, the Court of St. James,
and the marble arch in front of Buckingham Palace; to the left
Bird Cage Walk, and the Horse Guards, while stretching away
to the front was the enclosure with its beautiful shrubberies and
majestic trees, over the tops of which might be seen the square
towers of the Ancient Abbey of Westminster, and here and
there you could catch a glance of the ornamental waters, studded
with little islands, on which hundreds of foreign and domestic
water-fowl made their nests, and swam among the aquatic plants,
to the delight of the gay loungers, and troops of merry, laughing
children, who frequented that charming spot. A cheerful fire
blazed in the burnished grate, which imparted a feeling of
comfort to the apartment, in the corners of which were to be
seen cricket bats, balls, stumps, skates, fishing rods, and rifles,
with fencing foils and boxing-gloves. The side-table was strewn
with pets of the ballet, new music, pipes, meershaum and cutty,
cards and notes in profusion, and some unpaid tradesmen's bills; all
jumbled together in one confused mass. On the centre table were
newspapers, pamphlets, magazines, Coke upon Lyttleton, Parliamentary Blue Books, and other reading matter. I had just concluded my inspection when the owner of this miscellaneous
collection entered, in dressing gown and slippers. He was a good
looking young fellow, apparently about three and twenty, rather
above the middle height, with a fair complexion, dark blue eyes,
and a profusion of dark brown curly hair and whiskers. The

moustache, imperial or goatee, he did not affect, as in those days such appendages were only sported by men of the highest *ton*, the army and the numerous seedy-looking foreigners, who frequented the *Sablonnière*, and similar establishments in Leicester square and its vicinity. "By George," said he, laughing, as he dropped into an easy chair, "I fancy I was more frightened than hurt; but certainly, had it not been for your timely assistance, I should have been a fit subject for Highgate Cemetery, or the operator's knife. Do me the favor to lunch with me," he added, as a servant entered with a well-filled tray of Stilton cheese, ham sandwiches and cold chicken. "Try some sherry, or will you allow me to recommend some capital old ale to your notice—it always does me an immense amount of good when I feel a little shaky—it was some that my governor sent up; it was brewed when I was born, and not tapped until I came of age." I did try it, and certainly it was the best that had ever gone down my throat. Over our ale he informed me that he was the son of Sir Lewis Archer, of Stanley Hall, Sussex—a fine specimen of the real old English gentleman, who hated London cordially, but who nevertheless came up to town for a couple of months every year, that Lady Archer and her two daughters might enjoy the height of the season. "You see," said he, "that being an only son, Sir Lewis will not hear of my engaging in any profession, but being heir to Stanley Park, and its broad acres, he wishes me to enter Parliament, and sent me up here, where I have been for the last eighteen months cramming myself with legal and Parliamentary lore, for I am to stand for the county at the spring elections; a bore, is it not." "But you appear to relieve yourself from this drudgery, occasionally," replied I, pointing to the coloured engraving of the Pets, and other trifles before alluded to. He laughed a gay laugh, and with a courteous inclination of the head, said, "May I ask whom I have the honor of thanking for that good service." Pushing my chair a little round, I took up a pen, and wrote on a slip of paper, "E. W. Fortescue, Howard's

Hotel, Soho Square." "There," said I, "that address will always find me while in London; as for who I am, why, I am nobody. My family settled in Quebec, Lower Canada, some years ago. When I was about eighteen I conceived a desire to come and see the modern Babylon. My governor made no objections, and you behold me here ; I have done nearly all your public institutions, theatres, etc. ; but you English are such an exclusive set, that I cannot get an introduction into society. The only relations of my family in this country do not reside here ; besides, an old feud would prevent me from seeking their assistance for that purpose. We manage these things differently abroad." " My dear fellow, said he, "allow me to be your friend in this matter. I belong to an old English family, and I am proud to say that we still possess that unfashionable, though truly English feeling, family affection, and I am certain that Sir Lewis and Lady Archer, and my sister, would never forgive me if I did not allow them an opportunity of thanking you personally for the obligation rendered to myself." I had no intention of refusing his polite offer, so bowed an acknowledgment. " Her Ladyship gives one of her evenings to-morrow night. I will pick you up at Howard's at eight o'clock, and drive you to Portland Square, although they do not receive before nine. I wish to get the introduction and that sort of thing over before the crush comes," said he, as we parted. " Do tell me, Mr. Fortescue," said Lucy Archer, a pretty little brunette of seventeen, as we sat conversing together on a low ottoman, in the elegant drawing room of the mansion in Portland Square, some half-hour after my introduction to the family, "Is it true that the people in your country paint themselves before going into battle, like the ancient Britons we read about in our early history. When cousin John went out to join his regiment at Toronto, he sent us word that the ' red men,' as he called you, dressed themselves up in paint and feathers, and brandished their tomahawks to frighten our soldiers ; but I think he was only amusing himself at our expense ; he was such a dreadful old fellow." I endeavored to set her right by explaining the character of the Indian tribes, and to assure her that the Canadians, as a people, were as civilized and polished as their more favored neighbours in Europe. For in those days Canada and the Canadians were little understood by the generality of the people in England. "But," said I, as the band struck up, "the quadrilles are forming, permit me the pleasure of dancing the first set with you." She smiled an assent, and I led her to the ball room. Later in the evening as I sauntered through the card rooms, I stopped to look on at a table where Sir Lewis and Major Bradley, of the artillery, assisted by two elaborately turbaned dowagers, were engaged at whist. " You are a Canadian, I understand, sir," said the major to me, during the deal. "How are affairs going on in Canada ? Any probability of a general rising throughout the Province, and are more troops likely to be called for ?" " Not at all," replied I, " Her Majesty has not more loyal subjects than the Canadians in any part of the world. Some disaffection has shown itself in both sections, and collisions have taken place between the insurgents and the troops ; but the whole affair is now subsiding, and, in my opinion, would have died out long before this, but for the American element, which is ever ready to inflame the minds of the lower orders against the government, with a view to ultimate annexation ; but they will never succeed in that." Before leaving, I received a *carte blanche* to visit them, when I felt so disposed, and Sir Lewis insisted that I should spend a few weeks at his seat in Essex during the shooting season. I was likewise introduced, during the evening, to several other wealthy families, on whom I promised to call, dine, and so forth. This sort of thing lasted for about six weeks, and certainly I never experienced a more pleasant time. One evening, at a concert, I met my old schoolfellow, Charles Melton. We were equally pleased to meet again, not having seen each other for three or four years. After the concert I invited him to sup with me at the quiet coffee house.

4

Having no object in concealing from him my real position, I related to him what had happened to me since we both parted, and, in return, he informed me that his father had died, and left the business to his management; but having no taste for such matters his affairs became somewhat involved, and that he thought of selling off and engaging in some pursuit more congenial to his taste and habits. At an opposite table were seated a party of non-commissioned officers belonging to the East India Company's recruiting depot, Soho Square. One of whom, it appeared, was pointing out to a couple of country-looking lads the advantages that were to be gained by entering the military service of the said company; he concluded by saying, "a relative of mine enlisted and went out to India, remained there twenty-one years, then returned home with about a thousand pounds in cash, and a pension of eighty pounds per annum." At this juncture my friend Charley gave a prolonged whistle, then ejaculated something which sounded very much like "gammon." "Gentlemen," said another of the party, a grey-headed old veteran, who had noticed Melton's expression, "I can assure you that the statement is substantially correct. I do not know the party alluded to, but this I do know, that there is no service in the world which holds out such inducements for young men who have received a good education to enlist in its ranks. The advantages are, their relief from regimental duty, good staff appointments, such as riding masters of cavalry and artillery, barrack masters, conductors of ordnance, commissariat and cattle departments, head clerks of the Adjutant-General and Quarter-Master General's office—all of which are taken from the different regiments, and promoted to the rank of warrant officer; that is, they receive a warrant, or sort of commission, signed by the Governor in Council, and have all the privileges and allowances extended to a commissioned officer. The pay is, in many cases, superior to that of the regimental subaltern, and having none of those expenses, such as mess funds, subscription to band, and other deductions from their pay of a similar character; and living being remarkably reasonable, the careful warrant officer can save one-half of his pay and allowances, and on the completion of his service retire on an allowance of eighty pounds per annum. Besides these, there are a great many advantages for the deserving soldier, not to be met with in other services." The quiet and gentlemanly manner in which this statement was made, led me to believe there was some truth in it. It being now midnight my friend left, promising to meet me again in a few evenings for a night's amusement. The autumn now closing in, the Archers, and most of the families with whom I was acquainted had already left town, and the others were about to do so. I again began to feel what a very slight hold I had on the position of a gentleman. The pace at which, for the last few months, I had been going, totally unfitted me for the plodding humdrum routine of business life. One Saturday afternoon, on going to the counting-house I was informed that in consequence of the firm being about to dissolve partnership, my services in the establishment would be no longer required. This was as unexpected as inconvenient to me, for I much doubted if I could procure an appointment that would suit me as well as the one I was now leaving—and so it turned out—for a whole fortnight I sought with great diligence for some suitable employment, but without success. My funds were now getting low, and I knew that I could no longer keep up the appearance that I had hitherto done, and I resolved to do that which had more than once flashed across my mind since I had listened to the conversation of the recruiting party of the East India Company. But previous to carrying out this idea I determined to mix once more among the gay and glittering throng. I paid farewell visits to those of my acquaintances who still remained in town, and then drove down to Essex, where I was most hospitably received by the Archers at Stanley Hall. I found numerous guests, many of whom I had met in London. So what with shooting in the morning, riding parties in the afternoon and assemblages at night, my time was fully occupied, and in a manner which could not fail to give me the utmost satisfaction and delight. This sort of thing could not last long, so I made a virtue of necessity by informing my friends that I had received an appointment abroad, and must leave England in a few days. All expressed their regret at my short visit, but wished me every success in my voyage to the East. On reaching my lodgings in London, I sold off my wardrobe, with the exception of the suit I then wore, then sought out my friend Melton, and without mentioning my plans or intentions to him engaged him in a round of visits to our old haunts for a couple of nights; then saying it might be some time before we met again, I left him and seeking the sergeant-major of the recruiting depot, I enlisted in the Company's service, hoping by my general knowledge of the world, and the education I had received, to be able to carve out for myself a competency to fall back upon in my old age, should I survive the difficulties and dangers attending a military life for so long a period in that unhealthy climate. A few days after, behold me, with some score of others, embarking on board one of those small steamers that ply between London Bridge and Gravesend ; for we were bound to that port. With the early dawn set in a cold drizzling rain, rendering the street anything but pleasant to walk on. As the day grew older the sky became overcast with a dull leaden color, the rain came down in torrents, and the waters of the Thames looked black and swollen. There were few persons on the wharf to witness our departure. With the exception of a half-dozen watermen huddled for shelter under the protruding eaves of the old-fashioned warehouses that overhung the river, from the pointed gables of which the rain came down, drop, drop, drop, with a chilly monotonous sound, and those whose duty it was to attend to the unmooring of the vessel—not a soul was there to say a farewell word to those leaving that great city, perhaps for ever. A deck passage was all that was allowed by the authorities on this occasion, which, considering the heavy rainfall, was not the most comfortable quarter in the world. There is nothing like travel, it enables us to suit ourselves more contentendly with such situations as we may be placed in ; and I availed myself of the knowledge I had acquired by it to improve my personal comfort. Mentioning my idea to a tall, good-looking young man—whose well-worn garments of faded black were worn with the air of one that had seen better days, and from whose general appearance I felt inclined to know something more of—we sought out the purser, and by paying the difference between deck and cabin, soon found ourselves comfortably located in a snug little cabin, through the agency of a silver key. The steward produced two tumblers of that beverage known as hot gin toddy, and supplied us with a couple of dried cabbage-leaves, which the unsuspecting cockneys are deluded into believing to be nothing else but *real Cubas*. In this manner we sipped and whiled away the time, until we were informed that we were opposite Tilbury Fort, and that it was time to go on shore. Very little delay was made at Gravesend, and although the rain continued to fall, we started on our very disagreeable journey, hoping to reach our destination before night-fall. Wet through, spattered with mud from head to foot, and tired with our long tramp—for it was late in the evening before we entered the little town of Brompton, on the banks of the river Medway, in which place was located the depot of the Hon. East India Company—our party were billotted at the different public houses ; myself and three others finding comfortable quarters at a snug little tavern, whose creaking sign, as it swung backwards and forwards in the cold wind of that winter's night, informing all who cared to know that it was the "Shepherd and Shepherdess, kept by W. H. Brown," but we found that the said W. H. B. had been gathered to his fathers for some time, and that the establishment was presided over by his blooming widow, assisted by two very presentable daughters. Seated in the bar parlor, in which blazed a cheerful wood fire, we did ample justice to the meal that had been prepared for us, which, together with some good old ale, and the warmth of the logs completely dispelled the fatigue that we felt on our arrival. After a few games at cards we betook ourselves to bed, very well satisfied with our present quarters. The next morning, being Christmas Day, we were permitted to remain out of barracks, and enjoy the last day of our civil liberty in such a manner as would suit our tastes and pockets. After breakfast I and my three companions compared notes, and examined the contents of our purses, which being found sufficiently flourishing to warrant the outlay, we agreed to dine with our hostess and daughters, and, if possible, to have a regular jollification and keep up Christmas, perhaps for the last time in England, after the fashion and manner of good folks in English country towns. The necessary funds having been handed over to the landlady, we started out on a cruise through the town to take a look at the quarters we were to enter the next morning, and receive the first lesson in our new profession. We were very well pleased with our Christmas festivities. The dinner was all that could be desired, to say nothing of the plum-pudding, mince pies, fruit, nuts, and sweetmeats, nor was there any lack of wine and spirits. In the evening several neighbours and friends of the widow dropped in. One of these, who was no mean performer on the violin tendered his services which was duly accepted. Singing and dancing were kept up without intermission until daylight warned us to seek our beds for a few hours. After breakfast we were marched into barracks, inspected by the commandant, told off, and posted to our different companies. Then followed the hair-cutting, bathing, and shaving. The latter process, I must say, was much needed by the greater portion of our party. This business gone through, we donned the uniform, and were soon made to understand the utility of the goose step, extension motions, and setting up drill, and other positions thought necessary for the well-being of the recruit generally. From many of the fatigue duties incident to a military life, I managed to escape. The necessary, though to me disagreeable task of cooking I evaded by an exchange, preferring to mount guard to ruling the roast in the mess kitchen. Such labour and fatigue as carrying sand, I also escaped. This necessary article had to be brought from the opposite bank of the Medway. Here my nautical experience assisted me. The staff-sergeant of my company, learning that I had been at sea, appointed me coxswain. The only duty I had to do on these occasions was to steer, and take charge of the boat, while the others were digging and filling the bags. A short time after my arrival, while ascending the steps leading to my barrack room, after evening drill a voice exclaimed : " Can it be possible, is that Fortescue ? What on earth brought you to this place." I think I may ask you the same question, for I certainly never expected to see you here," said I, recognizing my old schoolfellow and friend Charley Melton. Mutual explanations followed, and we agreed to stand by one another as long as we should be in the service. At Chatham, which was about one mile from Brompton, were stationed two regiments of the line, between whom and us a great deal of good-natured chaffing went on, at each other's expense. We were provided with three good meals a day ; they only breakfast and dinner. The regiments of the Company's service never returned from India ; those of the line changed stations frequently. On meeting each other in the town the Royals would call out, "Halloo, Jack Company, when does your regiment come home ?" The usual response would be, "When your's gets its supper." I had been in barracks about five weeks when an order arrived to despatch a draught of recruits to India. A parade was ordered, and the requisite number called out from amongst those who had been longest at the depot, myself among the number. We were paid up and directed to hold ourselves in readiness to march to Gravesend next day.

CHAPTER IV.

It was a clear cold morning; a hoar frost hung on the trees and hedges, and the shrubs and nettles that grew by the way side were coated with tiny articles of ice that glittered and sparkled in the rays of the early sunlight. The road, a macada-mised one, was in excellent order, with many a bend and turn, disclosing here and there the ivy-mantled towers of some ancient church, or a view of the Thames, as it flowed onwards towards the sea. Our detachment consisted of two hundred and fifty-six men of all ranks, and had been accompanied to the outskirts of the town by the band of the depot, followed by the usual concourse of servant girls, young fellows, the acquaintances of an hour, and a crowd of boys, drawn together by the music, and the bustle and excitement of the scene. The distance to the place of embarcation was about twenty miles. Half-way we were halted at a little public-house on the roadside, and regaled with bread, cheese and beer in lieu of dinner. We then pushed on and arrived at Gravesend a little past mid-day. Here we were joined by the married men, their wives and families, and com-menced embarking immediately. As none but those belonging to the draught were allowed to go off to the ship, all leave-taking had to be got through prior to leaving the pier. Having no relative or friend to wish me God-speed, or say a farewell word, I sat down on a heap of baggage to wait for my turn for the boat, for I was glad to escape recognition by any passer-by. Here I witnessed several affecting separations, the parent looking on his child for the last time; sisters and brothers parting, perhaps, never again to meet. Few of all that throng now leaving, in the pride of their health and strength, would ever again set foot on their native shore. There was the careless, good-natured adieu, "Old fellow, I wish you good luck, of course you will write," of the schoolfellow or village friend; the boisterous grief of some Hibernians, who were kissing and hugging their kinsmen after the fashion of their country; and also that quiet undemonstrative sorrow that gives no utterance, and speaks no farewell; for as the old song says, "the heart feels most when the lips move not, and the eye speaks the gentle good bye." It was past two o'clock before we all got safely on board. For a time all was noise and confusion; messes being made up of six men to each, and quarters assigned to the married people. The orlop deck was divided into berths for the use of the remainder of the men; who were told off into squads under their respective non-commissioned officers, and a certain amount of order and discipline was soon established, which grew more effective and permanent as the voyage progressed. "Heave and haul," shouted the hoarse voice of the boatswain. The capstan bars flew round to the music of a violin, on which one of the crew was performing Jim Crow, and other popular airs. As the ponderous anchor rose slowly from its muddy bed, the jibs were run up, and the bow of the Indiaman swung round. The topsails were sheeted home, and the superb ship, with its living freight, dropped down the river, her white canvass swelled out by a light westerly wind that lifted and curled the sea-green waters into mimic waves. Shoals of porpoises bared their backs, and gamboled in the light of the setting sun, as we swept majestically on towards the Downs on our outward-bound passage to Bombay. At roll-call that evening Captain Woodgate, commanding the detachment, came between decks and enquired if there were any present who understood the slinging of hammocks; if so, to step out. "I can sling a hammock with the best man in the ship," replied I, in a confident tone, as I fell out and saluted the captain. He turned to me, saying, "Very good, my man; I wish you to commence at once and hang every man's hammock. Take six men, that the sergeant-

major will detail for that duty, **and** instruct them in **all that**
concerns it. Do this for two or three days, **I** will then order a
parade for the purpose of explaining to the detachment the way
it is to be done; after which every man must sling his own.
Pay attention to this, and you will find that you shall not be a
loser by your willingness to make yourself generally useful." On
the fourth evening I had been engaged with the hammocks, and
had nearly finished, when I had occasion to go on deck for a few
minutes. I called my friend Charley Melton, and asked him to
sling the rest. This he undertook to do. During my absence
Captain Woodgate **came below,** and going up to Melton said,
"Thank you, my man, I am much obliged to you for the trouble
you have taken; the men in future must do it themselves. What
is your name." It was accordingly given, **and** the Commanding
officer went to his cabin. **The next morning, at** ten o'clock the
sergeant-major read out the following **order:** " Private Charles
Melton to be corporal and lance sergeant, and to be borne on the
strength of the detachment, as such, until absorbed by casualty."
And thus, by a mere accident, I lost my first chance for promotion. **In the dusk** of the evening my friend Charles had been
mistaken for me, and to the day of his death nobody but
himself and I knew to what he owed his rise, or why I had been
passed over without some acknowledgment of my service. I of
course could have explained matters, and had the order cancelled;
but as it was my friend that derived the benefit I kept dark on
the subject. A few days after sea sickness made its appearance, prostrating the greater portion of the men, and putting
drill out of the question for a time. As for myself, having been
subjected to it previously, I was fortunately exempt. Nearly
three weeks passed before this malignant enemy disappeared.
One poor young fellow, named Stewart, of a very delicate constitution, **suffered** long and severely. Some other complaint seized
him before he recovered from sea-sickness ; and daily sank lower
and lower, until one morning he was reported dead by the medical

officer. All were sorry, for he had been a quiet, good-natured, harmless young fellow. Preparations were immediately made for the funeral service that evening : **the body** was sewn up in a hammock, leaving the face exposed to view, until the last moment; it was then placed on a grating and carried up to the forecastle, and partially covered with the Union Jack. At sunset the funeral service was to be read, and the body committed to the deep. All on board, not otherwise engaged, were at that time assembled to witness the last sad rites. The Commanding officer had opened the prayer-book when the sail-maker stepped forward to complete his work, that of the closing the open part of the hammock. In doing this, he drove his needle either by design or accident into the throat of poor Stewart. In an instant a convulsive movement was perceived in the body, and blood began to flow from the wound. Quick as lightning "Old Sails" ripped open the rough shroud, restoratives were immediately applied, and to the surprise and delight of all present, Stewart recovered consciousness, and was taken below. Before we had crossed the line he was reported fit for duty. Twenty years after I met him, a stout robust man, holding an appointment in the commissariat department. As we passed into warm latitudes various amusements were entered into for killing time. We had an excellent library on board, a weekly newspaper was started, cards, backgammon, and draughts were indulged in every afternoon and evening. Each man was allowed one quart of porter per diem ; lime juice was also issued daily. One afternoon a sudden excitement arose ; a sail had been reported in sight, and the officers had been on the look-out for her. "What is it ?" enquired Captain Morris, of the chief officer, **who, for,** several minutes had been intently gazing through his glass at a small object on the distant horizon. "I cannot quite make her out; she is evidently a small vessel, **but still too distant to** distinguish her course," he replied, as he closed his telescope." "Then jump aloft ; you will get a better view from the top-mast cross trees;" suggested his superior, who, by this time, had rested his own glass on the quarter boat, and brought it to bear on the object in question. He soon gave up the scrutiny, as he could discern no more than had been reported by Mr. Howard. "Well, could you make out anything more of her?" he continued, as that officer descended from the main rigging. "She is about four miles off on our weather quarter, has a large hull, and small sails, looks like a schooner, and is running parallel with us. There is a light fog rolling down towards us that will shut her out for a while, but when that clears we shall have a nearer sight of her, or I am mistaken," was his reply, as he descended the companion ladder, it not being his watch on deck. The appearance of a strange sail always creates a certain amount of excitement, especially on board a passenger or troop ship, and we were not the exception, for speculation was rife as to what sort of a craft she might turn out to be. The mate's words had been overheard by the sentry on the cabin door and duly promulgated through the ship; with a little addition, according to the inventive genius of the narrator, as it was handed about from one to the other. In about a couple of hours the fog lifted, and sure enough there was the schooner, a long, black, rakish-looking craft, with an immense hull, capable of holding a great number of men, and apparently pierced for ten guns; but her ports were closed. She was about two miles ahead on our weather bow, which she was crossing, and showed Swedish colors on her mizzen peak. "There she is, there she is," was shouted from a dozen voices from different parts of the ship, and immediately every glass was levelled at the stranger. Presently the boatswain, an old sailor, who had formerly served on board a man-of-war, after taking a good squint at her from the top-gallant forecastle, walked up to the captain and said, "That is the 'Tarentella,' commanded by the pirate Davoust. I know the cut of her jib, and trim of her sails, and many a chase we had after her when I was in the 'Wasp,' a ten-gun brig belonging to the West India squadron." "Are you quite certain," enquired his commander. "Quite certain, sir, there ain't another hull like that afloat," was the answer of the old salt. "Then tell the chief officer I wish to speak to him, and come yourself. I think we shall need your counsel." Captain Woodgate, with his subalterns, together with all the ship's officers, had assembled in the fore cabin by the request of Captain Morris, who thus addressed them : "Gentlemen," with your co-operation, I think we can have considerable amusement, and if the affair be managed carefully and quietly, some profit likewise, for there," said he, pointing through the open door of the cabin towards the schooner, which, by this time had tacked about, and was standing **towards** us," "that fellow, I am informed, is the celebrated pirate Davoust. He is a French creole, a native of Martinique, and possesses all the cruelty of the negro, with a strong dash of the polished cunning and knavery of his white associates. A large reward has been offered by the government for his capture or destruction ; either of these desirable events, I believe, we can attain, if we act promptly, **and** with caution. He evidently mistakes the character of our vessel, and fancies us unarmed, and, likely to become an easy prey. Mr. Block, the boatswain, knows his tactics and mode of attack. Now, to be forewarned is to be forearmed ; what say you, gentlemen ?" An unanimous approval followed this suggestion of the captain's, and several plans of attack were proposed, and the following was finally adopted. Under cover of the awnings, which were braced tightly down, two guns were to be got on the forecastle, loaded with round shot. Mr. Blocks was to take charge of these, and at the proper time open fire on the pirate, and endeavour **to** cripple her by cutting away her masts and rigging. **Two** other guns were to be placed on the orlop deck ; these were to be managed by some of the artillery recruits, many of whom had eighteen months gunnery practice at the depot previous to coming on board. Their instructions were to blaze away **at** sternpost and rudder, and try to knock them away, and thus render the vessel unmanageable ;

while the infantry, about two hundred and fifty strong, were
to sweep her decks by a continuous discharge of musketry.
Cutlasses, pistols, and boarding pikes, were served out to the crew,
who, under their officers, were to act on the defensive, if the
pirates should attempt to board us. If we were successful in
crippling the vessel, our vessel was to be jammed hard-a-port,
and we were to run her down by cutting her in two. Quietly,
and without noise or confusion, everything was got ready for the
reception of the sea-robbers. When within three-quarters of a
mile she showed her true character, clewed up her sails, hauled
down the Swedish colors, and ran up the piratical black flag,
with the famous death's-head and cross bones, opened her ports,
showed her teeth and fired a shot across our bows. "That is a
hint for us to heave to;" shall I give the order?" enquired
Mr. Howard. "Not yet," was the captain's reply ; "our object is to
get as near as possible to her before we appear to become aware
of her meaning or intention." "The next shot will be through our
mainsail," ejaculated the boatswain; and while he was speaking, a
puff of white smoke curled from the bow of the buccaneer; a
flash and report followed; and a round shot passed between our
fore and mainmasts doing us no damage, but burying itself in
the sea to windward. "Heave-to," shouted the captain at the
top of his voice. The seamen sprung to their stations, and the
ship was hove-to without further delay ; but although the
vessel's head-way was impeded, we were quietly drifting towards
the piratical schooner. Enthusiasm and excitement ran high
throughout the ship ; every one was anxious to secure the prize
that appeared now almost within our grasp ; yet everything was
carried on with perfect order, and there was nothing to indicate
externally that we were anything but what we appeared to be.
an outward-bound East Indiaman and unarmed. The pirates
seemed to be perfectly satisfied on this point, for they now
lowered a boat, which was soon filled with men armed to the
teeth, cut-throat looking dogs, doubtless, as those gentry usually

are ; but before they had pulled a stroke from the vessel's side, a violent commotion appeared to be spreading among the crew. They scrambled hurriedly on board, the boat was hauled up, the vessel's course altered, and in less time than I have taken to write this she was flying before the wind, with every stitch of canvas that could be set crowded on her. This was a contingency we had not anticipated—all our visions of prize money in doubloons quietly disposed of—but there was no help for it. Mr. Block treated them to a farewell salute from his two guns, one of which struck her bulwarks amidships, and sent the splinters flying in all directions—the other ploughed along her deck, but with what effect we could not find out. The two orlop guns likewise blazed away, but either from want of practice in naval gunnery, or that the distance was too great, they both fell short. And thus the affair ended, for by sunset not a vestige of the flying craft was to be seen, though the horizon was swept by some of our best glasses. During the evening the hasty and undig-nified flight of the pirates was thus accounted for. It transpired that one of the women, who was quite unaware of what was going on—for it was kept as quiet as possible from the soldiers' wives—was amusing herself by cleaning with pipe clay the red jacket of her husband, which, when completed, she thrust out of one of the port holes to dry in the sun, unintentionally attracting the notice of the pirates, who, at once discovered our true character, and hence their speedy retreat. Matters then fell into their ordinary routine. We had the usual amount of squalls and experienced some heavy weather, while rounding the Cape of Good Hope ; but on getting into the warmer latitudes, things wore a brighter aspect. As on all long voyages, a great deal of monotony was felt at times. However, an incident occurred one day, not long after our adventure with the pirates, that served to amuse us for the time being. The stiff breeze that had been blowing for several hours during the earlier part of the morning had lulled completely ; the mizzen had been brailed, the

mainsail clewed up; the heavy foresail hung down, occasionally flapping slowly against the mast; the huge sails creaked and
jarred as they swung backwards and forwards; the top sails were
of very little service, but the top-gallant sails and royals were
gently swelled by a light wind that impelled the vessel at about
three knots per hour, through the now calm and glittering waters,
from which ever and anon the albicore sparkling like molten silver,
would spring into the air in the morning sunlight. It was
Sunday, the ship's bell had just struck four bells, when our
commanding officer appeared on deck. " Captain Morris," said he,
"will you do me the favor to read the morning service to my
men. I am suffering from an attack of rheumatism, and Lieutenant
Roland is likewise somewhat indisposed this morning." "Certainly,
with much pleasure," replied the captain of the vessel. " Boatswain," continued he, addressing that functionary, " Pipe the
carpenter's crew aft and rig the quarter deck for church." Soon
the shrill notes of the old seaman's whistle rang through the
ship, the Union Jack was thrown over the capstan, and quite a
number of planks were made into seats by being placed on small
kegs. The bugle now sounded church parade, and in about a
quarter of an hour, all the men off duty, together with the
officers and ship's crew, took their seats. "Sergeant-major, are
all the married women present ? " enquired the commanding
officer. " I believe so, sir," he answered, glancing hurriedly over
the assembly, and saluting his superior officer. As Captain
Morris was about to open his book, and commence the morning
prayer, Mrs. Ann Reede, wife of one of the recruits, made her
appearance on deck from the fore-hatchway, dressed to kill, but
instead of coming towards us, she deliberately mounted the
forecastle steps, climbed on the bulwarks, and jumped overboard,
without uttering a single word or cry. So unexpected was the
act that for a moment no one stirred; then a simultaneous rush
was made; many ascending the rigging, while others crowded
the bulwarks, forecastle, and other favourable points that com-

manded a view of the floating object. " Cut away the life buoy ; back the fore and main yards ; clew up the top-gallant sails and royals," rang out the deep clear tones of **Captain** Morris's voice, with **that** coolness and promptitude so characteristic of the **practical** seaman. His orders were obeyed instantly, and the vessel's headway stopped ; then turning to the **second** mate, he said, " Lower away the quarter boat, take six men, pull astern, and endeavour to pick up the poor woman." The boat soon dropped from its davits, and was off on its way **to the** rescue. By this time she was half-a-mile astern, although scarcely ten minutes had elapsed since she made her flying leap into the deep. Considerable excitement was manifested during the absence of the boat, every glass brought into use, and from enquiries it was ascertained that some high words had taken place between Mrs. R. and her husband a few minutes prior to the bugle sounding for church parade. He was a stern, morose fellow, and somewhat jealous withal. It appeared that he had forbidden her to parade in certain feminine elegancies in the shape of bonnet ribbons or laces, which he asserted were not for him, but for the gratification of a blue jacket, with whom she was, as he said, on too familiar terms. The boat reached her just as she was sinking ; fortunately her skirts, which were rather extensive, supported her until help came, but she was brought on board in almost an exhausted condition. Being a fine, handsome woman, sympathy ran high in her favor. Restoratives, in the shape of hot brandy and water, and mulled wine, were administered to her, and she was soon all right again, but she was cautioned by the Commanding officer not to repeat the dangerous experiment. Of course she was the heroine of the hour among her companions. On the following Sunday morning, about the same time and place, namely the commencement of divine service, we **were** about to be treated to a similar scene, but unfortunately for the principal actress, it had a very different denouement. **A** sharp, ill-favoured little woman, whose ambition was greater than her stature, **became jealous of** the notoriety attained by her sister-in-law, and **was determined, if** possible, to bring herself to public notice by a similar act, in hopes, no doubt, of obtaining her share of the general patronage, and becoming the recipient of certain liquids known as "medical comforts," for which, if report spoke truly, she had a decided predilection. This little personage interrupted the morning service, precisely as the former party had done; but instead of mounting the bulwarks from the forecastle she made a sudden dart for the first open port, out of which she **thrust** herself. A seaman who was standing near seized hold of the skirts of **her** dress, and held on till assistance came, when she was hauled on board. The disappointed aspirant **for** fame struggled to free **herself from** the grasp of those that held her, but in vain, when she resorted to that feminine expedient, tears; but with as little success, for there was no fascination in her eye, no beauty in her cheek. "Make way there, **men,**" cried Captain Woodgate, and immediately **the** crowd fell back, as he appeared. "And so, madam, you thought to indulge in a little sea-bathing, at the risk of your life, and regardless of the trouble and annoyance it would create throughout the ship," said he, in the severest tones he could assume. Then, speaking to those who held her, said, "Lash her to yonder wooden grating, and lay her full-length on the deck." This was at once done. "Now pass along a dozen buckets of water." These were dashed full upon her to the no small mirth of many of the lookers-on. When thoroughly drenched, and half suffocated, she was released. "There, ma'am," said the commanding officer, "that will do you as much good as if you had been overboard for an hour. You may now go below. Quartermaster-sergeant, let her daily allowance of beer be discontinued for ten days." "Land ahoy," shouted the **look-out from** the mast-head—the blue waters assumed a **greenish** hue, sure indication of our proximity to land—and soon after the top of Peter Botte Mountain, on the Island of Madagascar, loomed up in the distance on our starboard bow.

CHAPTER V.

THE remainder of the day we ran along the coast, so close that we could see a great part of the island. Cattle were grazing or browsing on the hill-side, and in little shaded nooks there were huddled together quite a number of small bamboo huts, the inhabitants of which **would** hasten to the nearest point to look at our vessel, as she sailed past, the flag of Old England flying proudly from our mizzen peak. **As** the shades of night closed in, we lost sight of the island. The weather was now delightfully fine, being early in the month of June, **and** the evenings we usually spent on deck. Groups were formed in different parts of the ship, some engaged in smoking and listening **to** tough yarns from some old soldier **or sailor**; **in** another part the tones of the flute and violin, with the quick **stamp** of the foot announced that the jig or reel **were** in full operation. Some six or seven of our best singers would be on the quarter deck, performing a variety of songs in their usually happy style, for **the** cabin gentry; and in this manner we managed to while away the long evenings. One night while lying awake in my hammock, thinking of the land I had perhaps left for ever, and the one I was now so anxious to reach, I was aroused from my reverie by a great noise and shouting on deck. Wishing to know the cause, I hastened up the main hatchway laddder, and the first thing I noticed was an immense light, apparently at no very great distance, right ahead. This I soon learned was the light-house on the island of Colaba, at the entrance of the harbor of Bombay. Here was good news indeed; a long imprisonment within the wooden walls come to an end at last. As the captain had never been here before, **he** thought it advisable not to go in at night, so we stood off and on

until daylight, then ran in under easy sail. A pilot came out to
meet us, the boat was taken in tow, and that responsible officer
came on board and took charge of the ship. The boatmen, some
twelve or sixteen in number, Mahometans by caste, and naked
as they were born, with the exception of a small cloth scull cap,
and dripping like water spaniels, swarmed up the bulwarks and
squatted on the taffrail, chattering like monkeys. These were,
then specimens of the people among which, if I lived, I should
have to spend so many years. I must confess my first impression
of the natives were not favorable, but one gets accustomed to
almost anything, and the effect of their scanty clothing soon
passed away. We were now entering one of the finest and most
commodious harbors in the world. On our left lay the Island of
Colaba, connected with that of Bombay by a velard or causeway,
where, looming above the tall stately palm trees, was the light-
house, on a rock, at the base of which was placed a thirty-two
pounder signal gun, to warn off vessels that might be approaching
too close to a dangerous reef of sunken rocks called the Prongs,
that stretched across Back Bay to Malabar Point. This bay
is often taken for the harbor by persons who have not previously entered the port, and consequently many a vessel is
lost on that reef, by their commanders blundering in at night,
or without a pilot. Snugly embosomed among the cocoa nut
groves, could be seen the Infantry Barracks, the Observatory,
Gun-Carriage Manufactory, and that large range of buildings at
Artha Bunder called the Cotton Screws, where the cotton that comes
down from the interior loosely-packed is compressed or screwed
by hydraulic power into square bales for shipment to Europe.
On our right lie the Islands of Henry and Kenry. With a light
breeze and shortened sail, we were piloted through the numerous
shipping that lay at anchor in the stream. Passing the Dockyard,
Custom House, Castle, and Mint, we came to anchor in front of
the Artillery Barracks in Fort George, and nearly opposite the
Island of Elephanta. At no great distance was the main land—

the coast of Malabar—with its numerous peaks and **mountains,** rising apparently to the **clouds. As** our vessel had **been signalled** while entering the **harbor,** it was not **long before a** party of non-commissioned officers of the Artillery **came to take** charge and **conduct** us to their barracks. We landed at the Custom House Bunder, where a number of pack bullocks were waiting to carry our bedding and knapsacks. While passing one of these, the brute raised his foot and kicked me on the knee-cap, causing much pain. Mentally consigning the beast to a place much hotter than even Bombay, I limped away to purchase some milk, fruit, and other things, to which for so long a time I had been a stranger. As we entered the town, I was much struck with its crowded and ever-varying aspect—Banyans, Parsees, Persians, Arabs, and people of every caste and colour, in every variety of the Oriental costume—all so entirely new to me—winding their way quietly along, either for business or pleasure—the European merchant or staff officer dashing along in shigeorm or palkee to their country house **or** office, **as** the case might be—here and there a party of sailors on shore for a few **hours,** wandering about, following some crowing **native boy** that could speak a little English, to the different taverns, and such other places of resort, where sailors do most like to congregate. But there were none of the European fair sex to be seen, ladies never shewing themselves abroad until near sunset ; nor were the British soldiers allowed out between the hours of 10 a. m. and 4 p. m., except in cases of emergency, or duty, on account of the extreme heat. All the orderlies belonging to the different government or military officers, were men belonging to the native regiment stationed there, and very smart and soldier-like they looked, well set-up, and dressed in their best uniform. Passing along the principal bazaar, we reached Fort George, where we were to remain until our Indian clothing could be issued to us, for that which we had brought with us was unfitted for the climate. Likewise distribution rolls had to be made out for the various corps that required men to fill vacancies. Just at this period a new regiment was in process of formation,' and I, with nearly two-thirds of the draft, was posted to it, and ordered to proceed to head quarters at Poona, where a nucleus had already been formed by some officers and men from other corps. A few days previous to our leaving Bombay, we had a foretaste of the south-west monsoons. The day had been exceedingly hot and sultry, and when night flung her sable mantle over the earth, the atmosphere became thick, heavy, and oppressive. Neither moon or star lit up the dark vault of heaven ; a thick darkness prevailed, that could be almost felt. Towards midnight the heavy clouds parted, the rain descended in torrents, the vivid lightning flashed, and the thunder rolled, peal after peal vibrating among the neighbouring hills, like discharges from heavy artillery ; the wind swept up the narrow streets, and in at each portcullis embrasure with great violence, overturning sentry boxes, unroofing buildings, and moving all things portable. Our barrack-room commanded a view of the harbor, which was frequently lit up with flashes of broad sheet lightning, disclosing a wild scene. Vessels breaking from their moorings, and hurled by the violence of the storm against one another, or driven ashore on the sandy beach above the town. Minute guns, the signal of distress, were constantly heard from some unfortunate craft, and the gun at the light-house frequently boomed out to warn them to keep off from the dangerous reef of sunken rocks near the entrance of the harbor. I had been told that the monsoons lasted without intermission for about four months. " If," thought I, " this is a sample of the rainy season, what a delightful climate I have got into." The morning broke clear and bright, the storm had spent its fury, leaving in the sky no trace of its visit ; but on the coast a very different spectacle was to be seen. A little after daybreak orders were issued to the troops for every man off duty to be marched to the beach to render such assistance as might be required of them. Each one was directed to take what could be spared from their knapsacks in the shape of clothing, for the use of such of the unfortunate sufferers that might need them ; for by this time it became known that two large ships, the "Lord William Bentinck," with recruits from England, and the "Lord Castlereagh," from Karrack, in the Persian Gulf, had been wrecked on the Prongs during the fearful storm of the preceding night. All along the beach, from Artha Bunder to the rocks at Malabar Point, could be seen evidences of the ruin that had been wrought during that fearful gale. Broken masts, spars, barrels, bales, cabin furniture, ship's timbers, and hundreds of other articles, were strewn about in all directions ; but by far the most appalling sight was the numerous dead bodies that were constantly being discovered amongst the clefts of rocks or on the sands, some fearfully lacerated, and some without a bruise. The life-boats and catamarans of the pilot service—the said catamarans are bamboo rafts which can live in any sea—were successful in rescuing many a poor fellow from a watery grave, but not a single female was saved. One young lady, daughter of a rich old Nawab, who was returning from England, where she had been sent to finish her education, offered to give her whole fortune, and marry the man that would save her. Several tried hard for the prize, but perished in the attempt. Many were twice wrecked. The "Bentinck" went to pieces first, and several swam to the "Castlereagh," and were hauled on board, but in a very short time she also went to pieces, and thus they were again cast upon the treacherous bosom of the angry waters. Those who had been saved were at once sent to the hospital, and comfortably cared for. Several small guard rooms were converted into temporary dead houses to receive the bodies as they were brought in, until arrangements could be made for one general interment. A rather amusing incident occurred at one of these places. The body of one of the recruits had just been brought in and laid on the guard bed, and a sentry placed at the open door to prevent the corpses from being mutilated by rats or other vermin. He was walking quietly up and down his **beat** when a sepulchral voice from within called out: "Sentry, what o'clock is it?" Scared beyond measure, he fled to the guard-room and reported **what** he had heard, and of course got reprimanded and laughed at for his pains, and again placed on his post. The corporal looking into the room and finding the body in the same position it had been left returned to **his** guard. A few moments elapsed when the same voice cried out : "Sentry, give me a drink **of** water." The poor sentry could stand this no longer, and again bolted to the guard-room. The sergeant, thinking there must be something up, visited the place, and there sure enough was the supposed dead man sitting up straight, and calling for water. It appeared that on coming to, he had sat up, and, noticing the sentry, asked the time, but the exertion had been too much for him, and he had fallen back and fainted. **In a little while he** again came round and managed to assume the sitting position, in which he had been found by the sergeant ; and many a good laugh was afterwards had at the sentry's expense. The following **week we** received orders to start for Poona, and such of the "Bentinck" men as were sufficiently recovered joined our detachment. The first day's journey was performed in large covered boats up a beautiful river, winding in and out among the hills, and we arrived at Panwell, some seventy miles from Poona, and twenty from Bombay, late in the evening. Here we halted for the night, and at daybreak the following morning we commenced our first day's march to Choak, distant about ten miles. Next day we reached Campoola, **at** the foot of the Bore Ghaut, which forms a part of that range of mountains that runs throughout Western India, dividing the Dekan from the Conkas ; at which place we remained for a couple of days, in order to allow the baggage to go **forward** and **ascend the** steep and difficult road up the Ghaut, **the** height of which was several thousand feet above the level of the sea. The scenery was wild, grand, and romantic. On each side of the narrow road were deep ravines, with perpendicular scarps, and covered with thick jungle, the haunt of the tiger, and other wild animals, which, at that time, were very numerous, and committed great havoc among the droves of cattle that passed up and down the road, and not unfrequently carrying off some unfortunate native traveller. After some four hours' toiling up this rugged declivity, we arrived tired and foot-sore at Kandalla, the halting stage at the summit of the Ghaut. Here a magnificent scene burst upon our view. In the distance could be discerned the bright waters of the ocean; at our feet the fertile plains spotted with small villages, which looked like small specks in the distance. The remainder of the day and night sufficed to put us again in marching order, when we started *en route* for head-quarters, which we reached by easy marches, about ten miles per day, and then drill and discipline commenced in real earnest. The life of a recruit is anything but a sinecure in India, incessant drill and fatigues are his portion, until fit for duty, and long after, with the thermometer at ninety-six in the shade. Unfortunately I had almost double drill to go through, for I was no sooner acquainted with the mode of priming and loading, and other manœuvres of Brown Bess, as the old flint-lock weapon was called, when the new percussion musket was issued to us, and the new drill which this necessitated had to be mastered; this kept us hard at it for upwards of twelve months. I had entered the service with my head crammed full of romantic ideas of the glory and promotion that was to be attained by deeds of valor on the battle field, or the forlorn hope, and planting the flag of Old England on some Indian fortress. This I wildly fancied was all that was expected of us, but this notion was soon dispelled, and a round of parades, guard-mountings, and other duties, awoke me to the reality of my position; but there was no help for it, so I set to work with a good will and soon acquired a tolerable proficiency in my profession. Our station was one of the largest and most fashionable in the western division of the army, and what with amateur theatricals, races, cricket matches, and other

7

amusements, I soon brought myself to turn my thoughts away
from the home beyond the seas, and make myself as comfortable
as circumstances would allow in my new line of life. I had been
but little more than a year in the country when my regiment
was ordered to Bombay, where, after doing duty for some eight
months we were sent to Kurrachee, in Scinde, to assist in the
conquest of that country under the famous old warrior, Sir Charles
Napier. My regiment formed a part of the army of reserve
during the battles of Meanee and Hyderabad, graphic accounts of
which have already been given to the world, rendering any
comment of mine on the subject unnecessary. We remained in
Scinde several months, when we were relieved by the Seventy-
eighth Highlanders, and ordered to Belgaum, a most beautiful
locality in the southern Mahratta country; and right glad was I
to exchange the wild plains and barren sand hills of Kurrachee
for such delightful quarters. We had not been many months
here when the whole station was thrown into a state of excitement, intelligence having reached us that Babagee Nikum,
a Mahratta chieftain, who held large tracts of land under the
East India Company, subject to the usual conditions, had not
only refused to pay the annual tribute, but had resisted the
functionaries whose duty it was to collect the said revenue. He
had gathered his followers together, armed them, taken possession
of the strong fortress of Samunghur—long considered impregnable by the natives, situated on one of the largest of that range
of hills, about twenty miles north-east of Belgaum, near the
large native town of Sunkeshwa—and threatened to maltreat and
oppose any parties that might be sent to coerce him into pay-
ment. The news of those proceedings having reached the
government at Bombay, instructions were forwarded to the
military commandant at Belgaum to dispatch a force sufficient,
in his opinion, to support the civil authorities in carrying out
such measures as might be thought most expedient for the collection of the land dues; and if necessary, to escort the pugna-

cious Mahratta to the seat of government to answer in person
for having disturbed the public peace and violated the laws
of the country. At the time when the above occurred, the
native troops were noted for their obedience to their European
superiors, and the faith and loyalty of the Sepoy was proverbial.
The presence of a comparatively small number of British troops
only was necessary to keep up the pluck and stamina of that
army, whose prowess and achievements for the last hundred
years, had contributed so largely in placing the East India
Company in the proud position they then held, as masters and
rulers of a mighty empire. Little could imagination then picture
the scenes of outrage committed by those very troops some years
later, when rebellion, with all its horrors, swept the country like
a plague, leaving starvation and death in the place of peace and
plenty. The major-general commanding lost no time in putting
into execution the instructions he had received from government.
To carry out such an object a more efficient, zealous, and energetic
officer than General D—— could not have been applied to. His high
military qualications and long residence in India; his thorough
knowledge of the language, manners, customs, and habits of the
natives, rendered him more than usually competent in such a
case as the present to deal with the bold, unscrupulous, yet
haughty Mussulman descendants of a long line of Moslem con-
querors, but now dwindled down to mere petty rajahs, or with
the more subtle and crafty Brahmins, who—in their capacity of
priests and advisers—sway the minds of thousands of Hindoos of
all castes and classes, who acknowledge their influence, and render
implicit obedience to their behests. Orders were at once given
for the formation of a light brigade, to be composed of the following troops : one wing of my regiment—this young corps, for it
had scarcely been formed five years, was in a high state of
discipline; the men young, active, well-drilled, and burning with
impatience for an opportunity of distinguishing themselves in the
field, and earn the proud triumph of placing the first honor on

our yet maiden colors—a light field battery of four six-pounders, and two howitzers, with a company of the Madras European artillery, whose skill in evolutions, and rapidity and accuracy of fire, had often spread death and terror amid the ranks of the enemy; three squadrons of native cavalry ; a strong detachment of native rifles, and two battalions of Sepoys, the honors, emblems and devices on their standards and colors, shewing how oft and nobly these regiments had distinguished themselves on many a well-fought field. A party of native sappers and miners, under European commissioned and warrant officers, were likewise attached to the force, the whole strength of which amounted to about two thousand five hundred men, with their usual complement of officers, all under the command of Brigadier W——, an officer of great promise and undoubted courage. His orders were to hold himself in readiness to march at the shortest notice with this force, and after accomplishing the object of his mission, to return to quarters with as little delay as possible. Although the monsoons, or rainy season, was nearly over, the swollen conditions of the numerous small rivers which it was requisite we should cross to reach our destination, rendered the marching of our brigade exceedingly troublesome, and would cause much delay and inconvenience. While these warlike preparations were going forward, the political agent at Belgaum, made overtures to the Samunghur chief, to induce him to come to terms without the interference of the military ; he, over-confident, and fancying he could defy all authority, and acknowledge no will but his own, refused to listen. Many who were but ill-calculated to judge of the difficulties which would beset the party, predicted a six weeks' campaign. How far their conjectures were realized, the sequel will shew. This, thought I, is the opportunity which since entering the service I so ardently desired, and determined that no amount of danger should deter me from bringing myself to especial notice, should any engagement of importance take place between our forces and those of the rebellious chief of Samunghur.

CHAPTER VI.

THE good folks of Belgaum were roused from their **slumbers at** the first dawn of **day** by the booming of the station gun, **whose** echo had scarcely ceased to vibrate among the numerous neighboring hills, when might be heard borne on the morning air the sweet sound **of** many a popular melody pealed forth **by the** bands of the different regiments, which accompanied the corps and detachments to their place of rendezvous, a large open space. This was in front of the principal gate of the fort of Belgaum. As detachment after detachment arrived from their different quarters they were **drawn up in the** following order: my regiment in column of subdivisions, right in front; the two Sepoy **corps in** sections; the detachments of native Rifles in sections of fours; the light field Bullock Battery, then the light Cavalry in sections of threes. The party of Sappers and Miners had been sent on in advance at an earlier hour. As the sentry at the main guard struck the hour of five on the gurrie or gong, the sharp quick tones of the Brigadier's voice rang out; "The Brigade will come to attention and shoulder." The next order was, "Officers in command will take post at the head of their respective corps and detachments." A few minutes later, the bugle sounded the advance, and the force moved off, leaving many a sad heart behind them. Of those now going forth in all the joyousness of youthful spirit, who could tell how small might be the number permitted to return; and of all that mighty throng who stood to witness their departure, how different must have been the feelings with **which** they were affected—the soldier's wife standing with her young family around her endeavoring to stifle her sobs as she gazed with straining eyes and

sinking heart on the husband she might never behold in life again
—the fair young bride who but a few short weeks before had left
family and friends to follow the husband of her choice, finds him
borne away, and with scarcely any warning to scenes of danger
and perhaps death. Standing alone at a short distance from a
plain, though handsome carriage, from which she had but a few
moments before alighted, was a tall, elegant girl, fast verging
into womanhood, the affianced wife of an officer belonging to the
brigade. She had just received his last farewell, and stood
watching the receding troops as they disappeared on the distance
with what heartfelt anguish the tightly clasped hands and the
white quivering lips too plainly told. Nor were the friends
and comrades of those now leaving the station the only parties
interested in the above proceedings ; numbers of natives were
watching and making their comments thereon. A little in advance
of the crowd stood a tall, slight figure dressed in a white angraka,
or coat of long cloth, and a peculiar shaped turban. He is a
Parsee merchant, a dealer in wine, beer, and the general run of
articles which are sent out to India by such firms as Crosse and
Blackwell, for the use of the regimental messes ; looking on
with a speculative eye, and calculating on the chances that might
arise to his profit from the expedition. Some distance to the left
are a group of Banyans, persons who contract with government
for the supplies of forage, cattle and carriage, on occasions like
the present. They were no doubt discussing the probabilities of a
campaign, in which case they would be no inconsiderable gainers.
Yonder personage, mounted on a richly caparisoned elephant, is
evidently some petty rajah of a neighbouring Tallook, or Zilla,
watching, with deep interest, the troops as they pass before him,
and pondering on what may be the result to his brother chief. As
the crowd dispersed, there might be seen, driving in different
directions, the dashing English barouche, with its prancing high-
spirited horses and silver-mounted harness, of the military commander or rich civilian, the bullock gurrie or dumner of the

subaltern, and the boilee with its burden of native ladies **and**
children, **all** richly **bedizened in** silks **and** jewellery, but carefully
concealed from the gaze **of** the vulgar **crowd by** the purdah or
curtain which surrounded them, the vehicle, drawn by a pair
of Mysore bullocks. As the brigade **wended** its way across the
open plain it preserved all the discipline and precision of a
parade movement, but on its arrival at the boundary or camp
limits, the bugle sounded the "March at ease." The officers then
fell out, and mounting their tattoos, a species of pony peculiar to
the country, rode and chatted gaily with their friends, many of
whom accompanied them to their first camping **ground, to spend**
the last few hours with them, and at the same time to enjoy
some excellent sport, game in the adjacent hills being very
plentiful. The artillery and cavalry returned their swords to the
scabbard, and the infantry brought their muskets to the trail,
or carried them in such a manner as was most convenient to themselves. Pipes and tobacco were brought into active operation,
and soon the song, **with its** swelling chorus, burst forth amidst
peals of laughter at some sallies of Hibernian wit, at the expense
of some of their less fortunate comrades, whose unsteady gait,
repeated stumbles, and drowsy appearance, gave sufficient evi-
dence that they could not be classed among the disciples of
Father Matthew, proving that however fatiguing a day's march in
a climate like India may be to a soldier, it has not the power of
crushing that buoyancy of spirit which is so natural **to** the sons
of Albion. Nor were their dusky companions in **arms** a whit
behind them in mirth and spirits; an incessant chatter in almost
every dialect, from the high Bengalee **to the** low mongrel Madrassee proved this, and the Babel **of tongues,** although understood
by a few only, **was still** rendered sufficiently exciting by gesticulation to add interest to the **scene.** The route—for road there
was none—ran along the **foot of** a range of hills, which was in
many places intersected or covered by large nullahs, or water-
ways, formed by the rushing of water down the ravines, during

the rainy season. These obstructions caused considerable delay, and much exertion was needed to get the guns safely over. By the assistance of the Sappers and Miners, however, and the good-hearted pull altogether of the Europeans, these difficulties were soon overcome. It was now near nine o'clock, and the powerful rays of the sun began to tell upon all, when a shout from the head of the column drew the attention of many to a beautiful green spot about half a mile to our left front, where beneath some magnificent tamarind trees, the tents of the staff, which had already been pitched, were now distinctly visible. The commissariat, baggage and tents (as usual on leaving a station) had been sent on in advance the day previous. At a signal from the brigadier the officers dismounted and joined their various divisions, at the same time the men bringing their weapons to the slope, order was resumed, and in ten minutes the brigade was drawn up in lines on the different spots selected and marked off by the Quarter-Master General and his subordinates. The rolls having been called, and reports given in, the cavalry dismounted, and picketed their horses, artillery unlimbered and parked their guns; the infantry piled arms and took off their accoutrements. Now the welcome sound for grog rang out, and in a few minutes the orderly sergeant of companies were seen approaching from the direction of the commissariat, with large copper camp kettles filled with arrack, a spirit made from the fruit of the date tree, and resembling somewhat in flavor and color the rum used in the British navy. It is considered the most wholesome liquor in the country, and free from all deleterious ingredients, being manufactured by government expressly for the use of the European troops. Each man is allowed to receive one dram, about the fifth part of a pint; this he may drink neat; but if he wishes to dilute it, he must bring the water with him, as he is not permitted to take the liquor away, but may drink it in front of the sergeant. This appears rather an arbitrary measure, but it is done on the score of sobriety, as there are many men in a regiment who, not caring for spirits themselves, would draw their allowance, and sell it to their comrades, hence the restriction. This little affair being arranged, pitching of tents became the order of the day ; and as the reader may not be acquainted with the usual routine observed in the operation, it may be as well to give a slight idea of how it is done. The Indian tents for European troops are generally twenty feet square, with a pole in the centre, which supports the double top. The four walls, or sides, are attached to the inner top by loops, and the whole secured by cotton ropes made fast to wooden pegs, driven into the ground. The pole being in two pieces, is joined together with an iron socket in the centre. About three feet from the top there is a small ledge on which the inner cap fits, and the inner top rests ; two feet above that a second cap is placed which supports the outer top, two pegs being firmly driven into the earth, against which the heel of the pole is placed, and at a given signal, the tops are raised by means of double ropes at each corner, which are pegged down as before described. Six of these tents are issued per company, fifteen men to each. In what would appear to the uninitiated, in an incredibly short space of time, up sprang a town of canvas, beneath the cool shade of the surrounding trees. The routtee, or tent of the native soldiers, are differently constructed, and more easily pitched, the whole being in one piece. They are usually twenty feet by fourteen, supported by two uprights, about twelve feet apart, and joined in their centres with two iron sockets, the same as the Europeans, with a pole along the top, fastened to them with iron rings. The shape of the tent, when pitched, resembles the gable roof of a house, with triangular pieces attached to each end, one of which, opening up the centre and folding back, forms the entrance. The whole is firmly pegged down through loops hanging at intervals around the purda or curtain part of the tent. The noise made by the mallets in driving the tent pegs, and the shouts of the men, as some half-raised tent fell to the ground, made the place ring again. While matters were proceeding thus, the cooks, who were generally speaking natives of Goa, a Portuguese settlement, on the south-west coast near Bombay, were actively engaged in preparing breakfast, and in less than one hour from their arrival, the European portion of the brigade were comfortably discussing their matin meal. That part of the Sepoys' rations received from the Commissariat is always issued raw, as each man, according to his caste, cooks his own meal, at such time, place, and in such a manner as his religious observances demand of him. Near mid-day I took up a comfortable position on a sloping, grassy bank, beneath the shade of a neighbouring mango tree, and was indulging in the luxury of a few whiffs of the fragrant weed, when I observed a party of horsemen crossing the open space directly in front of the camp. A greater variety than these horsemen displayed, as regards dress, could scarcely be conceived. Shooting coats of every description and color, just as the wearer may have chanced to have had with him; high hunting boots of different shapes and make, from the rough untanned, samber-hide, to the highly polished English calf skin, were there to be seen. Many contented themselves with tucking their trowsers into their Wellingtons, and twisting the common white turban of the native round their foraging cap, while others, from their long residence in the country, and greater experience in all that pertains to the chase, wore leather hunting caps, incased with white cotton quilted covers, artistically bound round with silk puggaries, which effectually protected the head and neck from the burning heat of the sun. Each carried a steel-headed bamboo spear, about ten feet in length, and wore a creese in his belt, which at once convinced me that they were going in search of the wild boar of the jungle, or as the patrons of this sport term it, they were out on a pig-sticking expedition. As they disappeared in the jungle, the thought suddenly flashed upon me, that our own mess was unprovided with game of any description, and that I could not while away an hour more agreeably or profitably than by endeavoring to procure some. I therefore hurried to my tent, and put together a short but serviceable rifle presented to me some months previously by one of our officers, and now for convenience carried in my bed. Thrusting my pipe and a few pieces of biscuit into my haversack, I strolled forth, and passing through a small opening between two hills, a little to the right of the camp, soon found myself at the edge of a rivulet of no great breadth and very shallow, whose bright waters glittering in the sunlight, danced and rippled among the numberless stones which obstructed its course along its rocky bed. Following the windings of this stream for a considerable distance, without encountering any game worth throwing away a shot upon, I halted, and seating myself in a natural bower, partly formed by the mogree or wild jessamine bush, and partly by the overhanging branches of a large banian tree, which grew on the shelving bank, and whose fibres shooting downwards, had taken root in the earth; these were interwoven with various creeping plants indigenous to the country, and formed a delightful shade. I had not been many minutes in this position, when my attention was arrested by suddenly seeing a large black buck spring from a neighbouring thicket to the bank, some distance down on the opposite side. His intention evidently was to slake his thirst, but not liking the look of the water, or from some other cause, he turned towards the direction in which I was sitting, and trotted quietly along, stopping here and there to nibble at the fresh grass that grew at the water's edge. Another moment would have brought him within range of my rifle, when he suddenly stopped, tossed his antlers in the air, then glancing apparently at some object beyond me, turned sharply round and dashed into the jungle. At the same instant a grunting sound, accompanied by the clattering of a horse's hoofs behind, caused me to turn sufficiently round to enable me to observe a horseman making a thrust with his spear at a large jungle boar, when either miscalculating his distance, or not being expert enough he missed his point and drove the head of the spear into the earth with such force that he lost his balance and fell heavily to the ground. The infuriated animal seeing his antagonist placed *hors de combat*, was making rapidly toward him with headlong speed. Not an instant was to be lost ; quickly bringing the rifle to my shoulder, and taking as accurate an aim as circumstances would permit, I fired, and the ball entering behind the right ear, buried itself in the creature's brain, and thus saved the life of the young officer—for such he proved to be, and converted the jungle pig into pork. Hastily, but carefully reloading my rifle, I hurried to render assistance to the fallen horseman, who had, by this time, assumed a sitting position, and by his bewildered look was apparently endeavoring to realize something of the scene before him. Unscrewing the brandy flask which I observed slung across his shoulder, I poured some of the contents down his throat ; this appeared to invigorate him wonderfully, and rising to his legs, with my assistance, he soon became fully aware of the danger he had escaped. Warmly and heartily he thanked me for the prompt manner in which I had come to his rescue. The report of my rifle had been heard by his friends, who now came cantering up. Matters were explained, and they highly complimented me on the success of my shot, and seemed gratified at the exertion I had made on behalf of their friend, not forgetting at the same time to indulge in some good-natured jokes at his expense. The boar's head was cut off as a trophy, and they very kindly ordered two of their beaters to accompany me to camp with the remainder of the animal. I bid the party good morning, and returned quite as well satisfied with my morning's adventure, as my comrades were with the unexpected addition to their mess. I was engaged a short time after cleaning my gun, when Bob O'Toole, an old chum of mine, came in, bringing with him a very fine buck. The identical one, I have every reason to believe, that I had so anxiously watched in the morning, for my friend Bob informed me he had killed it within five hundred yards of the spot where it disappeared from my view ; so what with venison and pork, we fared sumptuously that evening. The sun was now sinking behind the distant mountains, and the gentlemen that had accompanied their friends in the morning were about returning to Belgaum, a distance of some fourteen miles. Videttes were thrown out, pickets posted, and all the usual precautions taken for the security of the camp. The shades of night were fast closing around us, as my friend Bob and I paid a visit to the canteen tent to indulge in a glass of grog, and enjoy our evening pipe. Somewhat fatigued with our morning's march, and afternoon's sport, we turned in, taking the precaution to wrap ourselves up in our camoleens—a thin kind of blanket, the manufacture of the country—as a protection against the night dews, which are very heavy about the hills at this season of the year, and quickly falling off to sleep we were soon in the land of dreams. There is, perhaps, no sound that grates more harshly on a soldier's ear, or one that he prepares to obey with so much reluctance as that of the "rouse," which breaks upon his slumbers, and warns him to prepare for an early march. Springing up at two o'clock on the following morning, with the sound of the various trumpets and bugles ringing in my ears, I hastened to perform my toilet, which, in general, is no very elaborate affair with a soldier, more especially on the line of march. A coarse towel, with a pot of water from the nearest stream, and a few passes of the comb through the hair, which the rules of the service did not at that time permit to be worn long, suffices, and the affair is concluded. Hastily slipping on my uniform, and accoutrements, I commenced securing my bed and knapsack, which for the present contained all my goods and chattels, and having arranged it safely on the hackery or common cart of the country, which was placed at our disposal for the conveyance of the baggage, I and my comrades commenced striking the tents. The walls are first taken down, rolled up carefully and put into bags made of gunny, a coarse kind of cloth. One man is then stationed at the double rope at each of the four corners; the intermediate ropes and pegs are carefully rolled up, and at a given signal the remainder is lowered, the pole meanwhile having been withdrawn. This is tied up in a similar manner, then handed over to the tent lascars and baggage guard, whose duty it is to see them properly placed on the camels and carried in safety to the next camp ground. Seating myself on the stump of a withered tree, I occupied the few moments that intervened previous to the sounding of the fall-in bugle by endeavoring to make out something of what was passing around me. The morning was very dark—no moon and not a star to be seen—but by the aid of the camp fires that blazed brightly in every direction, I noticed, not far off, a number of men, some standing, some sitting, others lying on the ground, but by far the greater part indulging themselves in drinking a villainous compound concocted and sold by the Madrassee camp followers, and generally composed of burnt rice, water from the first ditch and sweetened with "joggeree," the coarsest description of sugar which the country supplies; this has to pass muster and do duty for coffee, and is called by the venders, who loudly vociferate in their own peculiar manner, "Karfee, Sahib, karfee." At the same time, directly in front of me, I saw something that looked like two moving towers, but were in reality a couple of huge elephants laden with hospital tents and furniture, sweeping past with their usual stately step, to take their place in rear of the column. In another spot, by the lurid flame that shot brilliantly forth, illuminating all around, I observed a group of camels, some standing already loaded, and browsing quietly on the leaves of the young nym trees, with which the place abounded, while others patiently knelt to receive their burdens, the tents of the brigade. Behind them again were a string of spare ones, with their hoot wallas or drivers beside them. A loud roar of laughter now proclaims that some refractory pack bullocks do not appreciate the notion of suiting their backs to the burden, for off they fling their loads and with heads down and tails erect, —after the manner of a fly stampede among cattle—they kick and plunge about the camp, to the great amusement of many, and to the no small annoyance of those who are running, musket in hand, endeavouring to stop them, and who soon find themselves up in the air, their weapons flying from their grasp and, the next minute, sprawling on the ground midst the jeers of their comrades. The noise made by the native bullock-drivers in urging on the cattle of the deeply-laden baggage-wagons, the clashing of arms, rattle of accoutrements, and heavy rumbling sound of the artillery, as they move forward, all tend to create that tumult and confusion which to a young soldier unacquainted with camp life, appears almost bewildering.

CHAPTER VII.

THE assembly sounded, the brigade formed **up** in a manner similar to that **of the** previous day, with the exception that the cavalry took the lead. The different bands struck up some lively airs, and we moved off for the first mile with tolerable regularity. We **then** entered a dense jungle, commonly known **as** the Black Forest. **Here our** difficulties commenced. There was a **kind of wheel-track, but** the immense number of cattle that are **sent out** here to graze **during this season of** the year, had **completely** obliterated **all traces of a road, and** formed **innumerable paths in all directions ; this combined** with the **darkness of the morning, caused much confusion.** The heads of the various **detachments were constantly straying into different paths, so** much so, **that it was found necessary to keep** the **trumpets at the head of the column constantly going, and answered by each corps sounding their regimental call.** In this manner **the party was kept together.** This **jungle,** covering a space **of thirty miles in length by eight in** breadth, assumes every **variety of feature, and was at that time** infested with numerous **tigers, hyenas, bears, wild boars, and plenty of** shikar— small game—for **the sportman, in the shape of** deer, pea-fowl, &c. The government having **since then offered rewards** for the heads of different **wild animals, has thinned them** considerably, **and** they are now **rarely met with.** The smaller trees, such **as the mango, too well known to need description, and the thorny** barble, **interspersed with scrubby brush wood,** are most frequently found on the hills, **together with the tambool bush, which bears a** dark purple **olive-shaped plum, about an inch** in length ; also a very beautiful tree—the name of **which has** escaped **my** memory—the timber is very like rosewood in color, but much darker. The most fashionable furniture is made from this tree, and it is called blackwood. In the valleys, the larger trees, such as the banian, grow, whose branches, spreading in every direction, drop their fibres here and there, which take root as soon as they reach the ground, and quickly increase in size till they outgrow the parent trunk, and extend over a space almost incredible. The next tree to attract attention is the Jack; it resembles the English elm in size, but its chief peculiarity is the fruit. It is from twelve to eighteen inches in length, and twenty-four to thirty in circumference, of a greenish-yellow color, formed like a cucumber, but thickly covered with prickles, and often weighs twenty pounds ; but what strikes the beholder is the extreme smallness of the stalk of the fruit, which is four inches in length, and one-third of an inch in diameter. Then again, is seen the tall, majestic tamarind tree, with its fern-like leaves, and long rich clustering fruit, together with the wild fig, which, when ripe, bears a red fruit about the size of a marble ; on being opened it is found full of insects ; these are carefully knocked out and the fig-skin eaten by the native ; the leaves are similar to those of the cultivated fig, but smaller. These were the principal trees . that grew in the valleys through which we passed. There I noticed subsequently, while riding through the same jungle by daylight, the extreme beauty of the flowers, among which I observed the sweet scented jessamine, with its tiny white blossom ; the creeping convolvulus, with its soft-blue bell-like bloom ; together with the magnificent passion-flower, of various shades of purple, and hundreds of other beauteous flowers of every hue, that grew in wild luxuriance in the ravines, and along the borders of the numberless streams which flowed across the path. As we were crossing one of those streams the bugle sounded the halt. It was soon ascertained that the artillery in passing a similar place ahead, had forced one of the wheels of No. 2 gun, over a projecting piece of rock, capsizing the gun with a loud crash,

into a nullah five feet in depth, and drawing the bullocks after it.
The morning was so dark that it was found necessary to make a
large fire to enable the fatigue party to see to extricate it. As
the fire blazed and crackled up the sides of the ravine it caused
much heat and illuminated all around, rousing from its lair an
enormous tiger, who evidently not accustomed to that sort
of thing, and not liking the aspect of affairs, uttered a fearful
growl, and sprang towards the opposite bank. He endeavoured
in passing to carry off one of the leading bullocks of No. 1 gun ;
but the yoke chains proving too strong, he was compelled to
relinquish his prey, and escape into the jungle—not, however,
before he had lacerated the back of the animal in a frightful
manner. This, however, was not the worst part of the business,
for the other bullocks, although completely paralyzed during
the presence of their natural enemy, no sooner found themselves
free of the monster than they suddenly dashed forward with the
gun, the wheel of which struck one of the battery lascars,
knocked him down and passed over his body, breaking both his
thigh bones. He was immediately conveyed to the rear, where
his wounds were attended to, as far as circumstances would
permit, and placed in one of the doolies belonging to the hospital,
that followed the force ; but the poor fellow died a few hours
after reaching the camp. A spare bullock having taken the
place of the one injured, and the capsized gun righted, the
advance sounded, and we pursued our way. By the light of the
dawning day, we found ourselves emerging from the thick jungle.
Our road now lay down a sloping plain, thickly sprinkled with
loose stones, among which grew the silk cotton tree, and the
milk bush ; this last is altogether without leaves, and its long
green sprouting tubes when broken, are found to contain a milky
substance of a poisonous nature, and very dangerous should it
get into the eye. Here and there grew the kernee and curawander
bushes—the first bears a yellow kind of plum, oblong and about
the size of a cherry ; the other, when ripe, is the color of the

English damson, but in shape and size like a bullace, and is very delicious eating. Here **also, in** little clumps, grew the castor oil· tree and the prickly pear, or wild **cactus.** As the sun rose above the horizon, we arrived at the banks of the Sootgootee, and here we halted ; a party having been sent up **the river** to ascertain whether it was fordable for cavalry. They returned shortly, having discovered an available place. A **more** delightful or romantic spot could not have been selected ; it **was** about one hundred yards in breadth, and little more than three feet in depth, with a firm pebbly bottom. The river was **studded** with numerous small islands, on which grew the wild coffee and other bushes ; large slab-like stones covered **with** moss and lichen jutted out from the bank and formed little nooks of still waters, where flourished in all its queen-like beauty the snowy lily, with its golden petals, together with the Indian bulrush, and many other aquatic plants, in tropical luxuriance. The rich foliage of the trees that grew on either side, with their over-hanging boughs, as the river narrowed, nearly met, and as the morning sun played through the branches, revealed a quiet scene of rural beauty, undisturbed, except **by the** cackling of the water-hen, the whirr of the wild fowl, or **the** peculiar cry, " did you do it " of the grey plover, **as it** lazily flapped its wings. After resting for nearly an hour, the artillery, cavalry, heavy baggage, elephants and camels, commenced crossing, about a quarter of a mile above where the brigade had halted, and without accidents or difficulty got over. The Ooree Wallas now made their appearance, with five oorees or boats, the largest a sort of barge, with a square stern, sharp bow, **and** flat **bottom,** capable of con-taining one hundred men. This was **ferried** across with paddles by the native boatmen. The other four were round, made of a frame-work of bamboo, covered with hides, and each held twenty-five men. These were propelled **by means of a** long pole, placed in **a** sort of rowlock, and by certain peculiar movements of the arms, kept revolving until the boat reached the opposite side. The

scarcity of boats and length of time occupied in crossing, delayed
the infantry about three hours. The river at this point being
one hundred and fifty yards wide, and about eight feet deep,
much amusement was created by watching the antics of the pack
bullocks, as they swam over in droves of fifties; many, when
about half way, would turn suddenly round, make towards their
starting place, and scamper about the banks in spite of the exertions and vociferations of their drivers, and others engaged in
getting them across. By half-past seven we were again *en route;*
but now the face of the country assumed a very different aspect;
in the place of rugged rocks, steep hills, and dense jungle, our
path lay through beautiful undulating cultivated plains. On our
right, stretching away as far as the eye could reach, might be
seen the bright green rice growing in its watery bed, fields of
rich waving corn, with the scarlet poppy here and there interspersed, and the tall joaree, the grain of which is by the natives
made into chowpatties or bread, and the stalk used as forage
for elephants or camels; on our left were large plantations of
tobacco, reaching to the water's edge, sugar cane-brakes and
long rows of the chilli tree; hillocks covered with high feathery
grass, between which we observed large mango trees in topes or
groves. On reaching the outer edge of one of these, the havildar or
sergeant of the cavalry advance guard, was seen returning at full
gallop, with a report that a large party of horse, supposed to be
in the pay of Babagee Nikum—for we were now in his territory—
were approaching on our left flank, apparently gaining on us
from the direction of the river we had lately crossed. The
number of trees in the topes prevented our flank files or feelers
from discovering whether they were supported by infantry or
not. Preparations were immediately made to receive them.
The brigade changed front to the left; the rifles were thrown out
three hundred paces in advance to our new front, in skirmishing
order, with the howitzer, supported by two half-troops of cavalry.
The main body then deployed into line, on the Europeans, with

the remaining guns and cavalry on each flank. A strong reinforcement was also sent to the rear guard, for the protection of the hospital baggage, &c., and we were now all ready and eager for a dash at the foe. In this we were disappointed, for as soon as the commander of the party of horse caught sight of our line of skirmishers, he halted his men, lowered the standards, and galloped straight up to our brigadier, when it turned out that the supposed enemy was a regiment of Southern Mahratta irregular cavalry, sent to join us, by General D——, for out-post duties, guides, &c. They had missed us in the jungle, and crossed the river two miles to our left. The brigade having resumed its former order of march, we proceeded on our way, our new friends leading. The irregular corps are generally six hundred strong, with only two European officers, the first and second in command, the remainder are natives—respectively Russeldars, Jemadars, and Duffadars. It requires great interest to obtain command of these corps, as they are much sought after and highly valued. Recruits or volunteers for these regiments bring their own horses, saddles, and trappings with them, and receive pay monthly, according to the value of their horses, which they themselves have to feed and care for ; the uniforms, arms and equipments, are furnished by the State. They are dressed in dark-green tunics, pantaloons, high jack-boots, and red turbans, with a black pouch-belt across the shoulder, and armed with a double barrelled rifle, holster pistols, and native talwas or sabre. These men were very expert riders, I have seen many at full gallop bend lightly over on one side, and with the point of their sword, pick up from the ground, silk scarfs, or any other light article that might chance to be thrown in their path. The commissions of the native officers are usually obtained in the following manner :—the son of a Rajah, petty chief, or native gentleman, who can collect together fifty men, receives his appointment as a russeldar or captain; those who bring a lesser number of men, obtain subaltern rank. We had now been six hours on the march ; the obstructions and delays we had met with greatly fatigued the men, therefore, it was with much satisfaction that shortly after we perceived, snugly ensconced in a clump of trees, with its white walls gleaming in the sunlight, the small beechroer or tent of the commissariat conductor, who, with his stores, the quarter-master sergeants, line sergeants, camp color men and cooks, had started some hours in advance of us. The party being small, little delay was occasioned, as the goodly rows of spirit casks, bags of biscuit, rice, tea and sugar which were arranged, all ready for issue on our arrival, proved. The commissariat warrant officers, as a body, are a most intelligent, active, hard-working and thoroughly efficient class of men, selected from the European regiments for this department, in which they serve several years in their various grades, prior to receiving their warrant, necessarily, for although the commissariat officer has many highly important duties to perform, yet, on a campaign, the greater portion of the rough laborious part of the business devolves on the warrant officer, especially when they have to force provisions and forage, or press cattle or carriage, which involves great responsibility, and is at all times difficult to manage. Our camp this morning was pitched in the shape of a half-moon, or crescent, facing the road, with a fine mango tope at the rear, in which our baggage cattle were snugly tethered or picketed. An incident occurred to me in the afternoon, that nearly put a stop to all further recollections of this or any other campaign. A comrade who had been bathing in a small stream that ran through a shady dell, at the rear of the camp, informed me that he had noticed, on his way, a number of pea-fowl about the edges of the brook. This was sufficient inducement for me to visit the place. My chum, Bob O'Toole, delighted no doubt, with the idea of the chance of a good supper, gladly accompanied me. We soon came in sight of the game, which appeared rather timid, probably from the noise of the camp followers, who were stationed at no great distance from the locality. However, in a few minutes, a fine bird arose, at which Bob fired, knocking therefrom a quantity of feathers. The bird was wounded, but **not** sufficiently to prevent its reaching the upper branches of a tall tamarind tree, from whence it was unable to move. Being a better climber than my **companion**, I handed him my rifle, and quickly ascending the tree, soon got possession of the prize. While in the act of descending, I suddenly felt something touch me, and looking down, to my horror, found my legs encircled in the coils of a large hooded snake, the bite of which is said to be mortal. The creature's forked tongue **pro**truded from its mouth, with that peculiar hissing sound which it makes when about to strike its victim. Its wild glancing eyes were within a few inches of my throat, and in another second it would have been all over with me; but Providence willed it otherwise, for crack went the report of a rifle, and on the smoke clearing away, I found that my legs were again free, and the snake lying dead at the bottom of the tree. My friend Bob, as he was pleased to express it, had " taken the liberty of blowing the baste's head into smithereens." It was touch-and-go with me that time, but it did not, in the least, spoil my appetite that night for the **roast pea-fowl**, the obtaining of which had so nearly cost me my **life. Who** would be without a comrade in such a predicament. **I trust, in a** moment of danger, that I may always find at hand a Bob of the right kind; a brave, fearless, true-hearted Irishman, with a brogue thick and rich as buttermilk, although it was death, by the law, to even hint that he did not, to use his own words, "spake illegant English." He was rather above the middle height, a stout, well-proportioned figure, with handsome good-natured features; his hair was a bright red, but no one dared (on pain of excommunication,) insinuate such a thing; he always declared that " it was a rich and beautiful auburn, and much admired by the ladies." On the following morning the rouse or reveille did not sound until four o'clock, which we thought strange; but, from the unusual stir in the tents of the staff, it was evident that there was something in the wind, and so it turned out (for intelligence had been brought in during the previous night, by the party sent a few days before to endeavor to arrange matters with the rebel chief,) that the whole of the villages between the spot we occupied and Samunghur, had been compelled by their Rajahs to send all the men capable of bearing arms to serve under his standard, and that numbers of armed parties were moving about in the vicinity of the fort. Also, to our troops, the still more exciting news that the Samunghur chief intended to try his strength with us, never dreaming that he would have to contend with Europeans—much less with a force of such strength, and so well appointed. The commissariat stores, staff tents, private baggage and other things, that usually start some hours in advance, were now ordered to take their place in rear of the column, with the rest of the non-combatants, and securely guarded by a detachment of irregular cavalry, and two companies of native infantry. Our advance guard was likewise doubled, and every precaution taken against surprise. Ammunition was immediately served out—sixty rounds per man—to the infantry, with a liberal supply for the artillery. Officers exchanged their regulation swords for field sabres, and pistols appeared in the belts of many of the infantry. These warlike signs put us all in high spirits, and off we started in the full expectation of having a brush with the Mahrattas before the day was over. On this occasion we were not doomed to disappointment ; the villages that we passed on our way, confirmed what we had heard the night previous from the collector's party. With the exception of a few old men, and infirm women, they were otherwise deserted. I think we had marched some eight miles, when the brigadier, who, with his staff, had cantered on in advance, sent an aide-de-camp back at full speed, with an order for the rifles to move at the double to the front. The enemy were now in sight, and in a few minutes the sharp report of rifles plainly indicated that the game had commenced. The chief's men mustered pretty strong, and from the ridge of a hill, some half a mile from the fort, they kept up a smart fusilade for a short time with their matchlocks. But our fire soon began to tell upon them, and they gave way a little. The rifles were then ordered to charge, which they did in good style, driving the Mahrattas pell-mell before them. On the top of the ridge from which they had been driven, a 12-pound howitzer was put in position, supported by two companies of my regiment, but not in view of the enemy. Our commander did not wish them to know at that time that Europeans formed a portion of our force, in order to prevent them seeking the shelter of their fort before he could prove to them how dangerous a thing it was * to oppose disciplined soldiers, fully bent on conquest. At the same time, he determined to teach them a lesson they would not easily forget. The first shell from the howitzer nearly settled that point. A large party of the Rajah's principal officers and their friends had assembled on a small conical-shaped hill; they were quietly contemplating what was going on, and believed themselves beyond reach of our pieces, having no thought or anticipation of our artillery—the rifles alone being visible. This party soon caught the eye of our general, who ordered the howitzer to be laid for their especial benefit. This was done accordingly, and after a few minutes a mass of iron fell plump into the midst of the group, but without doing any direct damage, to the no small astonishment of the enemy, who, although startled at first, from their ignorance of artillery projectiles, doubtless concluded all danger was now over. They gathered around the treacherous shell, the fuse of which had been cut too long, and while yet burning one of the party held it up for the inspection of the others, when it suddenly exploded, killing thirteen, and wounding several. The remainder fled in great consternation to the fort, from which place they quickly returned the compliment by sending some round shot flying over our heads, but in such a wild manner that it was quite evident no aim had been taken. While we were thus engaged, our main

10

body were pitching camp a little to our right rear, but quite out of range of the guns of the fort; the tents of the Europeans being placed nearest to the scene of action. The fire from the fort soon ceased, as they became aware, how perfectly useless it was throwing their old iron about in that loose fashion. During the time we occupied the brow of the ridge the commissariat conductor made his appearance with some biscuit and a keg of arrack, which was very acceptable to the men, who had had nothing to eat since four o'clock the previous evening.

CHAPTER VIII.

WHEN the worthy warrant officer had finished **issuing an allow-ance** to each man, **and** was about packing up the overplus, a round shot from the enemy passed between him and one of his coolies, and so near **their heads** that they bolted off down the hill in great trepidation; indeed, as **though** his Satanic majesty was tripping at their heels. They went helter-skelter over stones and bushes, creeks and gutters, to the no small amusement of the lookers-on, who enjoyed their hasty and undignified flight. But our delight was much enhanced **by gaining possession** of the spirit cask, which in their speedy **departure they had** quite forgotten. We seized **it with great eagerness, and** soon made ourselves masters of **its contents.** Our matchlock-firing enemy, who for some time had been retiring, **keeping** up a desultory fire as they proceeded, and disappeared behind bushes and **huts,** situated within a **short distance of the walls of the fort.** For this reason it **was** not considered prudent just then to ad-vance any nearer. A large number of the enemy suddenly appeared on a sugar-loaf hill, to the right of the fort; they were amusing themselves by firing into our camp, and disturbing its serenity. We now got the opportunity we longed for. Two of our companies were ordered to take the hill at all hazards, in order to place a couple of guns in position on its top; for in this position they commanded the **fort as well as our camp.** Moving off at the double, in skirmishing **order,** we very nearly surrounded the base of the **hill, and at once opened a sharp fire on** the rascals, **who fell** in great numbers. **As** we steadily advanced towards **the top of** the hill, **they** gave **us a** parting volley, and endeavoured to gain **the** cover of their stronghold, but we were too sharp for them. Hastily closing on our centre, we gave them one volley, and afterwards charged. Our bayonets did fearful execution, and very few lived to gain the fort, from whence their friends viewed the scene in horror and dismay. Our loss was seven killed and nineteen wounded. After getting the guns into position, a party of native infantry relieved us, and we returned to camp pretty well tired with our day's work. The killed in the morning skirmish amounted to three privates of the rifles, one havildar, two nignes, and eight privates wounded. In the evening we performed the last sad rites for those who had fallen in the fore-part of the day. Those severely wounded were sent under escort without delay to Belgaum. The slightly wounded, after a short interval in our field hospital, (where every aid that skill or medicine could afford, was promptly and carefully administered), were soon about again. That night our camp was visited by one of those terrific storms which are only known to occur in tropical climates. The rain fell in torrents, causing a complete deluge; vivid flashes of lightning blazed forth, illuminating everything with startling brilliancy, followed by deafening peals of thunder, shaking the very earth, and vibrating for miles around. Combined with the wind, which at the time, blew a perfect hurricane, it compelled the stout soldiers' hearts to quake, as they stood wet and shivering, listening to the angry elements. Tents were blown down, and their contents scatterd far and near. Horses broke loose, terrified by the fearful uproar, and a scene of wild confusion ensued, that baffles all description. The storm having abated on the approach of daylight, we worked with right good will to arrange our things with something like order and comfort. Many a laugh and joke was indulged at the expense of some unfortunate comrade, who had been placed in some ludicrous position, or suffered more severely than the rest. In a few hours all effects of the storm had passed away, and the elements resumed their former quietude. Pickets were now established along the whole front, and right abreast of the fort. Our force divided into five flying camps, the better to observe the enemy, and to relieve our guards ; for it now appeared plain, that Babagee Nikum had no idea of surrendering, and we could make no impression on stone walls with our light guns. In reply to the General's despatch, he was informed that a complete breaching battery of eighteen pounders, together with nine mortars, scaling-ladders, and other requisites, would be sent out with as little delay as possible, and that he was to surround the fort, and prevent any relief reaching the besieged, as there were rumours of a general disaffection shewing itself throughout the Southern Mahratta country. We had now plenty to do to watch the fort, and scour the adjacent woods. One of our picket-houses, was called Picket Dangerous, from its exposed position, or Gun Picket— a long low building on the right hand side of the road leading to one of the principal gates of the fort, but too close to the walls to enable the enemy to depress their guns sufficiently to bear upon it. However, the enemy kept up such a constant matchlock fire from the loop-holes, that we lost during the four weeks that we held this position, no less than two officers, three sergeants, twenty-seven rank and file killed, one officer, two ser- geants, and thirty-two rank and file wounded. One of the officers killed, was the affianced husband of the young lady whose last farewell (for such it proved to be) we had witnessed on our leaving Belgaum. A sad trial for one so young ; deeply attached to him as she appeared to be. He was in the act of laying the gun at the picket-house, when he was shot through the head, and died instantly. Poor T—— was a great favorite with his brother officers, and they all felt sorry to lose him. Nor did our foes escape scot free, for no sooner did one of them appear at an embrasure, than he was made a target of; a great many were cut off in this way. Our guard consisted of two officers, two sergeants, and fifty-four rank and file, with eight artillery men, relieved every forty-eight hours. From the guard-room to the opposite side of the road we erected a sand bag battery ;

well do I remember its construction. It cost us fifteen killed and wounded. I was on guard at the time it was commenced. One pitch dark night, under the direction and guidance of one of the warrant officers of the Public Works Department, with a party of Sappers and Miners, had not been long at work when the rain fell heavily, accompanied by sheet lightning, which revealed occasionally our working party to the enemy. They immediately commenced, and kept up such a heavy fire from behind their stone walls, and as flash succeeded flash we had frequently to suspend all operations for a time. However, before daylight, the battery was completed, and the muzzle of a howitzer run through it. This was loaded with grape, in case of a sally from the gate. One evening, while on sentry over this gun, and just as it was getting dark, I fancied I heard a grinding sort of sound at one of the embrasures, just opposite the guard-room. As it continued for some time, I began to feel suspicious that the enemy were at some of their tricks, and cautiously creeping near enough to the wall, where I fancied the sound came from, perceived that a couple of large stones had been forced out of the lower face of the embrasure, which would enable them to bring a gun to bear on our picket. Regaining the cover of the battery, without being discovered, I alarmed the guard, and, while they were turning out, I watched the embrasure, and saw that they were loading a gun. While their gunner was in the act of ramming down the charge of powder, I took deliberate aim at him. I missed the man, but the ball struck the sponge-staff about the centre, cutting it completely in half. This, for a time, stopped the loading, and before they knew what to do, a shower of grape-shot from our howitzer fell amongst them, doing considerable damage. It was followed by a round shot, which struck the gun at the muzzle, dismounted it from its wooden carriage, and rendered it unfit, at least for a time, for further use. The following day, on the arrival of our relief, I was again on sentry at the gun ; the man that took my post, had scarcely been there a minute, indeed—I had not **reached the guard,** when I heard— him exclaim, " I have got it,"·and, **looking round,** saw him reel over inside the sand-bag battery. **It was** well for him that he did so, otherwise he would have been **completely** riddled before any assistance could have been rendered him. **The enemy were** more alert, and did greater execution during the time of our relieving guard, as during that time we were exposed to a flank fire from the numerous loop-holes in the walls. Two bullets struck him at the same instant ; one through the right arm, breaking the bone just above the elbow ; the other, in the fleshy part of the thigh ; on this man's recovery, he was sent to England, claiming a pension of nine pence per day. He had been five years in the service. The European portion of the brigade was now ordered to shift camp, and occupy ˙**a more** prominent position, on the right rear angle of **the fort, from** which spot it was intended we should **assault** the place, and effect a breach in the large round bastion at **that** point. **In** securing this position, we had **a very smart skirmish,** as there was a large petta or village running **from the rear gate to** the foot of the hill we wished to obtain. This was unknown to us until the morning in question ; it **was** occupied by the enemy, who gave us sharp work for a couple of hours, before we could **drive** them from the shelter of the houses. They then took refuge in the fort, the gate of which was opened to receive them. We were not strong enough to try the chance of entering and contesting the fort with them, therefore we contented ourselves with the capture of the petta, and the loot or plunder that fell into our hands, consisting principally of cash, brass and copper vessels, silk, grain, **&c.** We then established a couple of pickets, with a chain of sentries which reached round three sides of the place ; why the other angle was **not secured, I never** knew, but no doubt there **was** a sufficient reason for it. So much having been effected, we returned and pitched **our** camp on the plateau of the hill, **which** commanded **a fine** view of the stronghold and its surroundings.

Keeping watch and ward over the enemy's works proved rather a fatiguing affair, with little or no excitement, save the exchanging of shot with the people on the walls. A slight incident now and then occurred to relieve the dull monotony of routine; there was one which caused much laughter at the time. One day while pushing our pickets nearer to the rear gate, we came to a large house, and on forcing the door, the officer in command of the party fancied he heard a strange noise, which indicated that something was moving clumsily within. The idea immediately flashed across his mind that probably some of the enemy were concealed in the house; imagine his chagrin when ordering his men to fire a volley into the building, and on entering, the enemy turned out to be three fine bullocks that had been left there tied up by their owners, who, on hearing of our approach, had fled. A story never loses by repetition, and this shared the usual fate ; our encounter with the bullocks became a laugh and jest in the camp, and afterwards, whenever an enemy was seen, and aim about to be taken, the remark : " Are you certain it is not a bullock ?" was sure to follow. In the upper part of the house we found great quantities of onions, salt, and rice, together with a number of new chatties or earthen cooking pots. No sooner were we comfortably settled in our new position, than we killed and cut up one of the animals, made fires at the back part of the premises, and soon had a glorious supply of soup, and boiled meat. During the time that we remained here, one of our company, a fine young fellow named Matlow, a Herefordshire man, and a thorough soldier, had a narrow escape. As he was about to draw water from a well, in the next compound or garden, he was suddenly pounced upon by five Mahrattas, armed with the long two-handed swords of the country ; but little did they imagine what herculean strength and courage they had to contend with ; quite unprepared for such an attack, and alone as he stood, he was more than a match for them. Coolly raising his musket he shot the nearest, bayonetted the second, and then

clubbing his musket dashed out the brains of a third. **The other**
two simultaneously turned and fled, aghast at the fate of their
comrades ; it was well for the brave Matlow that they did **so,**
for he fell a short time afterwards, having fainted from loss of
blood. He received eleven wounds in different parts of his body ;
these, on examination, proved to be merely flesh wounds, and he
was soon all right again. I have related this brave act to show
the immense superiority of the European over the native, in
those most essential of all qualities in a soldier, viz., coolness and
courage. Our chain of sentries was composed of half European
and half native troops ; every alternate man being a Sepoy. One
day, when the bullets from the fort were rather more plentiful
than usual, a Sepoy, who was stationed between a man named
Hall, of our corps, and myself ; finding it getting too hot for
him, turned round and bolted towards camp ; but he did not run
far, for Hall deliberately faced about and shot him dead. The
act was a rash one, but the fellow's cowardice merited it, **and as**
none but myself saw the transaction, it passed without comment.
It was amusing to witness the expedients resorted to by our
cooks, to escape the fire from the fort, as they returned to camp
from the various guards. Many of them would tie the large flat
bottomed tops or dishes of the camp kettles on their back,
place the kettles over their heads, form up in Indian file,
and run off at full speed from the point of danger ; but as they
could not see before them they would frequently tumble one
over the other—roll and bawl in great terror—then regain their
legs, only to act the same farce over again, and in this grotesque
manner reach camp, to the no small amusement of the lookers-on,
who laughed and shouted, as they made their singular looking
summersaults. Many of them were wounded, but I do not
remember to have heard that any were killed, although daily
exposed to danger. They were hard worked, but received good
pay while on field service. At the foot of the hill, and immediately in rear of our camp, the country was covered with a

11

jungle of low thick brushwood, in which there were numerous
small wild pigs, striped somewhat like an Indian squirrel, varying
in weight from twelve to sixteen pounds ; these are considered
tolerably good eating. Now as nothing in the shape of food comes
amiss to a soldier on campaign, our men made great havoc
among them, and rare sport at times we had. I remember one
morning as some of our fellows were returning, laden with spoil,
two of the animals contrived to effect their escape, and ran, pursued by their late captors, into the lines of the native cavalry,
who were chiefly Mahommedans. Fancy the horror and indignation
of these men, for what pork is to a Jew, pig is to a Mussulman,
an utter abomination. It unfortunately happened that the per-
verse pigs would take to the forbidden ground, and dashed right
among a number of men engaged in cooking their morning
meal, upsetting everything right and left, to the no small consternation and dismay of the followers of Mahomed, who, on
seeing the Europeans close at their heels, fancied that it was a
planned affair, and immediately sprang away for their swords, to
revenge the supposed insult, and direful would have been the
consequences, but for the cool self-possession of a colour-sergeant
of ours, who happened to be passing at the time, he, at once fell
the men in, and before the troopers could return with their weapons
had doubled them back to our camp. The commanding offi ce
gave them a severe reprimand, and so ended the affair; but it
made our men more careful in future, how they approached too
near to the natives' cooking places. They are extremely particular
in cooking; each man clears a space of ground generally about
six yards in circumference; he, then, with earth and stones,
builds a fire-place, and the spot immediately around he spreads
over with a thin coating of cow dung, which the heat of the sun
bakes. The place is then carefully swept clean, and after
prayers it is consecrated for cooking, for they are so
bigoted that should the shadow of a Christian, whom they consider only one degree above a pig, fall on any of their culinary,

utensils, while using them, they will, if made of earthenware, break them, and if the implement is made of copper or brass, as is generally the case, they will throw **away** the food, and take the vessel to the river in order to wash and scour off the pollution. We now received intelligence that the siege train, so long looked for, was within eight miles of us, but stuck fast in the rice fields, the late rains having flooded them for miles. Fatigue parties from every corps were sent to assist in bringing in the long eighteen and thirty-two pounders. This was a severe tug, and had it not been for the assistance from our elephants, we should not have succeeded. It was managed in this way : four pair of spare bullocks were hooked to each gun ; two men placed at each wheel ; then one of the elephants marched up to the muzzle of the gun. He seemed then to understand what was expected of him, for at a certain motion from its mahout or driver, he would place his trunk round the mouth of the cannon, and lift it completely out of the mud ; at the same time the goad and lash **were** effectually applied **to** the bullocks, who, by this means were urged forward, dragging the gun about thirty yards to the front. By a repetition of these movements, the battery was at length got to the hard ground, at the foot of the hill, from which it was intended to open fire upon the walls of Samunghur. Many singular anecdotes of the surprising sagacity of the elephant had been related to me, by men who had lived the greater part of their lives in India. On one occasion I became an eye-witness to a remarkable instance of acuteness of observation in one of those usually docile animals. I had been conveying baggage belonging to some troops who were changing their station from Poona to Ahmednuggur, by means of elephants, camels and mules. One morning, on my return march, I had ridden on in advance of the cattle, for the purpose of procuring their forage, which arrangement having been effected, I betook myself to the Dawk Bungalo, or halting place **for** European travellers, to get breakfast, and during this time my cattle came in. Knowing

that there was plenty of game in the neighbourhood I threw my
gun across my shoulder and passed through the cattle lines on
my way to the nearest cover. On passing near the elephants,
one of them attracted my attention by a peculiar kind of scream;
on going up to the animal, he gently and quietly upset a
heap of flour cakes that had been set before him by his keeper.
The cakes rolled about at my feet, he at the same time uttering
another scream. Scarcely knowing what to make of this strange
conduct, I counted the cakes, and discovered that there were four
short of the usual complement. No sooner had I finished count-
ing them than the elephant turned slowly round to the keeper,
whose duty it was to prepare its food, and struck him to the
earth with his trunk, breaking two of his ribs; thus punishing the
man for depriving him of four pounds of cakes for his own
benefit. This he had in reality done. The animal then gave a
sort of grunt, as if quite satisfied with his performance; evidently
knowing that I was in authority over the keeper, he **eyed me**
with **a look,** as much as to indicate that he was able to
settle accounts with those who defrauded him; then gathering up
his cakes he quietly began his meal. It is almost needless to add
that the mahout or keeper was discharged on his recovery, and
before leaving confessed having taken the flour for his own
use. The daily food or rations of these animals are as follows:
two hundred pounds of forage, consisting chiefly of jowaree, the
green tops of the sugar cane, and branches of young jungle
trees; four ounces of ghee or clarified butter, two ounces of salt
and twenty-four pounds of flour, made up into one-pound cakes,
and for the baking of which fifteen pounds of wood was allowed
for one animal. At that time each elephant was allowed half-a-
gallon of proof arrack per day; but this the government discontinued of late years. Getting the breaching guns and mortar
battery up the hill, and into position was another long and hard
day's work, and was managed by means of fatigue parties; but as
patience and perseverance overcome many difficulties, every thing

was shortly in readiness to commence the assault on the fortress. The general now decided, as a preliminary measure, to shell the place, and this was effectively done by firing salvos from our mortars and howitzers every quarter of an hour during the night. Our officers observed, by means of their field-glasses, that in one part of the place there was a number of houses of a better description than the generality of native habitations; these they determined should be speedily destroyed. Accordingly, several live carcases, or hollow shells filled with combustible and inflammable matter, were discharged on the chupper or thatched roofs of the buildings, and in a short time a bright blaze shot up from several places at once, but the fire was put out by the inhabitants, who swarmed up in hundreds to extinguish the flames. However, we were not to be baffled in this way; therefore the remainder of the mortars and howitzers were laid for the dwellings—these were loaded with grape and canister. The carcases were first fired, then as the enemy were engaged in quenching the flames, the other missiles were sent with fatal precision among them, by which means hundreds were killed, and the remainder had the mortification of seeing their houses destroyed, or else risk their lives by endeavouring to save their property. The following day the large half-circular bastion at the left rear angle of the fort was selected as the spot where the the breach was to be made, and the batteries opened upon it in grand style, but after several hours practice it appeared to have suffered very little from the bombardment. It was now evening, and it became a question with the officers whether it would not be better to try the strength of one of the other towers. While they were discussing this important subject, a shot from one of the batteries hit the outer curve of the bastion, and glancing off, struck the curtain or wall about half-way between the two corner bastions and near the parapet, bringing down a great quantity of masonry ; this decided the question. A flag of truce was, at this juncture, seen on the battlement, and the Rajah sent to say that he requested a suspension of hostilities for forty-eight hours, to consider terms, with a view to surrender. Our reply granted twenty-four hours, and while waiting his answer we were joined by a regiment of native cavalry, and a troop of Madras European horse artillery, with six guns ; they also brought the news that several other petty States were in open revolt, and that a very large force was being assembled to reinforce us, and would join in a few days—as it was expected we should have to scour the Southern Mahratta country, from one end to the other. The truce on the part of the Rajah was only a *ruse* to gain time ; as we afterwards found out that he was in hourly expectation of a reinforcement of about two thousand men.

CHAPTER IX.

AT the expiration of the twenty-four hours, the fort opened
fire on our line of sentinels, upon which the whole of the breaching guns were turned on the curtain, to effect a new breach, and
our light artillery kept playing on the large bastion to deceive
the enemy into the belief that we intended storming in two
places. We battered away all that night, and by ten o'clock on
the following day, the reconnoitering party previously sent out,
returned, and the chief engineer reported the breach practicable.
Immediate preparations were now made for carrying the place
by storm. Our guards and pickets were strengthened, and the
line of sentries doubled during the night. The whole of the
cavalry formed a circle round the fortifications, just out of reach
of their guns, for the purpose of intercepting any that might
endeavour to escape during the assault. The rifles, with light
companies of the other native regiment, were stationed at the
foot of the hill, to the right and left of the breach, concealed from
the view of those on the walls, by a long hedge of tall, prickly
pear bushes. The storming party were told off, as follows :—
two hundred of my regiment leading, three hundred of each of
the native regiments, with about two hundred dismounted
troopers belonging to the cavalry. From this party, volunteers
were called out for the forlorn hope, as those that carry the
scaling ladders are called. The horse-artillery guns were so
placed that they could shower grape and canister into the breach,
directly over our heads, as we ascended. Now, we anxiously
awaited for daylight, to commence the attack. An order had
been issued that not a shot was to be fired on any account, by
any part of the force, until a given pre-concerted signal, which

was three blue lights, sent up in rapid succession from the top of
Sugar-loaf Hill, to the right of the fort.   During this time, the
enemy were not idle, for they anticipated our attack, and all their
available guns were brought to bear on the two breaches, loaded
with every description of missile—they used great quantities of
rod-iron, cut up into pieces about an inch in length.   All the
loopholes were bristling with matchlocks, and the battlements
were lined with hundreds of men armed with swords, pistols and
creeses.   Parties were also stationed in the barbican, with large
two-handed slings, for hurling pieces of rock and large stones
down on the heads of the storming party ; they had likewise
dug a mine beneath the breach of the large circular bastion,
believing that to be the place chosen for the grand attack.
In this they were sadly mistaken, and suffered severely at this
spot, as will be seen hereafter.   About half-past four in the
morning, the eagerly expected blue lights shot high into the air,
illuminating the whole scene for a few brief seconds—the old
fort with its frowning battlements, thickly lined with guns,
ready prepared to belch forth its murderous fire, and the dark
swarthy faces of its defenders, betraying an expression of eagerness and terror at the prospect of the swiftly approaching
conflict.   As their lights died out, the guard and pickets opened
a heavy fire upon the walls, the chain of sentries taking it up,
and blazing away at every form discernible to them during the
imperfect light of the early dawn.   The roar of our heavy
ordnance as it thundered forth from the height, pouring a
perfect hurricane of shot and shell into the fated place, seemed
to shake the very ground.   The storming party moved down to
the base of the hill, under cover of heavy volleys from the
rifles and light companies ; but, on reaching the foot of the
breach, we found that our ladders were not required, the breach
being so complete, that you might almost have driven an artillery
waggon through it with little or no difficulty ; therefore, casting
down the ladders, we prepared to ascend.   The guns of the horse

artillery sending a deadly shower of grape, canister, and spherical case over our heads, which would for a moment completely clear the mouth of the breach, and then began the tug of war. Fixing our bayonets, and with a shout or cheer, such as no native of whatever caste or color, can hear without terror ; up we dashed, and, as we advanced, the whole of this face of the fort became a perfect blaze of fire. Showers of shot swept through our ranks like hail, doing sad mischief; at the same time down came pieces of rock and large stones, crushing or mutilating many a fine fellow that the bullet had spared. The false attack at the large bastion was a complete success ; the party kept up a rolling fusilade from the base of the tower, without entering upon the breach. By this means, the enemy were divided, rendering the real attack less difficult. On our arrival at the top of the breach, there was a short hand-to-hand fight, but the swords of the Mahrattas gave way before the bayonets of the impetuous troops that formed the storming party. A large portion fell back on their reserve at the other bastion, while the remainder scattered through the fort, pursued in all directions by our men. On entering the fort, we divided into three parties ; one, the strongest, went to the left, to rout the foe at the bastion : another, to the front in pursuit of the Rajah and his principal officers ; and the third to the right, to clear the rampart and secure prisoners. I turned to the left, with my musket at the charge, and in passing a small watch tower, partially destroyed by a shell, I encountered a tall native, who had been hid behind a large stone, and who evidently thought my piece was unloaded, and under the impression that I would be an easy prey, boldly seized my musket with one hand, and deliberately unfixed the bayonet with the other, but he had " reckoned without his host," for I shot him through the head before he could raise his sword. Having replaced my bayonet, I pushed on without delay, for at that moment a terrific explosion shook this part of the fort. The mine that had been constructed for our reception had suddenly

12

exploded, by what means no one could tell, shattering the tower, and blowing into the air upwards of three hundred of the enemy, who had crowded into it. Our men continued to pour in an indiscriminate fire of musketry on the remnant of the foe. What was left of the tower and barbican was now covered with blood and full of the dead. The glare thrown by the flames of burning houses upon the ensanguined earth ; the powder besmeared faces of the combatants ; the groans of the dying; the clashing of weapons and the heart-breaking appeals for water or assistance of the severely wounded, pourtrayed a scene of horror to the young soldiers who, for the first time, were engaged in deadly conflict, not likely to be effaced from their recollection for many a month. By seven o'clock, the "cease fire" sounded, and the "assembly" rang out clear and loud from the large open square in the principal bazaar. There we found a large number of prisoners ; but Babagee Nikum and several other influential men had made their escape, when they found the day was going against them. They accomplished their flight by means of a subterranean passage that led from the Cutchiree, or principal house used by the chiefs while transacting business with the ryots or landholders under their rule, to a small Hindoo temple— an unsightly heap of ruins in the thickest part of the jungle— about half a mile to the rear of the fort, whose isolated position was its greatest protection, eliciting neither observation nor suspicion. Guards were now placed, and the dismounted troopers were stationed at the breaches to prevent the camp followers, who, for the sake of plunder, had entered in rear of us—but as may easily be imagined of such cowardly wretches—kept at a safe distance, anxiously waiting an opportunity to return to camp with their plunder, which, however, they were in most cases made to surrender. We remained about two hours in the fort, during which time I managed to pick up valuables to the amount of two hundred rupees, or £20 stg. A circumstance occurred upon our leaving the fortress, which will illustrate far better than any

lengthy description, how completely, any instructions given by a
European, in those days, were carried out by native soldiers,
no matter how inhuman the order might be, or just or unjust.
Quite a number of prisoners were being brought in from the
walls by a havildar's guard ; one of these fellows proved rather
restive, and was arguing with the commander. A sergeant of
ours, who happened to be passing at the time, noticed this, and
told them to move on, but the man would not go. " What shall I
do ?" cried the havildar. " Cut his head off," was the short reply of
the sergeant, as he left the spot. The order was decisive, and the
native non-commissioned officer drew his sword-bayonet, and in
an instant the head of the prisoner fell to the ground. By this
time the wounded of our party had been carefully conveyed to
the hospitals, and the bodies of those who had fallen were sent
to the camp for interment. We were now ordered to return to
our various quarters, and glad was I to escape from this place ;
for so many of the enemy had fallen during the siege, whose
bodies had been thrown into dry wells, for want of time to
burn or bury them, that the stench arising therefrom, was in-
tolerable. By ten, a.m., we were again in our tents, well satisfied
with our success, but of course much fatigued by our active exertions. On the same day, our guards, pickets, &c., were likewise
withdrawn from the outside of the walls, leaving but one strong
guard within the entrance of the principal gate. Fatigue parties were set to work, filling up with lime and earth the wells
into which the enemy's dead had been thrown, and such
other sanitary steps taken as were considered necessary on the
occasion ; and before nightfall, matters in the fort among the
native population, went on pretty much as usual. In our camp,
preparations were being made for the morning's meal. " Now,
Bob, my fine fellow, just step to the cook, and see what you can
obtain in the shape of breakfast. Here, take this rupee, it is one
that I got in the fort this morning. You know it is your turn
to forage, and in the meantime, as I am very hungry, I will

try if I can procure a couple of drams of arrack." " Musha, but it would be a quare male that I would go a hen's race for, this blessed morning, bedad, the trotters are knocked clane off me, crawling up to that infarnal houl in the wall, after them black-guard nagurs ; bad luck to them, every day they see a paving stone, and every day they don't. But Ned, avic, can you raise a golliogue, for I am dying for a toothful of the crature ?" exclaimed Bob, eyeing the rupee that I had thrown on the ground near him, but he did not move a peg. " I tell you what it is, my boy, if you don't find a beefsteak, or something of that sort pretty sharp, not a drop of grog do you get from me, as it is a scarce article in the camp to-day." " And if he does not, it will be the first time I ever knew O'Toole to refuse doing anything in reason, or out of it, when there is a chance of a glass of grog to be got by it," chimed in a comrade, as I rose and left the tent for the liquor, which I had been promised by the canteen sergeant, in exchange for a silver mounted creese, which I had taken from one of the enemy that morning. Returning shortly after, I found my chum fast asleep on a peg bag, underneath the outer flap of the tent ; I, therefore, carefully put away in my pouch one of the drams and drank the other, at the same time eating a few pieces of hard biscuit that I found in my haversack. I was about to visit the cook with a view to breakfast, when the " alarm " and " assembly" sounded, to turn out the whole, quickly followed by the " double." In a few minutes all was life and bustle ; each one was eager to know why we, who had been so hotly engaged all the morning, should not be allowed time to rest and get our breakfast in peace. It was soon explained. About two thousand of the enemy were approaching. This party had been sent by the Rajah of Kolapoor, a large independent State, some fifty miles distant, that had joined the standard of revolt, for the pur-pose of raising the siege, or in any other way to assist Babagee Nikum ; but they appeared a day after the fair, the place having fallen that morning. The advancing force was about

seven miles distant, marching through a long valley, but not
observable from our camp. The news had been brought in by our
cavalry scouts, and our General determined to meet them
in the open plain as soon as they should debouch from the
valley. Hence the alarm sounded, for it required great expedition
to enable us to reach the spot in time; but we turned out as sharp
as possible, some with, and others without, their morning meal;
myself amongst the latter. Our force consisted of one troop of
Madras Horse Artillery; one regiment of cavalry; about one
thousand native infantry; and three hundred of the second
Bombay European regiment. Within twenty minutes of the
sounding of the first bugle we were *en route*; the cavalry taking
their way through a deep nullah, or dry bed of a river, the high
banks of which hid them as they advanced; the artillery and
infantry availed themselves of the fields of jowaree, that stretched
out some miles to our right front, and completely screened us
from all observation. In this manner we proceeded until we
arrived at the banks of the river Gotoor, the opposite bank of
which was steep and rugged. A reconnoitering party was now
sent across to look out for the enemy, as well as to see how the
land lay. They soon returned, and from their information it was
determined to give them battle on the other side of the river.
They were not more than half a mile off, and it was evident from
the careless manner of their marching, that they were entirely
ignorant of our presence in their vicinity, believing us to be
actively engaged before Samunghur. The cavalry was first sent
across, with instructions to get to the rear of the Mahrattas if
possible, without being noticed, and follow them with a view of
driving them to cross the river, and, likewise, in case they should
discover us, to cut off their retreat, should they attempt to escape
before we could engage them. Our infantry then crossed, forming
upon the bank in columns of subdivisions, and advanced in a dia-
gonal direction to our right front some four hundred yards,
wheeled into line by subdivisions on the centre, right forward,

left back, which brought us under cover of a fine prickly pear
hedge, that effectually concealed us. The artillery, on crossing,
wheeled a little to the left, and advancing about one hundred
and twenty yards, entered a small opening surrounded by milk
bushes, and took up such a position as enabled them to open fire
on any body of troops who might attempt to cross the river in
the direction of Samunghur. Our reserve infantry and cavalry
did not cross, but was stationed in a corn field near the ford,
ready to act in any way, when called on. An aide-de-camp now
returned to say that the cavalry had succeeded without discovery
in gaining the position assigned to them; all was now completely
arranged, and the unconscious foe hurried on to their destruction.
The day was magnificent, and the scene as fair as may be, it was
just after the monsoon; the great thirst of nature had been
assuaged; the now refreshed earth teemed with vegetation,
which had burst forth with a rapidity known only in tropical
climates; thousands of parrots and bright coloured birds fluttered
from bough to bough in the mango topes, which dotted the
plain; whilst high in the air, like mere specks among the few
fleecy, lazily-drifting clouds, whirled here and there a kite, that
camp scavenger of the East, as if in anticipation of an approaching banquet. A gentle breeze rustled the bright green foliage,
impregnating the atmosphere with the perfume from blossoms
and flowers; the drowsy hum of myriads of insects, mingled
itself with the murmuring of the clear waters as they trickled
over their pebbly bed at the ford, producing a sensation of delicious languor and repose. I have it all before my mind's eye
now : alas, that so fair a landscape should be destined so soon to
be desecrated by a sanguinary drama. Were these my feelings
or my reflections then ? I regret to say they were not; my only
sensation at the time was that of a restless and feverish anxiety,
lest the foe should escape us. It was not until the enemy had
arrived within a hundred and fifty yards that they became
aware of their danger. Observing only the right wing of the

native infantry, they immediately formed in three lines—for they had no artillery or cavalry—and in this manner awaited our attack. They were not long kept in suspense, for we poured upon them a few volleys by companies from both flanks of the native regiments, followed by a heavy file firing from the muskets of three hundred of my regiment, which their first line replied to for a few minutes, by heavy discharges of their matchlocks; but no sooner did they observe the Europeans, than they appeared panic stricken and confused; their lines broke up, and they prepared to retreat. To their dismay, however, our light cavalry appeared in their rear; the open space in their front seeming clear, they at once dashed down to the river in hopes of getting the water between us and them, as the only evident means of escaping. This our General had foreseen, and this move was their destruction, for as soon as the first of the party had commenced crossing, our guns, which until then had remained silent, opened upon them with grape and canister, mowing them down like corn. The cavalry then swept through, sabreing all that came within their reach; it was a fearful slaughter. The remnant threw down their arms and crouched like beaten hounds at our feet; some two or three hundred, however, effected their escape through the rice fields. We left about seven hundred dead on the field, and forming into a hollow square, marched about five hundred prisoners back to camp. Our loss on this day was comparatively small, seventeen of all ranks killed; and one European officer, four native officers, thirteen sergeants and havildars, and fifty nine rank and file of all corps engaged, wounded. The return march sorely tried us all. Our morning's fatigue at the fort, and subsequent march and engagement without rest or food nearly knocked me up; indeed, were it not for the dram of arrack previously taken, I think I should have succumbed. O'Toole had fallen out to obtain a drink of water, as he was almost exhausted, and he was fortunate enough to get a lift nearly all the way back on one of the artillery limbers. It is a trite and hackneyed remark regarding excitement, that it is wonderful how soon hunger, thirst and fatigue, are forgotten, whilst under its influence in an engagement or pursuit, and in proportion to the intensity of the feeling the more terrible is the reaction. Our prisoners suffered severely ; they had been making forced marches, and now, with the prospect of a gaol before them; numbers wounded, and sinking with exhaustion, their state must have been anything but enviable. They were a heterogeneous throng ; some small farmers holding their land under the Kolapoor Rajah, and bound to assist him in his forays, no matter against whom ; field labourers and hundreds of bud-mashes or lazy, evil-disposed persons, who have everything to gain by rebellion, and nothing to lose, except their worthless lives ; plunder being their chief means of support. It was past seven in the evening before we got to our tents, and after a good meal, and glass of grog, it was not long till rest and sleep rendered us for a time oblivious of the stirring scenes of the day. The time we remained here, after the reduction of the place, was occupied by the Sappers and Miners, assisted by large parties from the different corps, in dismantling the fort and rendering it useless as an asylum to the rebellious or disaffected, who might seek its shelter on our quitting that part of the country. In about ten days we received orders to pass on to a fort called, if I remember right, Ang-Ghur ; it was small, and situated on a hill some twenty miles to the south-east of Samunghur. A number of rebels, probably those that escaped from the plain amongst them, had established themselves there, and were rava-ging the country in its immediate vicinity ; plundering and burn-ing the small villages and dwellings of the more peaceably inclined inhabitants, who had as yet taken no part in the rebellion. The Mahratta country, previous to its subjugation by the East India Company, was in a state somewhat similar to our own during the feudal ages, when every baron or chief held his own by virtue of his sword, accepted terms at his gate, and made war on his weaker **neighbour when** avarice or personal revenge prompted him to do so. Hence the number of forts or strongholds that are to be seen on nearly every range of hills throughout the country. The East India Company, after conquering these petty princes individually, confirmed them in their authority, upon their paying tribute, allowing them to make war on each other as they thought proper, and in no way interfering, unless specially called on by some weaker Rajah for assistance and protection against the raids of some stronger neighbour—for which assistance you may depend, the Rajah had to pay in good round terms. At last the Samunghur Rajah having subdued all the neighbouring principalities, began, as het hought, to feel himself sufficiently powerful to resist the authority of the East India Company itself, set it at defiance, and save an immense yearly tax; hence the Mahratta war. In two days we **reached** the place, but the birds had flown; doubtless **the** recollection of their late disaster had led them to think that discretion was the better part of valor, for they had hastily evacuated the fort, and dispersing, sought their individual safety as best they could. We halted here for a week, spiked the few remaining guns; burnt the carriages, blew up the magazine, and threw all the shot that **we** found into the valley at the rear of the hill, it being perfectly useless to us, or, in fact, to any body as a projectile. This little affair having been brought to a conclusion, we again started in pursuit of more of these gentry that were disturbing the country in the direction of the large fortified village of Neepanee on the road to Kolapore. Three days after leaving this place we camped near the plain where our late fight had taken place; the prowling hyena and barking jackal had, with the assistance **of** the carrion **kite,** performed their work effectually. Human **bones laid in all** directions, and ghastly grinning **skulls, some of which** still retained the long scalp lock. These alone marked the spot where so many had perished, only three short weeks before, and where man had been busily engaged in

13

the annihilation of his brother man. We were here joined by four companies of the Native Rifles, one wing 20th Native Infantry, and the 4th Company, 21st battalion Bombay Artillery. A large force under Major General —— was to meet us in a few days, for the whole country was by this time tainted with the contagion of rebellion, and likely to give considerable trouble, ere it could be effectually and entirely put down. At this point, our route was changed, as information was brought that the enemy, in large force, under experienced leaders, were advancing from the Fortress of Baddaghur, with a view of intercepting or delaying our march towards Kolapoor, and so afford time for the chief of that district to prepare for our reception, by fortifying the city, and placing the whole of the forts in its vicinity in such a state of defense as time and circumstances would admit of.

CHAPTER X.

THE probability of again meeting the insurgents in large numbers on the plain, away from the shelter of their strongholds, was to us a source of great satisfaction, and the new line of march was taken up with that enthusiasm so peculiar to the British soldier, when on the right track, and eager to meet the enemy he is pursuing. A very absurd and highly ludicrous occurrence took place at this time, and which, but for the unfortunate way it terminated, would have been heartily enjoyed by all. We were ascending a small but very steep hill in order to gain some table land, where it was intended that we should camp. A road had been made up to this place by our sappers the day previous; about half-way from the top this road rounded a sort of projecting point. This portion was very narrow, and on the left hand side the ground was rugged and covered with thick brushwood; a deep ravine occupied the right. The day was just dawning, when we reached this locality, and the light was of that peculiar hazy kind that renders objects at a short distance shadowy and indistinct. The artillery were in front, and between them and the infantry rode the General and his staff; suddenly an aid-de-camp wheeled his horse to the left, and cantered into the jungle; returning in a few seconds, he reported to the General that he had seen a number of the enemy enter a clump of trees a few hundred yards in front of the guns. To this the General gave no credence, for a circumstance of that nature could not have escaped the notice of our advanced guard, and they had not signalized; but the young aid-de-camp declared he could not have been mistaken, and offered to lead a company to dislodge them. Our commander called a halt, directed him to take the right subdivision of the leading company of infantry, and scour the jungle to our left front ; this was done, I believe, more to convince the young officer of his error than any other motive. Away the party went in the direction indicated, and on being within a hundred yards of the spot, sent in a volley, when lo and behold, the smoke clearing off, instead of the enemy, out dashed about fifty large monkeys! They came shrieking, yelling and howling, like so many satyrs or wood demons. The shouts of laughter that burst from all that witnessed this unexpected event, may be easily imagined, and the little party on their return were greeted with all manner of jokes and fun ; the Lieutenant came in for his share of chaff, and had to run the gauntlet of his jesting friends, which he did, joining good naturedly in the laugh against himself ; it was fortunate that he did so, otherwise he would have been continually tormented. As a matter of course, the story spread like wildfire over the whole Presidency ; and I have often since heard him greeted with— " I say A——, what is the price of nuts ?" or, " How is cocoa ?" which he would ward off with, " No more of that, Hal, an' thou lovest me," or something of that sort. Had the affair ended here, all would have been well, but it was not so, for the terrified monkeys, many of which had been hit, frantically leaped from the high bank into the road, a few yards in front of the artillery : the horses startled at their unexpected appearance, and frightened at the fearful din, became unmanageable. Just then a large snake was seen to glide across the road, and pass under the horses ; unfortunately one of them trod upon it ; in an instant it darted at and bit him in the shoulder, fastening its fangs on it. The poor brute writhing in agony, kicked and plunged violently in his efforts to shake off the reptile. The other horses rendered desperate by the cries and struggles of the bitten horse, reared, backed, and before anything could be done to avert it, gun, limber, horses and men, were hurled over the edge of the road, tearing and dashing through the brushwood and decayed stumps, in their passage down the steep sides of the ravine. The gun,

which was a brass six-pounder, fortunately got entangled and
jammed in the branches and roots of a banyan tree, which stopped
its further downward progress. Assistance was promptly given,
and the party rescued from their perilous position. It was then
discovered that one of the horses had been killed, and one of the
drivers so severely crushed, that he only survived a few hours ;
the remainder escaped with some slight contusions and a few
ugly looking scratches. A fatigue party was despatched to get
up the gun, the rear guard received orders to see it brought
into camp, and we again moved forward. An hour later the
staff who had ridden on with the advance guard, were seen
returning at a smart canter, and the General addressing several
of the officers that were riding together said, pointing to an
eminence in front, " Gentlemen, there is your camping ground,
but you must fight for every inch of it, as the enemy have possession, and are in great numbers, therefore you may expect
warm work." He then passed on to the centre, to give instructions for an attack on the foe. The cavalry were ordered into
the valleys and nullahs, and large parties of infantry, each accompanied by a light gun to assist in the work of destruction, were
soon seen swarming up and over the numerous hills and ridges
with which the country abounded, whilst the main body or
reserve followed close up, relieving or reinforcing the skirmishers
from time to time, as circumstances required. It was a lovely
morning ; the sun that had been obscured during the earlier
hours, now shone forth in all its brilliancy, dispelling the misty
and vapour-like clouds that floated among the hills, disclosing a
magnificent panorama of wood, water, valley and mountain. The
dark blue range of the western Ghauts being distinctly visible,
stretching away to the left, as far as the eye could reach, seemed
to disappear among the clouds. The pleasing effect of the picture
was considerably heightened by the events that were now passing.
Here and there might be seen small parties of our cavalry, who,
while sweeping round the base of the different acclivities came

occasionally upon some of the enemy's horse, when a hand to
hand encounter would take place, resulting generally in the
defeat of the latter ; while the artillery from various prominent spots, opened a conversation with the rebels from the brazen
throats of their guns, in a language not at all appreciated
by, but painfully felt by many of them, as their mangled
remains testified. Then again, the advancing lines of our skirmishers driving the Mahrattas before them like scared sheep, the
green and scarlet uniforms of our rifles and infantry contrasting
strangely with the loose white clothing and brightly burnished
weapons of the flying foe, formed, with our reserve, for a fore-
ground, a grand tableau, that would have made the fortune of
any good artist, could he have placed it on canvas for exhibition.
It was quite evident, from the obstinate way in which many parts
of the ground were contested, and the orderly manner in which
large parties of the enemy made good their retreat, that they had
a leader among them of no mean capacity, and well skilled in
military tactics ; and so it turned out, for as our main body was
pursuing its way along the foot of a steep acclivity, the spur or
rocky point of which hung over the path at no great distance in
front, there suddenly appeared on its extreme summit the tall
figure of a man, whose dress, features, and general appearance as
he stood out in bold relief against the sky, plainly indicated that
he was of European birth. He waved his sword several times,
either in defiance of us, or as a signal to his followers, of our
approach in that direction. The quick eye of our Brigadier
measured at a glance the distance between them, and turning to
his orderly, a non-commissioned officer of the rifles, who constantly
attended him, said : " You are reckoned the best shot in your
regiment, I believe ; do you think you could hit yonder figure ? "
" The distance is great, but if the Sahib wishes it, I will try my
best," replied the havildar ; " it is not more than six hundred
yards in a straight line, remarked the commander, and if you
succeed, I will give you five rupees ; but you must be quick." The

soldier stepped a few paces to the right, then dropping his rifle into the forked prong of a wild guava tree, took deliberate aim and fired. The man was seen to spring apparently about six feet into the air, then turning a somersault, came down headlong into the jungle below. It was a splendid shot, for there were no Enfield or minie rifles in the army in those days. Then, to hit a target the size of a man, at 300 yards, was considered **good** shooting. The body was discovered, and, on examination, proved to be that of a man named Lowengholm, a Norwegian, who had entered the service of the East India Company, and deserted from the horse artillery at Poona, about two years before. It was afterwards ascertained that he had been employed by the Rajah of Sattara, as a sort of generalissimo of his forces, and sent by that intriguing native prince to assist the insurgent chiefs; hence his presence on the battle ground. **On the** fall of **their** leader, the rebels gave up the contest, broke **into small** parties, and fled through the jungle, seeking the shelter of the fortress of Baddaghur, which **their superior** knowledge **of the** country enabled them to attain, in defiance of our light troops who followed them as best they could, but only in time to witness the massive gates of the fort close on the last party of the fugitives. We had the satisfaction, however, of seeing the white flag of truce or surrender, flying from the tower of the principal entrance, and a great satisfaction it was; for a thirty mile march in a country like India, through thick jungle, with a running fight for **the** last fifteen miles, beneath a noon-day sun, is no joke, and quite enough for one day, especially for infantry. **On the** arrival of the remainder of the brigade, we commenced making ourselves comfortable and snug in the valley at the **foot of the** hill on which Baddaghur **was** built, at a distance of about **four hundred** yards. Rolls were called, **arms piled, and some of the** tents **of** the staff in course of erection. I threw myself on the ground, awaiting the arrival of the grog, beneath the shade of a cur-rawa bush, where I soon fell asleep, but **I did not long** enjoy the

exquisite luxury, having been awakened by a lot of earth or dirt
which struck my face. I sprang up, highly indignant, as I
fancied some of my comrades had been playing a practical joke
upon me. The booming of artillery at once silenced me. The
white flag had been hauled down, and the fort suddenly opened
fire upon us, sending their old iron flying through our camp in a
most uncomfortable manner. The first shot, a thirty-two pounder,
struck close to where my head laid, covering me with earth, then
ricochetting over a pile of arms, passed through the officers' mess
tent, and finally lodged in the lap of an old woman, a Madrassee
camp follower, who was vending cowheel curry to a group of
hungry soldiers. The poor old creature was cut completely in
two, to the no small surprise of her customers. I had a narrow
escape that time ; but " a miss is as good as a mile." We had to
cut and run to get out of range of the guns of our treacherous
foe ; which we did without loss, pitching our camp on a piece of
table-land, about the same height as that on which the fort stood,
and about sixteen hundred yards distant, with the valley between
us and the enemy, who discontinued their fire as soon as we got
out of range. We then commenced in good earnest to make
ourselves comfortable, and got our breakfast, dinner and supper,
three meals in one, and as the foe did not further molest us, we
did not interfere with them. Burying the slain, bringing in
the wounded, and securing our camp for the night, every one
was fully employed that evening, all being anxious to avail
themselves of the chance of a good night's rest, and feeling
satisfied that tough work would be cut out for us on the morrow.
As I said before—at the period of which I am writing—the
East India Company was in its palmiest days, trusted and
yet envied by the European powers, and feared and respected by
its native subjects. Just prior to the outbreak of the present
campaign, its already large army had been strengthened by three
European regiments of infantry, and several battalions of Sepoys,
while the complement of native artillery and irregular cavalry

had been largely augmented. These troops were all thoroughly drilled, and in a high state of discipline, ready and anxious to be led to any point or against any foe, no matter of what creed or denomination—for the material of which the native army was then composed looked down with sovereign contempt on all those who followed any other occupation than that of the noble profession of arms. As the grey dawn of day lit up the eastern horizon, and ere the world's great luminary had blazed forth upon the scene, all was bustle and preparation in the camp. Large parties of men on fatigue, from the various corps, were hurrying here and there ; earth-works were being thrown up, breaching batteries got into position, and mortar-beds laid ; whilst those gentlemen of the scientific branch of the service —as the field engineers are usually styled—were busily engaged ascertaining by means of theodolites **and other** instruments, the correct distance between our position and the Fort, the height of its walls, and such other information as they deemed necessary for the work in hand. To one of these look-out points, where the theodolite was in full operation, my friend Bob and myself not being required for duty, made our way, and having some slight acquaintance with the European sergeant who had charge of the instrument, I obtained permission to take a peep at the enemy's works. Having satisfied my curiosity I beckoned my comrade to approach, who, believing it to be nothing more than a large telescope, was impatient to look through it. He had not been more than five seconds at the glass, when he exclaimed, " Arrah, Ned, avic, sure the place is upside down, why don't the nagers fall out," then shifting his head on one side he looked steadily at the fort, and finding it in its usual position, called out : " By the piper that played before Moses, and sure he was a musical man, **it's mighty** quare any how." " Thereupon I endeavoured to explain to him the use, construction, and peculiarities of the glass, but I fear with little success, for it was evident by the quiet way in which he retired, that

14

he was not at all satisfied in his own mind, but that his
Satanic Majesty had some hand in the construction of the instrument in question. This incident brings to my mind a story that
was related to me by one of the Royal Engineers. It appears my
friend was engaged in surveying a portion of a country road
somewhere in the south of England, and had just commenced
work, when a party of young ladies from a neighbouring boarding
school, of various ages, from the infant prodigy of eight to the
blushing maiden of seventeen, were seen approaching ; they were
headed by a tall thin vinegar-visaged female, the peculiar rustle
of whose stiff silk, together with the primness of her general
costume, clearly indicated that she had never loved, or had loved and
sighed in vain. As they drew near, he advanced, cap in hand, to
meet them, and with a politeness for which he was proverbial, ·
offered to use his scientific apparatus for their amusement. This
proposal was received with delight by all, but to the unloving
governess, the theodolite had no charms. Indeed, she was superior
to such things. However, she offered no objection to the scheme,
and in a few minutes distant scenes were brought near. Cottages,
gates, trees, and other objects, were turned upside down, to the
wonder and astonishment of the party. When all had been
satisfied, our hero, with a spice of that mischief for which he was
noted, turned the glass full on the group, saying, with a wicked
smile, " Ladies, as I have afforded you a little pleasure, it is
nothing but fair that you should contribute a little to mine ;" so
I am about to turn you all upside down." At this remark a
terrible commotion seized them. The antique lady of the Academy
believing the glass to be levelled solely at her, uttered a scream
of terror, and fled for refuge behind a clump of laburnums,
which effectually screened her from view. Some of the maidens
performed a manœuvre known to the initiated as " making a
cheese," formed by ladies dropping on their knees, compressing
their garments closely around them. While they remained
huddled together in little groups, each holding the bottoms of

their petticoats firmly with **both** hands to **the** ground, uttering piteous exclamations, **such as** "Well, I never;" "Did you ever;" "Oh, **please,** don't, Mr. Man;" "Take **away that** nasty thing." **The** scene was ludicrous in the extreme. **At** this juncture, three **of the** elder pupils who had loitered **behind, fern-gathering,** now **came** up, and it so happened that **they had brothers,** who were surveying students. These ladies were perfectly *au fait* with the theodolite, and its peculiarities; therefore the meaning of the scene burst upon them at a glance, and being no longer able to control their risible faculties, broke forth into **a** peal **of** merry laughter, which instantly communicated itself to the little tremblers, and tended to reassure them. At the same time the head of the glass swung round **in** an opposite direction, and now **all** was fun and good humour again. But the shouts of laughter **were** too much for the stately dame, who now advanced, **and** with scathing words of reproof **at** what she termed **the** levity of their behaviour, hurried them quickly away; casting a withering look of scorn and indignation at the man **of** chains and **links,** she was soon lost in the distance.

Our belligerent neighbours opposite paid **us** little attention during the early part **of the** morning, save treating us to **an** occasional round shot from one or the other of their bastions, **and us** in each case, they fell short, shewing **they** had no gun **of** sufficient calibre to pitch a shot into our camp, while we intended, in a very short time, by means of our eighteen and long thirty-two pounders, and eleven and-a-half inch mortars, **to** make their fort too hot to hold them. Things remained **in** this state until about **eleven** o'clock, when a violent commotion **was** observed going on in the fort. Numerous matchlocks were fired; flames shot up here **and there, and the** Mahratta **sword** blades were distinctly seen **flashing in the** sunlight. This **lasted** about half **an** hour, when all **was** again silent. The crimson and yellow war banner **of** the insurgents, which had been proudly floating over the principal gate, **was** now hauled down, and a white flag of truce substituted; but our general, recollecting the manœuvre that had been practiced at Samunghur, continued his preparations for the attack. About four o'clock in the afternoon, one of the cavalry that had been posted on an eminence midway between us and the fort, dashed into camp with information that a single horseman, with a numerous guard, on foot, with one of the number in front, bearing a flag of truce, had left the fort, and was coming in the direction of our camp. This caused considerable stir among us, and preparations were made to receive this dignitary. A lane was formed through which he had to pass on his way to the general's quarters. Every available gun was brought up to the front, and our whole strength united in several divisions along the front, and we made as good a display of our force as possible, in order to convince the foe that we were prepared to take by force what they might at first not feel inclined to concede. These arrangements had scarcely been completed, when the party arrived. A man carrying a white banner, protected by two matchlock men, headed the party; then came, mounted on a superb cream-coloured charger, the appointments of which were of velvet, covered in many places with silver stars or roses, the keladar or governor of the fort, for such he proved to be. He was a fine looking man about fifty, by caste a Brahmin, he wore a yellow satin quilted dugla or surcoat, with pagamas of the same material coming down as far as the knees; a pale blue turban, with a deep border of kinkob or cloth of gold, formed his head dress; a magnificent Cashmere shawl was round his waist, into which was thrust a silver-mounted pistol, and a double handled Mahratta creese; a profusion of jewellery ornamented his person, and a golden amulet was suspended from his neck by a number of curiously worked chains. But for such of my fair readers who have a weakness for long boots, I must confess that his pedal extremities were innocent of covering from the knee downwards; his naked feet rested in silver clogs, affixed to the stirrup irons. On each side a man walked, supporting, by means of a bamboo pole, an enormous umbrella of crimson satin, with a deep fringe of **green silk**, which effectually protected the horseman from the scorching rays of the sun. His followers, **to** the number of one hundred **and** fifty, were armed some with matchlock and creese; others with long swords and shields of hides, studded with iron, brass or silver knobs, according to the fancy or wealth of the owner. They **wore no** sort of uniform, but were dressed in the usual dress of the country; though all had sandals on their feet. On reaching the general's quarters, the keladar dismounted, and was conducted by our commander, who had met him at the entrance, to a small tent, that had been prepared for his reception, and here the business on which he came was transacted. In about an hour the Council broke up, and this important personage departed with his dusky attendants, in the same order as he came. It soon became known throughout camp that the fort had surrendered, and that two companies were to go in the evening to take formal possession. The cause of the disturbance in the morning also came to our knowledge; it appears there was a war and a peace party amongst them. At first the war party were in the ascendant, but on learning our strength many had succumbed, when a contest ensued between them, in which several were killed and wounded. The pugnacious few were overpowered and **driven** beyond the walls through one of the rear gates, and left to shift for themselves as best they could. My company and one of the rifles were ordered out for duty at the fort, which place we soon reached; guards were placed at the different gates, and the Union Jack hoisted. We then proceeded to make ourselves comfortable in the Cutcheree, a large public building near the principal entrance. The officer of the rifles being senior, had command of both companies, and previous to dismissing us, said **that as** the place had been surrendered, no looting would be **allowed, at** the same time taking down from **the** wall of **the** room a pair of handsome peacock fans, set in wrought silver frames, which he concealed in his bedding. Understanding perfectly what he meant, we acted accordingly. During the evening I passed a large temple, and on entering was asked by the Brahmin priest if I was an officer. Anxious to learn his reason for the enquiry, I replied in the affirmative. He then asked if I would furnish a guard to protect his temple. On enquiring his reason for this request, he drew back a bamboo screen exhibiting a rough stone altar, which supported a massive silver idol, about three feet in height, with the head and trunk of an elephant. I remarked that it appeared to me to be a fixture which could not be easily removed. Not so, he replied, the figure is put together by pieces fitting one into another, which can be instantly taken apart, at the same time lifting the head and trunk in order to convince me of the fact. I turned away apparently satisfied, promising to return with a guard in half-an-hour. On my way back I conceived a plan of converting this idol into rupees, and hailing Bob O'Toole and two others on whom I could depend, at once communicated my design, which pleased them mightily. Stealing out quietly with our muskets, we met in rear of our quarters, where we fell in and marched down to the Temple. On our arrival we halted and planted a sentry at the entrance; then piled arms. The Brahmin was highly satisfied with this arrangement, and shortly after left for the Petta. He had not been gone long ere we took his elephantship down a peg or two, divided it amongst us—myself, as leader of the expedition, taking the largest share—and returned to our quarters with the booty, and without detection. Thus, like the Israelites of old, we entered the temples of the heathen, and despoiled them of their idols. The next morning, at daylight, a company of Sappers and Miners, with a detachment of Native Infantry, arrived for the purpose of dismantling the fort, and we were ordered to return to camp forthwith.

CHAPTER XI.

THE arrival of this party to take our **place was exactly** what
we desired, for most of us had managed **to** pick up some memento
by which we could remember our visit to Baddaghur. A day or
two after our return to camp, Bob, myself, and several **others**
of our company **were warned** for duty **at** the look-out picket;
a guard that **had been** stationed at the extreme end of the piece
of table land, on which our camp had been pitched. It commanded
a **view of** all roads leading to and from the fort, and the sentry
could, either by day, or on moonlight nights, observe any body of
troops, or others, moving either way. This **guard was in** great
repute amongst our men, for various **reasons.** It was sufficiently
distant from head-quarters to **avoid the surveillance** of the
sergeant-major, or his subordinates, and relieving those on duty
there from the many harrassing fatigues incidental to camp
life. The guard being a strong one, and mounting but few sentries ; each man had **but** two hours duty to perform ; **and if**
cards, dice, backgammon, and **other** games, were not **exactly**
allowed, they were at all events winked at, and most decidedly
practised to a great extent. The day had drawn to a close,
cribbage, all-fours and twenty-fives had been given up ; the moon
had just risen in all its splendor ; and the men had gathered round
in a circle—some smoking and conversing, others lying on their
beds, ready to listen **to** any song or story that their comrades
might indulge in—such **being the usual way** in which our time
was spent, between sunset and tattoo-beating. **The scene, on**
this occasion was opened by some one asking the O'Toole to spin
a yarn or sing a song. " And is it me ye mane ?" replied the
Hibernian, "the devil a **yarn** have I at all, at all, and as for
singing, sure the voice of the bullfrog would **be music** compared

to mine, but if I can't sing, bedad, I am the purtiest whistler as
ever cocked a lip." Thereupon he executed a number of **jigs** and
reels with surprising correctness as to time **and cadence,** to the
no small astonishment of those who were unacquainted with his
ability in that line. When he concluded, he turned to me,
and said, " Musha, Ned, but it is yourself that ought to know
about singing, by my sowl that's a mighty nate ditty consarning
the colleen that dhramed she was going to be kissed, but
woke too soon. Ye might give us a taste of that same, so you
might." Knowing that my audience were in no way particular,
and that anything about love and ladies, &c., is always acceptable
in a guard-tent, I responded to my friend's request, and with the
best voice then at command, sang the following lines to the air
of " **Marble Halls**":—

ELLA'S DREAM.

I dream't I was dancing in old white halls,
    With an ebon haired youth by my side,
And as we were waltzing along the hall,
    He asked me to become his bride.
He told me of castles and wide domains
    In merry Northumberlandshire,
But I told him that love only counted its **gains**
    When the object it worshipped was near.
        CHORUS—Was near, was near,
            When the object it worshipped was near.

And the time flew quickly and pleasingly past,
    And the festival drew to a close,
When he won with soft seductive arts,
    A maiden her love to disclose.
Half laughing, half sighing, I cried, "I'm thine";
    When goodness, how strange it did seem,
For just as his lips were approaching to mine,
I awoke, and 'twas only a dream.
        CHORUS—Only a dream, only a dream,
          I awoke, and 'twas only a dream.

" Bravo, bravo, bravo, repeated several voices," as I concluded.
" Did the young lady compose herself to sleep again ?" mildly

enquired the corporal. "**Be the powers, if** I had been there, I
would have kissed her any way—sleeping or waking, it's all one
to the O'Tooles." "That is something new; I do not remember
having heard that sung before," remarked the sergeant of the
guard. "No, perhaps not. It is a conceit of my own; I wrote it
some time ago, for our amateur theatre, but it is your turn now,
I suppose you will have no objection **to** assist **us with** your
voice." "Well," replied the sergeant, "to tell the truth, I do not
profess to be a singer; neither can I whistle like **O'Toole, but if**
a story will suffice, **I** will try my best to amuse you, and **as the**
yarn is about love and soldiers, it may pass muster." A general
shout of approbation ensued, and he commenced as follows:
"Zillapoore was one of the best stations in Rajahpootanna. It
had been previously the head-quarters of a native contingent,
but for some reason the Nawab had given it up; and the
Bombay Government knowing the salubrity of the climate, at
once seized upon it as a station for European troops. It was most
beautifully situated, and fountains, tanks, aqueducts, temples, and
gardens, the usual surrounding to the whereabouts of a native
prince, were still to be seen at every turn. A commodious
barrack had been erected, and a number of bungalows had been
put up, of various sizes, for the officers and petty staff, in the
beautiful gardens adjoining the old palace. In one of those
dwellings, a small and compact one, nearest to the barracks, but
screened from view by creeping plants and the outspreading
branches **of** some magnificent gold mohur trees, sat, or rather
reclined **in** a luxurious easy chair, a young man, apparently
about six and twenty, remarkably good looking, with an open
and intelligent countenance, a fair complexion, with eyes of the
deepest blue, and light brown wavy hair. **The** golden chevrons
on the sleeves **of** a scarlet jacket, which had been thrown care-
lessly on the back of **a** lounge, denoted his rank; that of quarter-
master sergeant, for such was the position held by Herbert Grey
in his regiment. He was puffing away a few clouds of fragrant

tobacco, through the velvet snake of a handsome glass silver-mounted hooka, when he was disturbed by some one entering the veranda. "Who is there," enquired Herbert, half rising, as the tall handsome figure of Walter Cressingham, in the uniform of a color sergeant, advanced through the open doorway. "Oh, is that you, Walter, come in, old fellow; how are you. What is the news. "I see you have the order book; do we march on Friday, or is it postponed until Monday." "As I anticipated, neither one or the other," replied Cressingham—throwing him-self at full length on the lounge before alluded to—but some-thing, I fancy, will suit you much better," at the same time glancing round the comfortably furnished apartment. The order for marching has been countermanded. A new regiment has arrived from Europe, and they are to take the place of the one we were to relieve at Dessa ; therefore we are to remain here for the next two years, and if all I have heard be true, before that period arrives you will receive your commission as Lieute-nant and Quartermaster." "Well, by Jove, that is news indeed, and to tell the truth, I do not care to leave the place at present, it is a pleasant station ; I have snug quarters, and if I only had some little divinity in petticoats, to aid me in whiling away the leisure hours, and to keep the servants in order, I should be quite contented to wait for the promotion, but one might as well expect a major-generalship as a wife, in this part of the world; indeed, I do not believe there is an available female within five hundred miles of the station ; beautiful country, is it not?" "And if there were," rejoined his companion, without apparently noticing the fling at the country, "nothing under the rank of a commissioned officer would have the least chance; but however, be that as it may, I must be off to my company and promulgate the orders ;" rising, as he spoke, to depart. "Wait a little, my dear fellow, I must go and speak to the quartermaster about unpacking the stores, and if you will take a glass of brandy Pannee, while I am dressing, I will walk up to the barracks with you." Herbert was not long at his toilet, and then, taking a little of the *eau-de-vie*, for which the good news was a sufficient excuse, the two friends passed out together. The following afternoon, as Herbert Grey was returning from the stores, he was accosted by an orderly, with, " Sir, Sergeant Cressingham says he would feel obliged if you would go over to his room after evening parade, he wishes to see you particularly." " Very good, Green, tell him I will call and see him, " Is there anything the matter." Not that I am positively aware of, but he received a letter from Europe this morning, and he appears out of spirits ever since," replied the soldier, saluting as he moved off. According to promise, Herbert paid his **friend** a visit during the evening. On entering he found Walter seated at a small table, covered with writing materials; an open letter lay before him, and from the numerous pieces of torn paper lying around him on the floor, it was evident that he had not been successful in framing a suitable answer. After the usual salutation, Walter proceeded to give his reasons for sending for him. "Herbert," said he, " I have requested your presence, for advice and assistance on a subject of the utmost importance. I do not remember that I ever mentioned to you any portion of my early history. To be brief, my father was a lieutenant in the Royal Navy, and was killed several years ago in an engagement with some pirates off one of the West India Islands. At his death he left a widow and two children, to be provided for out of the small income of his rank, allowed by the Government. I was then about fifteen, and my sister was ten years of age. After the loss of my father, my mother and sister went to reside in a small cottage on the sea coast, in the South of England, but I was kept at school near London. My aunt, my mother's sister, a maiden lady receiving a small annuity, kindly paid for my education there. I remained **until** I was eighteen, when my aunt died. I had then to leave school, and being unfit for a trade, and having no interest to procure **an** appointment abroad, I entered the service and joined this regiment. The rest you know. This morning I received the announcement of my mother's death, which from long illness and other causes, I have been led to expect for some time past; but the unhappy position in which my poor sister is left, is to me a source of great anxiety and uneasiness. How I am to relieve her from her present embarrassment, and care for her future welfare, is the cause of my seeking your friendly counsel and assistance. Read her letter; it will explain matters better than I can." Herbert took the letter in silence, and moving to an open window, read as follows:

" Dear Brother—

" The blow has at last fallen, our poor dear mother is now no more, and we are orphans. She died on the fifteenth of this month; oh how fervently she prayed that she might be spared until your return, but it could not be. She died, blessing us both, and the last word she uttered, was your name. You are aware that her income was drawn in advance, and died with her, and as she expired a few days prior to pay-day, there is nothing to receive on that account; and after the funeral expenses were defrayed, there remained but a few shillings. The landlord, a hard, cruel man, seized and sold the furniture for some arrears of rent that was due; thus at one stroke I was rendered motherless and houseless; and thrown on the cold charity of the world. What I should have done, I know not, but for the kindness of a poor neighbour, who has given me shelter for the present. Our dear mother spared no pains with my education, and I believe myself competent to perform the duties of a governess, or school teacher ; but alas, there are hundreds of better qualified persons seeking for such appointments daily without success. Dearest **Walter, I know** that the kindness of your heart will prompt you **to do all in** your power for me ; but oh, if you could remit a little money, **to** repay **these** poor people **that** have sheltered me, and can ill afford to do so, it may **be an** inducement to them to extend it until something turns up. I am too much overpowered by our loss and my sad situation to say more at present, but oh, do write soon, and relieve the anxiety and suspense of your affectionate sister.

ALICE CRESSINGHAM."

Herbert quietly refolded the letter, and for a few moments made no reply, but continued to pace up and down the room in thought. Suddenly he confronted Walter and said, " Cressingham, we have been friends since you entered the service; you know my present position, and future prospects; you have asked my advice, and I **now** give it frankly and unhesitatingly. I have a sum of money in the paymaster's hands, a portion of which I would willingly lend **you** for your sister, but this would not be exactly what is now required, and you will be unable from your rank in the regiment, to spare a sufficient sum to support her. I see but one way to obviate this difficulty, that is, to write a line and explain exactly how you are situated—our long friendship—and tell her that I will, if she wishes it, remit to England a sufficient amount to pay her outfit and passage to join you, and that on her arrival at this station, I will make her my wife, and sweep away the present difficulties. The suddenness of this proposition may at first startle her somewhat, but calm reflection will shew **her,** I think, that the offer is made in all sincerity, and with the **best** of motives. Now, Walter, what do you say on the subject ?"
" My dear Herbert," he replied, shaking his friend warmly by the hand, " I sincerely thank you for your generous offer, and I can assure you that nothing will give me greater pleasure than to see you united to my sister ; it shall be as you propose. I will write, and explain all to Alice, and leave it to her good sense for the acceptance of your kind suggestion in our behalf." The next morning a letter was despatched to Alice, in which Herbert enclosed a draft on **Forbes & Co.**, London, of sufficient amount to **meet** all requirements. In **a few months,** Alice's answer was received by her brother, in which she had consented to entrust her happiness to the keeping of her brother's friend. She had

procured a passage on board the "Seringapatam," East Indiaman,
which vessel was expected to arrive at Bombay about the middle
of the ensuing January. It was now late in November; Cressingham lost no time in communicating the news to Herbert
Grey, and it was soon arranged that Walter should at once obtain
leave of absence, and proceed to the Presidency, to await the
arrival of Alice. On his reaching Bombay, he found that the
"Seringapatam" had arrived, and that Alice had been fortunate
enough while on board to make the acquaintance of an officer's
family who were to remain a few weeks at Bombay, prior to
their journey up country, and that they had invited her to
stay with them until her brother could fetch her. This was all
very satisfactory to Walter, and after visiting the fire Temples of
the Parsees, the Towers of the Silence, as their burial places are
very appropriately named, and other places of interest on the
island, they set forth on their long and tedious journey to
Zillapoore. One morning, after having been ten days on the road,
on entering the Dawk Bungalow, they found one of the rooms
occupied by Henry Dashville, sergeant-major of Walter's regiment,
who had also been on furlough, and like themselves was on his
way to rejoin. This was indeed a fortunate event; Walter introduced him to Alice, and he was invited to dine and spend the
day with them, when it was arranged that they should perform
the rest of the journey together. During the evening, as the young
men were lounging and smoking in the veranda, Dashville said,
as he drew a letter from his pocket, " Here is something that I
had forgotten until now ; it will, I think, surprise you very
much—it is from sergeant Winter—read the concluding paragraph," handing the letter as he spoke to Walter, who, glancing
over it, read aloud the following lines :—" The only news of
interest here is, that your friend, Herbert, the quarter-master
sergeant, was detected in an intrigue with one of the women of
the regiment, by her husband ; of course Herbert was arrested,
tried by a court martial, and reduced to the ranks ; this affair

caused quite a sensation in camp." **Walter was thunderstruck ;**
he could scarcely believe the statement; he read, and re-read the
few lines, and each time he did so, he felt the more **confused ;**
he apologized to Dashville for leaving him, **and** sought his sister.
She met him at the door of her room, and noticing his agitation,
said ; " Calm yourself, dearest Walter ; seated, **reading** at an
open window, I became unintentionally a listener,and have heard
all. You take this matter too much **to** heart, for a man who
could be guilty of such baseness is unworthy of your confidence,
or my love, and he shall never be the husband of Alice Cressingham." Her cheeks flushed, and her eyes flashed with indignation
as she spoke. It must be remembered that Alice had not seen
Herbert, and knew nothing of him more than he was her brother's friend, and therefore she had but little difficulty in dismissing him from her thoughts. But not so with Cressingham, they
had been so long acquainted, and to think that he should have so
acted when his intended wife was within a few hundred miles of
him, stung him to the quick. It was an insult to both, and it
was several hours before he could compose himself sufficiently to
reason calmly on the strange turn events had taken. They did
not proceed on their journey until the following evening. The
beauty and quiet manners of Alice made a deep impression **on**
Henry Dashville, as was evident by the marked attention he paid
her during the journey. In crossing the fords, and as the roads
were almost impassable he was ever ready to assist and anticipate
her slightest wish, paying those delicate attentions so pleasing to
females in general. During the beautiful moonlight evenings, she
would alight, and in company with her brother, but leaning on
the proffered arm of Dashville, walk on a considerable distance,
Dashville endeavouring to interest and **amuse her.** Although
young, he had seen a great deal of the world, besides possessing a
fund of anecdote and agreeable rattle, and the happy knack of
suiting his conversation to the circumstances and place. These
attentions were not lost upon Alice Cressingham. On one occasion

having been compelled to go to the rear in order to give instructions to the servant concerning the baggage, Dashville embraced the opportunity of declaring his attachment, at the same time **making** Alice an offer of his hand and heart; and the appeal was made so ardently and eloquently **that** she consented, provided he **would** speak to her brother on the subject. Dashville took advantage of the first opportunity to speak to Walter on the matter, but the latter demurred at first. However, when Dashville assured him that he would, on reaching camp, refund the amount which Herbert had advanced, he hesitated no longer, and finally consented. On their arrival at Mow, a large military station, about ninety miles from Zillapoore, they were united; this entailed a delay of a few days, and the trio then resumed their journey. It was a beautiful morning, the sun had scarcely **risen,** the heavy dew being upon the hedges, plants and grass, which sparkled and glittered like diamonds in the sunlight ; the air was impregnated with the odour of roses, jessamines and other flowers that bloomed in great beauty in the surrounding gardens. There had been a full-dress parade, and the officers were returning to their quarters, as our travellers entered the cantonment. Walter **and** Dashville had alighted, and were walking in advance of the garrie, and on turning the corner of a compound they came suddenly upon Herbert in the full dress of his rank, a quartermaster sergeant. "Oh Cressingham, I expected you in this morning, glad to see that all is safe," said he, bowing politely to Mrs. Dashville, as she drove past. "Dashville, you look well after your trip. The colonel has been enquiring about you ; he says the regiment is getting quite slack since you left ; that is **a** feather in your cap, I can tell you. What is the matter with Cressingham ? he spoke little, and seemed quite confused," continued Herbert, looking after Walter, who had followed the garrie and was **conversing** with his sister, as they proceeded onwards. "There **has** been a great mistake made somewhere," said Dashville, "look at those lines," he resumed, at the same time handing him the letter he had received from Sergeant Winter. " Well," replied Herbert Grey, "what has Charles Herbert's reduction to do with it ; he has left the Native Infantry and joined his former regiment, but how that can affect Cressingham I cannot understand ?" "But," said Dashville, "we all thought it was you, and as you may well imagine, felt much concerned about it ; however, it gives me great pleasure to find you are all right again. You will excuse me, for I must overtake my wife." "Your wife!" " Yes, I married Cressingham's sister at Mow, a few days since ; come up in the evening, and I will introduce you," said he, walking rapidly away. Herbert Grey seemed almost dumbfoundered for a few moments, then advanced slowly towards his quarters. It was great satisfaction to Walter to learn, that instead of his friend it proved to be a quarter-master sergeant named Charles Herbert, of the Native Infantry, that had been reduced to the ranks, and he blamed himself for being so hasty ; indeed, he sincerely regretted the unlucky moment that placed Dashville in his way. An explanation and apology was due to Herbert, and that evening Walter wrote a full account of the whole affair, and sent it to him. The next morning he visited Herbert, who was a good man, and too generous to bear a profound resentment ; and they parted, as on former occasions, nothing appearing or transpiring to interrupt their friendship. Alice felt considerable embarrassment on her first introduction to Herbert Grey, but her anxiety was modified by his quiet, gentlemanly manner, and while on after-visits, which were frequent, she endeavoured, by courtesy and pleasing attentions to convince him that she was not unmindful of the generous effort he had made in her behalf. Some months later, Herbert received his commission as lieutenant and quarter-master, and was sent to Bombay, on some duty connected with his office. Before his return, Dashville had been promoted as lieutenant and adjutant, and Cressingham, to the vacant sergeant-majorship. Dashville, poor fellow, did not long enjoy his rank, for at the first brigade parade, at which he acted as marker to the regiment, he was thrown from his horse and died before he could be removed to his bungalow. This was quite a severe blow to Alice and her brother, and cast a deep gloom over their little circle. A short time after her husband's funeral, Alice, by the advice of her brother, paid a visit to some friends at Mow, who had invited her to stay with them during the first few weeks of her bereavement, in hopes that time and change of scene would in some degree alleviate her sorrow and assuage her grief. "Where are we now?" exclaimed the occupant, aroused from his slumbers, by the sudden sloping of the "dumny." On the banks of the river Taptee," replied the driver, as the traveller descended from the vehicle. "Hand me my rifle," said Herbert Grey, for he was on his way back to join his regiment. He carefully examined his weapons, for it was at such places that the tiger and cheeta lurked, ready to pounce upon the droves of cattle as they crossed the river.   Descending the steep path that led to the water's edge, by the light of the moon, and aid of the stepping stones, that were placed at regular intervals, he succeeded in crossing the broad but shallow stream, dryshod.   Silently ascending the opposite bank, he was about emerging from the deep shadow of the overhanging trees, when, on the road, at a little distance in front, and beneath the broad moonlight, he observed a party of Bheels, (robbers) in the act of plundering a bullock garrie. He pondered for a moment whether to advance singly or to await the arrival of his servants, when instantly a fresh object met his view, a little to the right of the road. On the high bank, apparently engaged in stripping the jewellery from the prostrate form of what appeared to be a European lady, was a ferocious looking Bheel. At this instant a loud shriek broke the stillness of the night, and while the ruffian's bright creese glittered in the moonbeams, while in the act of plunging it into the heart of his victim, a bullet from Herbert's rifle brought him to the ground, and he rolled over the edge of the bank and into the river beneath. At the report of the rifle and the appearance of the Sahib, the other Bheels fled to the jungle, and on Herbert's advancing he recognised the beautiful features of Alice Dashville, who lay almost lifeless before him. His servants now came up, and he procured some stimulants, which served to restore her to consciousness; then lifting her gently in his arms, she was conveyed to the garrie. When sufficiently recovered, she informed him that she was on her way back to Zillapoore, when they were attacked. She was dragged out, half-fainting, and thrown upon the bank; her quick ear having caught the sound of wheels crossing the river, she uttered that scream, which, but for the trusty aid of Herbert Grey, would have been her last. Her driver and the two chaprassees or native policemen, that had been sent to protect her, but who, as usual, had run on the first appearance of the Bheels, now came from their hiding places, and with the assistance of the other servants, soon set matters right again, and under the protection and friendly escort of Herbert, they reached their station in safety. After a suitable time elapsed, Herbert sought her love, and again made her an offer of marriage. Grateful for the preservation of her life, and no doubt impelled by a deeper feeling towards him, Alice accepted his offer and became his wife. All the *elite* of Zillapoore were present at the wedding, for Alice's story, like most things of the kind, had leaked out, and all were anxious to be introduced to the beautiful and interesting heroine. Not a great while after this event, in looking over the orders, I noticed the following: "Sergeant-major W. Cressingham to be lieutenant without purchase, *vice* Sterling, promoted." Thus, the two friends are now both officers, and Alice is as happy as she could wish. "I wish promotion would only go as fast in our regiment as it did in that one," growled out an old soldier, who had lost his chance, by his great predilection for strong drink. "An' if it did, sure it's Captain O'Toole I would be this blessed night, with an Alice of my own, whose Christian name would be Biddy!" responded the incorrigible Bob, knocking the ashes out of his pipe and preparing to re-fill it. "Well, boys," said the sergeant, consulting an old fash-ioned silver watch, "it is nearly 'sentry go,' but I think there is time for another song before planting the relief, and the bugler, here, if I mistake not, is a famous singer, so come, Green, lay aside your bugle and see what you can do." The individual alluded to, who for the last half-hour, had been smoking a short black pipe, which he seemed to enjoy very much, now came for-ward, and seating himself on the end of a peg mallet in such a posi-tion that the light fell on his features, without further preface or delay, and with a serio-comic expression of countenance that was perfectly irresistible, chanted the following lines:

THE LEGEND OF HAMLET THE DANE.

A long time ago lived a monarch
In an outlandish place in the north,
Who, some folks supposed killed his brother,
For a crown, which was all he was worth;
If he did, he made fine reparation,
For the crime he committed, do you see;
For he invited the wife to supper,
After giving her husband his tea.

CHORUS.

Now, just pay attention a minute,
All you that would knowledge obtain,
And I'll shew you, or the devil is in it;
The Legend of Hamlet the Dane.

Now, this brother was a cunning old fellow
And so he contrived his plans,
To send his relation to heaven
Without blood or staining his hands;
For stealing one day into his compound
When slumber did over him creep
He poured something into his ear-hole
Which served to continue his sleep.

CHORUS.

Now, just pay attention a minute, &c.

Now the king who was killed, left behind him,
A son who became all the talk ;
For his learning and various acquirements
Had made him cock of the walk ;
He could read all the stars and converse in
Hebrew, Soomallee, and Dutch ;
He could whistle his own native lingo,
And sneeze in most excellent Scotch.

CHORUS.
Now, just pay attention a minute, &c.

Now one night when Prince Hamlet was on duty,
In charge of an officer's guard,
He prowled like a sick wolf round the ramparts,
It is mentioned by Shakespeare the Bard ;
Th ith e Ghost of his father having opened
His tomb with a skeleton key
Came forth to divulge a grave secret
Which preyed on his spirits, do you see.

Now, what the precise nature of the secret which the spirit of Hamlet's defunct papa had to communicate, we were not then destined to learn, for at that moment we heard the sentry's loud, "Who goes there?" which made the guard turn out quickly, and caused us to spring to our arms in a hurry. Our steps were accelerated by the report of his musket, which was immediately replied to by half a dozen carbine shots that whistled over and around our tent, cutting leaves and branches from the trees which partially concealed it.

CHAPTER XII.

"HALT that guard," shouted an officer, riding up from the rear; "You are off the track, sir," said he, addressing the Soobadar in charge; "What was the meaning of that firing?" "We were fired upon from the top of yonder hill, and I returned it," replied the native officer, lowering the point of his sword as a token of respect to his European superior. "One would have thought that with your thirty years service, you would have been able to distinguish the difference between the report of a musket and that of a matchlock, it was one of our European pickets, and the wonder is that you have not drawn the fire of the whole guard upon you. We distinctly heard the sentry challenge from the head of the column! fall to the rear and give up your sword to the Jemadar adjutant, consider yourself under arrest, and should any casualty have occurred through your carelessness and stupidity, you will have to answer for it before a general court martial;" then, turning to the guard, said, "Take ground to the left in file, and follow me," and he lead the way through a narrow cart-track. As they merged from the deep shadow of the dark jungle, they were brought to a halt, on a sandy road, beneath the broad moonlight, by the quick sharp challenge of a sentry "Who goes there," from a rocky point that jutted out from the table land to their right front. "Advance guard of the heavy brigade," responded the deep voice of the aide-de-camp. "Pass guard, all's well," replied the sentry, at the same time bringing his piece from the port to the shoulder, with a ringing sound that was heard by all. "Keep that road," said the aid to the havildar, indicating, as he spoke, the direction with his sword; "move slowly on, and I will send you an officer in a few minutes;" then wheeling his horse to the rear he galloped off to make his report. This force was the heavy brigade that we had been expecting for some days past; it consisted of five squadrons of European dragoons, the same number of native cavalry, two regiments of Her Majesty's foot, several corps of sepoys, some heavy and light artillery, and an efficient siege train ; likewise a detachment of Sappers and Miners, with all their usual accompaniments ; our total strength amounted to upwards of eleven thousand of all arms. A number of men from the various head-quarters of the several detachments of our light brigade also arrived, to fill vacancies caused by death or other casualties, and the brigade was soon as effective as ever. After a few days we broke up our camp and took up the line of march for Kolapoor, on the banks of the Kisthna. The evening before our departure from Baddaghur, there was a general chevo throughout the force, which was entered into, more or less, I believe, by all ; from the General in command to the youngest drummer boy. Many an unfortunate dragoon had to pay the penalty for his too frequent libations to the rosy god, by being com- pelled to carry his saddle and trappings on his head, and lead his horse fourteen miles the next morning's march. On our approach to Kolapoor, it was ascertained that the Rajah and his fighting men had left the town, and established themselves at Punella and Pawanghur, two forts situated on a range of hills, with a small valley dividing them, a few miles distant, on the opposite side of the river. Just prior to crossing, our chief received notice from the Rajah, that he had made a prisoner of Colonel O——, staff officer of the Bengal army, while passing Punella, and that if we crossed the river in the direction of his fort, he would cut him into quarters and hang him over the principal entrance ; and that all persons that might fall into his hands would be served in like manner. The bearer likewise brought a com- munication from Colonel O——, requesting our commander to push on without delay, as the threat of the rebel chief was only a *ruse* to gain time, he being in hourly expectation of

receiving reinforcements, both in men and provisions; that there
was a peace-party in the council, who, though not strong enough
to induce the chief to surrender, had sufficient influence to prevent him from committing any violent or outrageous act, and that
this same party were now devising means for his (Colonel Ovens')
escape, understanding of course that certain immunities would
be granted them, should they be successful in so doing. Upon
this hint the General acted; his answer was brief, and to this
purport—"that if the Rajah should hurt a hair of his prisoner's
head, or failed to surrender within three days, he would batter
down the Fort; and any prisoners—persons of note—irrespective
of caste, who might be captured, should be blown from the mouth
of a gun, and their remains swept up into one common grave by
the bungys or sweepers of the camp." This alternative, terrible
as it was, to the Hindoos, and natives generally, was not in this
instance put into execution; though some years after, during the
Sepoy mutiny, it had to be enforced. After dispatching his reply,
our General waited for no further parley, but moved on in the
direction of Punella. The river was crossed by means of pontoons,
without opposition from the enemy, and before eight o'clock the
following morning, we had established ourselves on various
positions, around the base of the hills on which the forts stood,
completely surrounding them. The ground in our immediate
vicinity was of a very different nature from that of Samunghur
or Baddaghur, it being an open plain, without any elevation of
sufficient height to be available for artillery purposes during the
siege. It was soon discovered by means of field-glasses, that there
were at least three pettas or villages, outside the walls; one was
in the valley, directly between the two forts, the other appeared
to be built on the slopes leading up to the principal gates. These
villages were swarming with insurgents, who might give us
considerable annoyance while we were engaged throwing up the
necessary earth-works. Therefore, it was deemed advisable to
occupy these places without delay, or render them untenable by

means of our shells, so that they could form no cover for the enemy. The petta in the valley was soon taken possession of by a detachment of dragoons, who made it their head-quarters, and effectually cut off all communication between the two forts. The capture of the others was a far more tedious and difficult affair. Several companies of one of Her Majesty's regiments were ordered for this duty; but it was not until after a very severe and obstinate struggle that they succeeded in driving out the foe, who took refuge in their forts; but they were only enabled to hold them for a short time, as during the night the rebels suddenly sallied out in large numbers, and after a desperate contest our men were obliged to fall back, leaving not only the villages, but their knapsacks and great-coats in the hands of the enemy. They were not long left in peaceful possession; fire was opened upon them from one of our mortar batteries, and both villages were soon reduced to ashes. This had scarcely been effected, when a native made his appearance in our camp, requesting to see the General in command. He was the bearer of a letter from Colonel O——, from which it appeared that he, the Colonel, was a prisoner, but at large within the fort, under the surveillance of a small guard; that he had had two or three interviews with the rebel chief, and was of opinion that the place would be defended to the last, as the Rajah evinced no sign of a change of purpose respecting a surrender, although strongly urged to do so by the peace party. But the latter being in the minority had but little influence with the chief; they were therefore determined, from private reasons of their own, to aid and assist him in making his escape, suggesting that the following means should be adopted: That the General should make a sudden demonstration during the night on one particular part of the fort pointed out by them; they would then be enabled to bribe or overpower the guard during the uproar and confusion which must necessarily ensue, and lower him safely from the walls into the hands of any party that might be sent to meet him

Steps were immediately taken to carry out this idea, a battery
of artillery and a detail of infantry were moved up to the point
indicated, and having, under the cover of night, and unseen,
approached as near the walls as was deemed necessary, the
guns opened a fierce cannonade, followed by a rolling fire of
musketry, to the great alarm and consternation of the insurgents, who, although taken completely by surprise were alive to
their danger, and made simultaneously to the part threatened.
This was exactly what had been anticipated by the projectors of
the plan. The small party of infantry, to whom had been
entrusted the duty of receiving Colonel O—— and covering his
escape, silently and without delay, made their way up the steep
sides of the hill in the direction of the ruined village, near the
main entrance. The large boulders and stunted jungle screening
the party from the observation of those who might be on the
look-out from the walls, enabling them to reach the desired spot
without accident of any kind. They patiently waited for a
further development of the plan, nor were they long kept in
suspense, for the booming of the distant guns of our heavy
battery announced to them that the time for action had arrived.
Pieces of dry timber, brush and other light material was hurriedly gathered together, and thrown into a pile in order to form
a sort of bonfire within the walls of the roofless houses, ready for
use, when required. In a few minutes afterwards a bright blue
light shot up from one of the embrasures, about forty paces in
front of the concealed party ; this light illuminated the locality
for several seconds, and again all was shrouded in darkness. The
Commander, who had been anxiously watching for this signal,
now gave orders to fire the pile, which soon blazed forth, and the
light from the flames disclosed a large portion of the angle of the
wall. There we discerned the form of the Colonel slung in a sort
of bamboo frame-work or basket, being lowered carefully from the
mouth of the embrasure, from which he alighted without accident,
and in less time than I have taken to relate it, the fire was extin-

guished, **and the** little party were making their way back to camp.
On arriving at head-quarters **a rocket was sent up, as** this was the
sign agreed upon, for the discontinuance **of the false** attack ; the
whole party then quietly returned to quarters, without loss of **life**
or accident of any kind on our side. A great deal of useful and
necessary information was furnished by Colonel O——; no
further delay was made, and active preparations now began for
for the reduction of the place in good earnest. A slight sketch **of**
the country surrounding Punnalla and Powanghur may be interesting to my reader, **and at** the same time enable him
more readily to follow me **in** my description of the siege. **For**
miles round the forts the country was a flat open plain, in a
high state of cultivation, bounded on one side by the river
Kishna, on the banks of which stood the large city of Kolpoor;
and on the other, far away in the distance, a dark line could be
distinguished, which marked the commencement **of a dense**
jungle, the haunt of the tiger, **cheeta, and** wild boar, and where
many a venomous reptile **and** poisonous **snake** raised its hideous
head at **the** approach of man, or any other enemy. The forts
stood on **a** long high hill, separated from each other by a valley,
Punalla, the largest, occupied two-thirds of the hill ; this fortress
was in the form of a large parallelogram, and it stood considerably higher than Powanghur, (thereby commanding it **for all**
military purposes), and divided from it by a valley extending
down, yet not reaching the base of the hill, save by a rugged
ravine. For a quarter of a mile ere a person commenced the
ascent, it was a barren, rocky, desolate soil, but as one toiled
upwards it gradually merged into a tangled mass of stunted
brushwood, and immense boulders, afterwards to arrive upon a
large plateau, on various parts of which patches of joarree, gram,
and other grains, had **been cultivated** by the inhabitants of the
villages. On the ascent—for unlike the small farmers of other
countries, they do not live on their farms, but huddle together,
in villages for mutual protection—you would then find your way

impeded, by a bluff rock, or scarp, that almost defied further
progress, winding round which the path leads through brushwood, and over boulders, till another plateau is gained ; and thus,
by tiresome winding and climbing the summit is finally
reached, from which a magnificent panorama of the surrounding country bursts upon the view. The bright waters
of the Kishna, glittering and sparkling in the sunlight, while
winding its serpent-like course ; the waving fields of yellow
grain in the plains below ; the neighbouring city of Kolapoor,
with its sea of palaces and temples ; and, stretching away
in the distance, as far as the eye can reach, the dark jungle, with
its lofty background, the Ram Ghaut mountains, standing out
in bold relief, towering thousands of feet above the level of the
sea. The singular manner in which the Hindoo devotees bathe
or wash themselves must have been a source of amusement to
many. It is somewhat after the following fashion, and could
easily be seen (with the aid of a glass) by any one standing in
either of the forts. A cluster of some four or five temples stood
near the river, in the city of Kolapoor, from one of which a flight
of stone steps descended into the water ; at the foot of these
steps the natives, some standing, some sitting, would stoop down,
and with their brass, or silver lotas, scoop up the water, hold
it above their head, and pour it over their person, at the same
time the Brahmin priests stand at the door of the temple, chant-
ing prayers in a low monotonous voice. After the bathing process is over, they prostrate themselves before their idols, which is
considered a necessary duty before their usual daily work. Some
of the temples are very beautiful, being carved all over with
grotesque figures, in every imaginable attitude. The cupolas are
covered with chunam, a white polished substance that gleams in
the bright sunlight, like burnished silver. Hauling our heavy bat-
tering trains of long eighteen and thirty-two pounders, together
with eleven and a half-inch mortars, up the steep and rugged
side of the hill was both a difficult and fatiguing task, which

had to be effected during the **short** Indian night, as to have attempted it in broad daylight, beneath a scorching sun, would not only unnecessarily expose our **men to that intense** heat, so fatal to Europeans, but **to a** concentrated fire from the Fort; therefore, it was resolved not to commence the work until Sol had set in its golden splendour, behind the distant **hills.** He no sooner disappeared beneath the western horizon than the numerous fatigue parties from the different corps commenced their arduous and somewhat difficult and dangerous duty, in placing **the** guns in their different positions, on the several plateaus; but we were not long allowed to pursue our work undisturbed, for we had scarcely gained the first ridge, when the pale silvery moon rose majestically, shedding its refulgent light, on camp, tower and tree, pouring a flood of moonlight on the long row of white tents, in our now nearly deserted camp, where nought but the measured tread of the sentry, and the footfall of the horse of the cavalry vidette broke upon the silence of **the** night; all was calm, clear and quiet. **Far above** us frowned the dark fortress, with its embattled towers, ramparted curtains, and numerous bastions, from the **deep** mouthed embrasures of which bristled many an old fashioned cannon, the whole pile standing out in bold relief against the clear and almost cloudless sky. Those on the walls were no doubt watching our movements with some anxiety, but as we made no attack upon them, they did not deem it necessary to arouse the whole garrison, when no immediate danger threatened, but contented themselves **by** treating us to an occasional round shot, and keeping up a desultory fire from every available jingal or wall piece, that could be brought **to bear** upon our batteries. These jingals carry one ball each, **of** various sizes, weighing from twelve **to** twenty-two ounces, **and** they gave us considerable annoyance, wounding many, but I do not remember that any were **killed. Our men** worked energetically, and with good will; and, by day, light every gun and mortar had been dragged up, over the numerous obstacles that impeded our way, and all got into position. The Sappers and Miners had, at the same time, thrown up the necessary earthworks, and all was now ready to commence the assault by breaching. At six o'clock our batteries opened a heavy fire upon the walls, with a view of testing their solidity, in order to ascertain the most vulnerable part for the main breach. After a couple of hours of severe cannonading on different parts of the place, the second embrasure from the principal entrance was decided upon for the real breach, and now the fire of our heaviest metal was brought to bear on that spot, while the lighter guns kept up a continuous bombardment at other places, to deceive the enemy as to our real point of attack. From our mortars we sent shot into every part of the fort, waking up the Mahrattas from their peaceful slumbers, and sending many to that last sleep from which there is no awaking. Being on the plain we had not the same opportunity we had in the Fort of Samunghur, or Baddaghur, of witnessing the effect of our shells. Not many of those missiles had been thrown in when a terrific explosion took place. High in the air were hurled pieces of stone, earth, timber, and human beings, in one heterogeneous mass ; some of which fell inside and outside of the place ; here and there a leg, or arm, or head, scorched out of all semblance of a human being, while at a short distance lay the blackened and shapeless trunk, frightful to look upon; one of their magazines had blown up, producing great noise, confusion and death. All that day and night we kept pounding away at different parts of the walls, to prevent the enemy from filling them up to any extent. Next morning the bombardment was recommenced with redoubled energy, and about eleven o'clock the besieged appeared to have divined our plan to effect a breach or entrance point, and directly opposite to it, they commenced to erect a work, half barrier, half stockade, and right ably did they work away, despite the shower of spherical case, canister, and round shot, that we hurled amidst them. They were under the direction of a tall, fine looking Mahratta chief, who, standing on the rampart, near the great gate, with the upper part of his person exposed to our view, being either unconscious or indifferent to the danger in which his prominent position placed him, while skilfully directing and commanding his men by word and gesticulation, to complete their work. All thought of self seemed banished from his mind, his bright scarlet cloak and white turban, presented a fair target, and when the breeze occasionally swept away the cloud of smoke and dust by which he was enveloped, many a pot shot was taken at him from the muskets or rifles of the infantry, some of which had crept up within a short distance of the wall, but to no purpose, he seemed to bear a charmed life. At length a sergeant-major of a battery of brass nine pounders, that were engaged in pitching spherical case at the new work in progress, asked and obtained permission to try a shot at him. After carefully laying his gun, he gave the word " fire," the cloak and turban disappeared, the work ceased to progress, and in half an hour afterwards, not a vestige of it remained. On entering we found the body of this brave fellow lying on the rampart, it had been cut completely in two by the sergeant-major's shot. By mid-day the principal breach was reported practicable ; dinner was hurried through, which, to many a poor fellow, proved a last meal, and at one o'clock the general assembly sounded, and out turned the whole force; volunteers from all corps were now called, to form the storming party that were to force their way through a murderous fire into the stronghold of rebellion.

CHAPTER XIII.

THE hour of four in the afternoon was the time appointed for the grand attack, and seven hundred were the number required for the forlorn hope, (as this desperate service is usually termed,) and for such duty many men from our regiment offered themselves, myself among the number. Smaller parties were also told off for the minor breaches, to act as false attacks or decoys, in order to draw numbers of the besieged from the real point of attack. All our guns were brought into play; the cavalry surrounded the entire base of the hill, and four thousand infantry swarmed up the slopes, taking advantage of every stone or bush that offered a sufficient cover. At four, p. m., the order to advance was given, and the whole force moved forward to perform the various duties assigned them, under a terrific fire from every species of artillery, while the infantry poured an unceasing hail of musketry, sweeping away everything human that presented itself on the ramparts. Nor were the insurgents (now rendered desperate by the almost hopelessness of their situation) a whit behind us; every embrasure belched forth its dire messenger of death; the loopholes, walls and towers, flashed out a murderous fusilade from matchlocks and jingals, while huge masses of stone were hurled from the ramparts, crashing from rock to boulder, and in their descent frightfully mangling and killing many of our poor men. As the colonel of a native regiment was cheering on his men to advance, a round shot from one of the bastions struck him, taking off his right leg, then passing through the body of his horse, carried away the left. Whether the unfortunate officer survived this terrible dismemberment, I am unprepared to say. The band of stormers consisted of men from every regiment in the force; native and European, formed up in columns of sections, those of Her Majesty's regiments claiming the honor of leading. These were all fine sturdy men, of long service, cool and determined. Next followed those of my own regiment, all high-spirited young soldiers, and being on their first campaign, eager to compete in the coming struggle with those of the line. Then came the Sepoys, zealously pressing forward to support their white brethren in arms. All were under the command of Colonel B——, of Her Majesty's —— Foot, the insignia of whose regiment was " the Lamb and Flag." At four p. m., the order for our advance was given, and up we sprang, through bush and over boulder ; from steep to steep, as best we could. The enemy had been watching our approach with intense anxiety, and no sooner did we arrive within range of their fire, than a perfect shower from matchlocks, together with ball, and grape, round shot, and every description of projectile, mingled with pieces of rock, swept through our ranks, crushing, wounding and killing in every direction, thinning our party fearfully, yet onward we rushed. Our artillery sent shells of all sizes into the breach—over our heads—as we advanced. These for an instant would clear all before them ; but again the foe would rush to the great gap only to be hurled back with greater slaughter. We had nearly gained the uppermost plateau, when we were brought to a momentary stand still by a perpendicular scarp of rock, some fifteen feet in height. Noticing a narrow path, a little way to the left, I went with eight or ten others and hurried up into it. There was an officer of the —— Foot with us, who, after proceeding upwards a little way, turned round in search of his own men, and exclaimed, " O, where are my lambs, where are my lambs ?" " Grazing at the foot of the hill," I replied, as I passed him with a bound. This pert reply elicited quite a shout of laughter from my comrades. A few steps onward almost brought me to grief. A comrade, having been a little way in advance, was shot down and fell immediately before me, so close that I stumbled and fell over his dead body, and in so doing, my bayonet fell out of the

18

scabbard, where it was lost among the stones and grass, while the shot fell fast and thick about me. To remain in this position was extremely perilous, and to go into the fort without my bayonet was equally so. I had no alternative but to secure the one belonging to the fallen man, and rushed upwards. I soon gained the wall at the foot of the breach, where I found some officers and a few men close to the wall, and out of the line of fire, the enemy not being able to depress their guns sufficiently to hurt them. They were consulting as to whether they should make a dash into the breach or wait for more men to come up. " Gentlemen, it is better to make a rush than remain here to be crushed to death ; a large mass of stone is on the rampart above our heads, which in a few seconds will be hurled upon us ; I am for a dash," I said, at the same time preparing to advance. "You do not go in alone," cried the Colonel, springing to my side ; and up we went, followed by the remainder. It now became a race between us, as to who should achieve the proud and glorious distinction of being the first man in all that gallant band of stormers to stand on the summit of the deadly breach, and leap into the stronghold of the enemy. This proud triumph fell to me. Just as we reached the top, a piece of rock struck the Colonel on the shoulder, at the same time another hit him on the side of his head ; he would have fallen, had I not caught him, having been completely stunned by the blow. Seizing my musket by the barrel, with the butt I dealt a crushing blow on the chest of a native, who was making a downward cut at my head, that sent him reeling to the earth ; and amid the fire and smoke of a thousand matchlocks, and with a wild hurrah, leaped into the fort ; throwing the Colonel between my legs, I used my bayonet to some purpose among the rebels. By this time a greater portion of the storming party had entered, and now the conflict became more general, fierce and bloody, for the Mahrattas fought with the valor of desperation, defending each position with an obstinacy and energy worthy of a better cause.

But what chance had they in a hand-to-hand encounter with troops before whom the well disciplined soldiers of France and every other European nation had quailed. Standing across the prostrate form of the Colonel, I took several shots at the flying foe, as they crossed before me from bastion to tower. I had just brought down my fifth man, when an officer of Engineers exclaimed : "Capital shooting, by thunder ; but who have we here ?" pointing to the Colonel, who now attempted to rise. I assisted him, and in a few seconds he came to himself. " Where am I ? How did I get here ?" " You owe your safety to this good soldier, my dear Colonel," said an aide-de-camp, who now joined us. " We saw the whole affair from the principal battery, and the General will not forget him." "Oh, I remember it all now; let me have your name and regiment, my brave man. After this affair is over, you shall find that I too will not forget you." I saluted and turned away. By this time the principal part of the fighting was over ; numbers of the Mahrattas had, by means of their turbans, lowered themselves from the walls, in order to escape, but they all fell into the hands of the cavalry, or parties of infantry, who were on the look-out for them. But there still remained many on the walls, and in other parts of the fort that kept up the contest. Passing a look-out station on the wall, which was roofless, I saw the turban of a rebel just above the top, and fancying that the head could not be far off, I sent a shot at it. The bullet being a jagged one, caught in the fabric, carrying it out to its full length, some fifteen yards, exposing to my view the bare scalp of the wearer. While reloading I observed a flight of steps leading up to the ramparts, which commanded a full view of my gentleman ; up these I ran, and faced him ; at the same moment up went both our pieces, and the triggers of both pulled at the same time, the whizz of his bullet sounded very unpleasantly as it passed my ear. My hammer came down, but no report followed. In my hurry I had forgotten to cap, therefore, bounding up to him, and before he could raise his pistol, I sent

my bayonet directly through him. He must have been a person
of some note, for on him I found a very handsome kurgoota, or
silver waist chain (usually worn by persons of rank), five gold
finger-rings, a few rupees, and a magnificent silver hilted sword
and pistol. Taking possession of these, I went on my way
rejoicing; but while passing a small dark archway, a man fired at
me, cutting the pouch off my belt, but doing me no injury.
Flinging down his matchlock, he took his sword in hand and
sprang upon me, but ere he could reach me, my bullet went
crashing through his brain. Crossing towards the centre, I came
upon a very fine looking temple, which, on entering, to my
surprise, I found several of my comrades busily engaged in
digging up with the point of their bayonets something from the
floor. On examination it proved to be rupees, with which the
floor was paved; they had been let into the chunam or plaster
which formed the floor. Taking from my waist-belt a small axe or
tomahawk that I had picked up, I lost no time in following their
example, and succeeded in collecting eighty-four of these pieces
of silver. The ornaments or valuables had been removed before
my arrival. As I left the spot the "general assembly" rang out in
different parts of the place, the firing had ceased, and the fort
was entirely in our possession. The men were collected together;
no further looting or pillage being allowed. By this time it was
nearly dark, and the greater portion of the men were ordered to
return to camp, leaving a sufficient number to guard the mint
and other places, to prevent robbery by friend or foe, during the
night. A prize agent was immediately appointed, and many had
to give up their spoil for the general good. It being necessary
to send an orderly to camp to warn the quarter-master-sergeant
to furnish rations for such of our men as were ordered to
remain in the fort or on sentry, and being on good terms with the
acting sergeant-major, I prevailed upon him to dispatch me for
this duty. By this means I passed out through one of the
smaller breaches with all my booty, prior to the guard being

placed whose duty it was to search all parties leaving the place, to prevent any spoil being carried off. On reaching the camp I sought out the quarter-master sergeant, and gave him the order concerning the rations. Then looking over my booty, I found it to consist of twelve silver-mounted swords, one silver mounted pistol, eleven kurgootas, eight gold finger rings ; and one hundred and two rupees in cash. I went immediately to the bazaar, disposed of all my valuable articles, and being first in the market, obtained a better price for them than those who came after me on a similar errand. I raised in all, cash included, three hundred and thirty rupees—not a bad afternoon's work. During the heat of the engagement at Punella, a party of infantry stole up from the ravine, unobserved, to one of the rear gates of Powenghur. This gate, like all the others, was strongly barricaded on the inside, but it had a small postern, or wicket, which was securely fastened with a large ancient Mahratta barrel-bolt, the staple or fastening of which came through the door, and was secured on the outside by an iron nut or boss ; the whole door was covered with these bosses, which rendered it a difficult matter to decide by a casual observer which one covered the lock. My comrade, Bob O'Toole, who was one of the party, and who had some knowledge of this description of lock (by what means I know not) seized a piece of rock, and dashing it with great force against the nut, which age and exposure had completely rusted through, broke it off, the bolt gave way, and the wicket flew open. Bob jumped in, followed by the rest of the party, to the terror and consternation of the small guard, for there were not many in the archway ; most of them being on a rampart that commanded a view of Punella, watching our operations during the assault. A few shots were fired by both parties ; a short hand-to-hand conflict ensued, but they were soon overpowered—the remainder surrendered at discretion—and long ere night had spread her sable mantle over the earth, the red cross of St. George was proudly floating from the towers of both the rebel strongholds. The fall of the Forts Punella and Powenghur had both a powerful and salutary effect on the insurgents generally. The capture of the Rajah of Kolapoor and his principal officers, not only deterred others from joining the standard of revolt, but was the means of inducing many to desert the cause, and to return to their allegiance. Thus peace and quietness was restored to that section of the country where rebellion first unfurled its defiant flag. But it still existed deep in the Sawent Warree Jungle, and in the immediate vicinity of the chain of Ghauts, which run through the whole country, from east to west, dividing the Deccan from the Conkan, where, trusting to the natural fortifications and the difficulty of access for large bodies of troops—there being no made route but a mere track through the dense jungle—many had sought refuge within its recesses, and set the government at defiance. The day succeeding that of the siege was one of frolic and amusement; there were no parades or roll calls until tattoo. Those who had fallen during the engagement had been interred with all the solemnity befitting the occasion. At an early hour in the morning all was now life and glee; men of different regiments visited and congratulated each other on their safety, the dangers they had escaped, or the booty they had obtained. My companion, Bob, and myself received an invitation to a chevo, given by some of the Dragoons, with whom we had become acquainted some years previous, while at Poona, and right glad were we to avail ourselves of their kind invitation. About six o'clock in the evening we strolled over to their lines. In a large well-lighted double-poled tent were assembled some ten or twelve soldiers of different corps. The fun had began before our arrival, judging from the peals of merry laughter that rang in our ears as we approached. On entering we were greeted with a rousing cheer. My friend Vincent, a sergeant of Dragoons, and who had been for many years manager of their amateur theatre, had been installed Master of the revel, and being principal improviser, was seated on a throne, or dais, erected for the occasion out of an empty beer barrel, with a shabrug thrown over it ; the rest of the company were seated in rows to the right and left of him on saddles, or anything that could support them. Vincent, like the King in Bombastes Furioso, had a foaming pot of porter before him ; a long clay pipe protruded from his lips, from between which volumes of smoke came puff—puff—puff—and as it curled and rolled upwards, mingling with the fumes from the various pipes smoked by his companions (from the aristocratic meer-schaum, to the short black dudeen), floated above the heads of the assembly like vapours on a sunny morn. He stood up, and like that sapient monarch welcomed us right bombastically. " My brave associates, companions of my toil, my pleasure and my fame, behold," said he, majestically waving his long clay pipe in our direction, " behold the men whom the General delighteth to honor. Fill, fill your goblets to the brim, my bold cavaliers, and drink welcome and success to yonder braves—the leader of the forlorn hope, and the heroes of yesterday's fight. Take your time from me, my worthy men at arms," and raising his pot of foaming heavy wet to his lips, took a deep and mighty draught ; his companions following his example in a most laudable manner, and then followed three hearty cheers that made the place ring again. " Most puissant Sir Knight of the sabre, and gentlemen all," I replied, stepping forward, and bowing with most profound mock gravity, " many thanks for the high compliment which you have been pleased to bestow upon myself and comrade. I do not possess sufficient eloquence to reply in suitable terms, for indeed I am no speaker, and not much blessed with eloquent phrases, therefore little shall I grace the cause in speaking for myself, but by your leave I will transfer the grave but pleasing responsibility to my friend and chum, the immortal Bob, the last of the O'Tooles, and lineal descendant of the King of Munster." " Oh, Ned, ye villain of the world, is it me that is to be speechifying. Oh, ochone, the devil a word can I say, baring that

its mighty dacent of yees all, gentlemen, so it is, to trate us in
this fashion, and I'll remember it two years after I'm dead, and
if any man or mother's son, after this, should say, black's the
white of your eye, be all the crosses in a yard of check, I'd take
the measure of his eye for a shute of mourning," and he sat down
amidst a torrent of acclamations, completely overcome by his
feelings. A jorum of steaming arrack punch was now handed to
us from a large camp kettle, in which there appeared to be about
three gallons of this highly spiced, and very tempting tipple. Two
large kettles of commissariat porter graced the floor, there
being neither board or table to be had. Filling our pipes, we
seated ourselves in the most convenient places we could find,
and the convivialities of the evening commenced in right earnest. Songs, yarns, and anecdotes, followed each other in rapid
succession, and although it is now over twenty years since this
occurrence, I will endeavour to relate a few of them, in their own
words, as near as I can remember. " Talking of ventriloquists,"
said an old trooper, in answer to some remark that had just
been made, " we had one in our troop, though no one knew it
until the day after he obtained his discharge. It was old Joe
Brown. I remember a very good joke that he played off some
years ago on one of our non-commissioned officers; he was a very
young sergeant, who had been promoted in consequence of some
letters of introduction he had brought from an unpaid tailor,
bootmaker, or somebody of that sort, and he was very generally
noted for being very pompous, dictatorial and authoritative
when on duty as barrack orderly, or sergeant of the day, consequently, he was not at all a favourite with the men of his
troop, but being of a vindictive disposition, no one cared to
play off any joke upon him. Well, on one occasion he gave
some cause of umbrage to old Joe, and the latter determined to
pay him off the first opportunity, which, to one possessing
his peculiar gift, was not long in occurring. You know
that in the barrack rooms at Kurkee, there stands a wooden

horse about eight feet high, between each man's cot, and
on which the bridle, saddle, and trappings are hung; now,
opposite to old Joe's cot, there slept a man named Nelson, a
regular *bon vivant*, and devil-may-care sort of a fellow. It so
happened that Nelson was on leave for the day at Poona on the
next occasion that young Sparks was sergeant of the day.
Old Joe knew that he would be absent without leave, and he
embraced this good opportunity to take the pompous young
sergeant down a peg. After sundown, and prior to the closing
of the canteen, Joe managed to make a stuffed figure, and dress
it in some of Nelson's clothes, with his full-dress shako on its
head, and a short pipe stuck in the mouth. He placed it on the
saddle, and by the uncertain light of the barrack room, it had
all the appearance of a half-drunken trooper. He succeeded in
effecting this without being observed by any one, for the room
was usually vacant at that time in the evening, and then getting
quietly into his cot, waited patiently the approach of the non-
commissioned officer in question. Soon after tattoo the clanking
of spurs, and clatter of sabre were heard, and the pompous
sergeant strutted into the room. "Where is trooper Nelson?"
said he, standing at the foot of his cot. No response. "Where
is trooper Nelson?" he again demanded, in a stern authoritative
tone. "Here I am, old buffer," said the figure on the saddle,
"what's the row?" "I will let you know to your cost, if
you do not immediately come down; none of your rustical
rigadoons with me, or I'll find another place for you," replied the
sergeant. "You be hanged, you can't do as you like, if your
father did make the major's breeches." A suppressed titter was
heard throughout the room. "You shall have some extra rough
riding drill for this, you blackguard." "I don't ride like a tailor,
as you do, any how." This was a severe cut for young Sparks,
for he was a good horseman, and rather prided himself on his
personal appearance when mounted. Here several horse laughs
broke out in different parts of the room. "Fall in, a couple of

19

troopers, pull yonder fellow down, and take him to the guard," exclaimed the now thoroughly exasperated sergeant. Up jumped the troopers, and down came not Nelson, but the stuffed figure. "It's a dummy," cried one. "It spoke out pretty plainly, any way," cried the other. The shouts of laughter that followed this discovery may be more easily imagined than described ; and the crest-fallen sergeant was only too happy to escape from the room as quietly as possible. Old Joe's practical joke had succeeded to perfection.

CHAPTER XIV.

THERE were various comments made at the conclusion of the trooper's yarn narrated in the last chapter. "Brown must have had a great deal of impudence to treat his superior officer in that manner," remarked young Sims, a cockney, and a corporal of some three weeks standing. "When a non-commissioned officer makes himself ridiculous, as a great many young ones frequently do, by their pomposity and arrogance, they must expect to be laughed at," remarked Sergeant Vincent, with a a meaning look towards young Sims, but he continued, "there is a good deal of fun and frolic to be met with in all ranks of the service." "That there is," I responded, and I will relate what once occurred to myself, while on leave at Bombay. I was in the habit of daily frequenting the "Crown and Anchor," which no doubt many of you know well. They had a capital billiard table, which was the inducement that drew me there. I here met and became on very friendly terms with a midshipman of the Indian navy, who, for some wild prank had been suspended from rank and pay for six months, and sent on shore to rusticate. He was an Englishman by birth, and a native of London, and we often amused ourselves by relating the different scrapes and frolics we had gone through in different parts of the world, for you must know that I was several months at sea prior to entering the army. One afternoon, when I called upon him to have our usual game of billiards, he said : "Now Ned if you are the fellow that I take you to be, you can have some capital fun to-night, it will require some cool impudence, however, but where

is there a soldier worth anything without it. But to my plans ;
a very rich Hindoo named Jaggurnath Sunkersett, living at
Girgaum, gives a ball and supper in a most magnificent and
Oriental style, and has given a general invitation to all officers,
both military and naval, together with all the civil grandees in
Bombay, and it is, I believe, to eclipse anything that has been
seen in the island for years." " But what is all this to me ; I
cannot go, not being either an officer or a grandee, nor have I a
ticket of admission ; I do not see clearly what part I can play
in this pageant." "Then, you must be duller to-day than usual ;
but I will turn on the gas a little ; listen, come to my room
about six this evening, slip on my uniform, it will fit you to a
hair ; jump into a palkee, and off you go. On arrival, wait until
you see a knot of our fellows, follow them in, and when once
inside, you can easily carry on for the remainder of the night, or
I am no judge of horse-flesh." The scheme pleased me exceedingly ; it would enable me once more to mix in decent society,
though under false colors, and anything that promised fun or
excitement, though attended with some risk to my personal liberty,
for I knew that if discovered it would lead to my arrest, was
of itself sufficient inducement for me to accept the offer. My palkee arrived at the principal entrance just as a number of naval
officers came up laughing and jesting among themselves, seemingly in high glee. With this party I entered, and in five
seconds found myself unquestioned in a spacious reception hall ;
directly in front of the splendid mansion of the host, upon the
marble steps of which he stood, surrounded by his dusky friends,
magnificently attired in their Oriental costume, Sunkersett
himself bowing a welcome to all that entered. On my right,
beneath a double row of picturesque looking palm trees, the leaves
of which waved and rustled in the evening breeze, imparting a
delicious coolness to the place, was erected the supper
saloon, it was formed of tent walls, festooned with gorgeous flags and evergreens, with a long table running down the

centre, brilliantly illuminated, and redolent with splendour, consisting of gold, silver, flowers, and cut glass. On the left, reached by a flight of broad stairs, handsomely carpeted, the niches of the walls, on each side, filled with elegant figures in gold, silver, and marble, fantastically supporting wax lights, in every position that grace or fancy could dictate, was the ball-room. It was superb, with its beautiful canopy of white glazed cloth, studded with gold stars, and roses, and supported by fifty-four fluted columns of burnished silver, the reflection of which was seen in the enormous mirrors that were placed between each of the pillars, lending a feeling of enchantment to the scene; sofas, lounges, and ottomans were innumerable in the verandah outside the pillars, into which the pale moon threw its soft light, while the interior or dancing hall, was lighted by numerous wax tapers in massive candelabras. Scattered over the grounds were iron cressets, filled with blazing cocoa nut shell, and Chinese lanterns of many colors were suspended from the numerous orange and pomegranate trees, the whole forming a splendid *coup-d'œil*. Putting a bold face on the matter, I sprang lightly up the steps, just as the first set of quadrilles were forming, and stepping quickly up to a fair young girl, of about nineteen summers, solicited and obtained her for my partner, and was soon lost in the mazes of the dance. At the conclusion of the set I led my fair friend to a seat, placed myself by her side, and was not long in finding out who she was. Chancing to glance to my right, I saw, to my confusion, seated on the same ottoman as myself, a lady flirting violently with no less a personage than the colonel of my own regiment. " I am in for it now," thought I; but fortunately, a young middy was too unimportant a personage to attract the attention of the gorgeously apparelled field officer. I saw that he did not recognize me, and in a moment I was myself again, and blossoming out in trope and metaphor to the little divinity by my side. Waltz succeeded gallop, and quadrilles followed in turn; there was no lack of partners, thanks to my own assu-

rance. I flirted first with one, then another, told innumerable
stories and escapes from storm and wreck in the Persian Gulf,
to elderly ladies and cavalry griffins. Drank as much champagne
as would have floored any one possessing a softer head than
mine, and in fact enjoyed both myself and supper amazingly.
About two in the morning while I was crossing from the salle à
manger to the ball-room, an officer came suddenly to me, and
touching me on the shoulder, said, " Step this way, sir, a few
words with you, if you please," leading the way, as he spoke,
towards an orange grove. I followed, " I am done for now,"
said I, half aloud ; for, by the light of a Chinese lantern, I recognized the uniform of my regiment. When beyond ear-shot of
the gay throng, he halted and turned towards me. By the
moonbeams that played upon his countenance, I discovered much
to my relief, the features of Captain C——, the wildest, hand-
somest, and certainly the most popular officer in the regiment,
and with whom I was on easy terms, having played on several
occasions at our theatre in many of the pieces in which he took a
part. He had recognized me from the fact of my having played
Lieutenant Wilder to his "Red Rover," some four months previous,
in a uniform similar to the one I then wore. "Upon my word,
youngster, you possess no small amount of cheek to present
yourself in that character in this brilliant assembly. I knew
you the moment you entered, and have had my eye on you all
night ; the wonder is that the Colonel did not twig you, for you
sat awkwardly close to him in the early part of the evening, but
he has not the slightest suspicion, nor any one else, as far as I
can learn ; but if the Major had been here, you would have been
cooling your heels in the guard room long ere this. You have
been pulling pretty heavy at the champagne, or I would
not have spoken to you until you were about to leave, but you
do not appear to be the least affected by it ; mind, keep sober, and
you are all right. I see that you can behave like a gentleman,
but this I suspected before, or I could not have allowed you to

remain five minutes after your arrival ;" then laughing heartily at what he was pleased to call my taking a cheerful rise out of the grandees generally, he left me, and turned into a large octagon shaped tent, fitted up as a smoking divan, where the Bengal cheroot, and trichanopolly cigar, were in vogue, and that Oriental luxury, the silver-mounted glass hooker with its velvet snake, was to be had in true Mahommedan style, but in those days the odour of lavender mille-flower, or otto of roses, had more charms for me than garraco or tobacco; therefore I did not follow but returned to the ball-room, nor did I again leave the gay and festive throng until the boom of a gun announced that the festival was about to close with a grand display of fireworks, which were to be seen from different parts of the grounds. And anything more magnificent or grandly beautiful can scarcely be conceived ; countless meteor stars, serpents, rockets, blue lights, and every description of fireworks, shot high into the air, in one simultaneous mass, spreading beneath the sky brilliant shades of every tint and hue, reflecting back again their tinge on water, wood and temple, like a magic scene in fairy land ; lighting up the whole country for miles around the harbour, wherein lay a fleet of vessels, from whose masts floated the flags of all nations. The rugged rocks of Malabar Point, with its temples, mosques, and the far-famed towers of silence, or burial places of the Parsees, on the extreme right. On the left the wildly picturesque island of Elephanta, celebrated for its magnificent caves, and directly opposite, with silent and deserted like appearance, stood Colaba lighthouse; all were brought in vivid and startling beauty before us by the dazzling and brilliant light of the fireworks. At the close I helped myself to a bumper of champagne, and ere the crush came, jumped into a palkee, and was fast asleep before I reached my friend's bungalow. "By George, I would have laid in the guard room for a month, to have had such a glorious spree as that," said one of the party, as I concluded ; "but you must have been used to that sort of thing, or you never could have carried it out so cleverly." "I thought that your regiment was stationed at Poona. How was it that so many of your officers were at the ball," enquired another. "Our head-quarter wing was there; the other under the command of the major at Colaba," I replied: "But why did not he attend, and why would he have recognized you more than any of the others?" "Well, you must know that our second in command was one of those sanctimonious, praise God bare-bones sort of men, who pretend to have a perfect horror of balls, parties, theatricals, and such like vanities, as he termed them. He had many peculiarities, both of speech and manner, which I used to mimic on our stage to the no small delight of my audience. This, of course, came to his ears, hence his dislike to me. He had evidently mistaken his vocation by entering the army instead of the church ; not that I think the ecclesiastical body would have benefitted by his admission ; far otherwise, but had he abstained from entering the service," "I fancy that his absence would have been mighty good company," put in the O'Toole, finishing the sentence for me, at which there was a general burst of laughter. "I should say by the way your friend Bob handles his pipe, and takes his grog, that he could spin a good yarn for us," suggested Sergeant Vincent. "No doubt of it," cried several voices, "let's have a twister from the hero of Powenghur." "Faith, it's little I know about spinning yarns and the like as you call it, however, I'll tell ye's an anecdote I had wid a black divil of a bear in Ameriky." "In America, I did not know that you had been such a traveller, Bob," "Arrah, hould yer whisht, Corporal Sims, for a meddlesome cockney that ye are ; it's many more things ye don't know, nor ever will. Do you remember, Ned, avic, where I first met ye?" "Yes, I remember very well," was my reply, "it was at Quebec." "Well, then, I'll tell ye how I got there. My father was what they call one of the better class of immigrants ; that is to say, he had a few sovereigns in the heel of an ould stocking, whun he wint to Canada, where he was to get ever so much land just for the axing, and live like a foin gintleman as the O'Tooles used to do, when they were kings of Munster, arrah, but it's little he knew what a devil's own hole we wor going to. Well, to make a long story short, from Quebec we were forwarded to Toranto, and then to a place called Barrie, and from there to our estate, in the township of Wasanagus ; faith, it was well named, for we were all like to die with the ague there ; devil a fut of dry land was there in it, but what was under wather. What is ye'es laughing at, ye devils ?" "Never mind, go on, Bob, said I. "After a while," continued Bob, "we get up a bit of a log shanty, wid a shed at the ind of it for a cow, and a tranneen of a pig, and began to feel a little comfortable like, altho 'twas awful lonely. Be this and be that, I often think of that same cow, boys, and give her a blessing, for she was the cause of all my trouble wid the bear. There was a beaver dam, and a meadow some distance from our lot, and the little cow would often stray away there, bad cess to her, and stay until I fetched her back. One day I was after the cow, and not far from the meadow, when I heard a kind of shuffling noise behind me. When I looked round, be the mortal, but there was a big brown bear hot foot after me. Ye's have seen me run a race, boys, but ye never seen me run in airnest ; bedad, I run that time, and sure it was no kind of use at all, at all ; the shuffling came nearer and nearer. "Well, jist forninst me, I seen a hollow log about twelve feet long, wid a hole in it that a bit of a gossoon could crawl into ; so bedad in I went ; faith 'twas time, for the next minute I felt the claws of the baste tickling the soles of my feet ; the brute was too big to get in. Arrah, but he was mad ; I could hear him tearing and biting at the ind of the log. Presently, the other ind of the log got dark-ened, and the bear poked in his head, champing and foaming like a mad wild boar ; musha, but it makes me shiver yet when I think how I could feel the hot breath of him in amongst me hair. Round and round the log he wint, from one ind to the other ;

20

says he, at last, ' this will never do, I must get the boy out of that.'" "What, do bears speak in America ?" said the unfortunate corporal. " Shure, was'nt he thinking it, and is'nt it all as one, ye omadahon ye," said Bob. " To be sure," said I, " go on Bob." " All of a suddint I felt my feet rising up in the air, till I was standing on my head, houlding on for dear life, be the knots and rough places inside the hollow log, which the baste commenced shaking and pommeling on the ground, for all the wurld like a pavier bating paving stones, and whin he thought he had loosened me hould, he let the log go down with a bang that fairly shuck the breath out of me, and quick as thought made a dive at the ind of the log, but I was as far from him as ever. Well, presently the head ris up, and by this and by that, the black divil took me in his arms, log and all, and began walking away wid me, till I felt him splashing in the water. Tare and ages, sis I, I'm kilt now entirely ; he manes to droun me, and shure inough he rolled the log in till it was under wather. Well, boys, it's well I can swim like a duck, and can bate any stone at diving. So before I was quite smothered, I took a deep breath, floated quietly out of me hiding place, and dived clane acrost the pond, till I kim up amongst the rushes, on the other side, thin I took courage to raise me head and take a look. There sat me gentleman on the top of the log to keep it down, looking as knowing as you plase, and whin he thought he'd kept me there long inough to drown me, he rowls the log out and looked in at the ind of it. Ye'd have kilt your- self laughing, to have seen the look he put on, whin he found me gone ; he was fairly puzzled. But bears, me lads, is cute things, and this one bate Banagher for cuteness ; he began now to walk round the pond, and af course whin he kim forninst me, I put my head under wather, and kept it there too till he wint by. Well, when he had done sniffing and looking after my dead body, thinks he, ' his body must be at the bottom of the pond,' and would ye's believe it, boys, he began tearing away the dam wid

the big paws of him, to draw the water off, and soon had it
running like mad through the sluice. Then he began walking
round the pond again. 'Holy Virgin, shure, I am lost now,' says I.
I took **another** dive for the sluice, and down I wint with the
stream, and kim up just below a bind in the creek, where I
landed and away for the bare life, towards a small Indian
encampment, that I knew was on the banks of the river, not
far off. Jist as I got within sight of the wigwams, as they call
them, I heard the same noise again, and be all that's great,
there was the bear after me again, but bedad he was too late
this time; I gave a yell ye'd have heard a mile off. The Indians
kim running out, and in less than half an hour they had the
divil kilt and the skin off him. A few days after, my father,
may the Heavens be his bed, sent me to Barrie, for something
was wanting, and somehow I thought I'd had enough of Canada,
and that me little brother Tim wid be the better of the estate, so
I made my way to Quebec, and from there to the ould country,
where I listed, and here I am, and," added O'Toole, reflectively,
"**if,** as some of yees says, there is the laste taste of **rid in**
my hair, by this and by that, it's that same fright I got wid
the bear turned it that color." Such exclamations as "Bravo,
bravo," "More power to your elbow;" "That you may never die,"
and others of a similar nature that burst from his amused hear-
ers, shewed with what satisfaction he had been listened **to.**
"That is a very good story of yours, and you had a narrow escape
from a watery grave, but there is an ancient proverb, that the
man who is born to be hanged will never be drowned," maliciously
remarked Corporal Sims. "Oh thin, you are a purty boy, corporal dear, has your mother any more like ye ; but the divil
a fear of your being hurt, had ye been in my place." "For
what reason, Bob," said I, the whole group looking enquiringly
towards him. "Arrah, gintlemen, shure the bears in Canada
don't ate carrion," was the response. The unfortunate man of
two chevrons wished he had kept his ancient proverb to himself,
the laugh had been so cleverly turned against him.

CHAPTER XV.

AFTER the roars of laughter, had somewhat subsided, which had greeted the yarn of the immortal Bob, Sergeant Vincent immersed his moustache in some of Barkley and Perkins' dark-looking fluid, greatly to his satisfaction, and having laid aside his long clay pipe, began as follows : " I suppose you all know the black jungle near Belgaum ; it was, and in fact is now, the favorite shooting ground for the officers and men at that station ; principally because in addition to deer, peacock, partridge, duck, and other game of a similar nature, there are still to be met with, the tiger, cheeta, hyena, and not unfrequently the brown bear. Many a trophy has been brought in from there, and many a narrow escape from loss of life and limb has been related by parties on their return from a hunting expedition in the thickets of this jungle. What I am about to relate, happened to two men belonging to a company of artillery that were doing duty at the fort, and who had obtained leave of absence to go on a shooting excursion within the jungle in question. They had very fair sport up to about four, p.m., as their game-bag amply testified. They had quietly seated themselves to take some refreshments, beneath the shade of some bushes that grew near the bank of a small stream, which ran rippling and murmuring with a cool refreshing sound through the little valley where they halted. Both were tall, well-made, muscular men, between thirty and forty years of age, and they were dressed in shooting coats and overalls of checked cotton, the manufacture of the country, with high hunting boots, stout leather belts round their waists, while their heads were protected from the **heat of** the sun by broad-leaved felt hats, around which was twisted the common turban of India. One carried a double barreled shot-gun, and a long stout hunting knife, stuck in his belt , the other had a carbine loaded with ball, as was likewise the regulation holster pistol that he wore in his waist belt. They had finished their meal ; one had filled his pipe and commenced smoking, the other had gone to the stream to slake his thirst with some of the clear element. As he was about to rise from his kneeling position, he observed a pair of fierce gleaming eyeballs fixed upon him from amidst the bushes that grew on the opposite bank of the narrow rivulet. He had barely time to rise, and draw his knife, when the creature, a monstrous hyena, sprang upon him—a frightful struggle ensued. Several times did he bury his knife in the body of the animal, but to no purpose ; the savage beast seemed to heed them not, but fixing his immense paws on the man's right shoulder, tearing off the flesh in one piece, down to the elbow ; the pain was so intense, that with a shriek of anguish, the poor fellow sank fainting to the ground. The cry aroused the attention of his comrade, who sprang forward, and seeing the fate of his friend, levelled his carbine, and fired at the creature, his shot taking effect in its neck. Turning from the man with a hideous laugh, for which that beast is noted, he sprang at the throat of the other, who, clubbing his weapon, dealt many a heavy blow on the head of the brute, but unfortunately in so doing, the carbine broke short off at the small part of the stock. Dropping the now useless weapon, he felt for his pistol, but to his dismay, he found that during the struggle it had fallen from his belt, and lay at some distance from him ; he was now powerless, but, in desperation, he, with both hands, seized the brute by the head, and endeavored to shake himself free from its grasp. But, alas ! he was but an infant in strength compared with his enemy. He was nearly exhausted ; his clothes had been torn to shreds, and blood issued profusely from many a ghastly wound, inflicted by the teeth and claws of the monster, on different parts of his body. At this critical moment, a double report was heard quite close to the scene of action, the hyena grinned horribly, and with a convul-

sive gasp relaxed his hold, and fell dead, pierced through the
side by a couple of rifle bullets. Fortunately the captain of the
men's company likewise sought game in that neighborhood, and
had witnessed the first encounter from a slight eminence, at a
short distance. Rapidly, but without noise, he approached close
enough to the spot, under cover of the adjacent bushes, to make
sure of his aim, then fired, with the effect above related. After
some stimulants had been administered, both the men recovered
sufficiently to walk home. A few weeks' attendance at the
hospital enabled them to resume their duties ; it was a narrow
escape for them." " But what became of the hyena," I enquired.
" He was brought into camp during the evening by some natives,
who had been sent out for that purpose by the captain. He had
it skinned and stuffed, and it was usually kept in the Orderly
Room, and for all I know may be there to this day," he replied.
" Bedad, but it's mighty quare that I did not hear of that same
baste's story before," hiccuped the O'Toole, as he buried his
glowing visage in a porter pot. "Hark," said Sergeant Vincent,
" the trumpets are sounding off the first post, fill up my boys,
and let's drink the Queen's health, and confusion to her enemies,"
which was done right loyally. " Long life to John Company, and
bad luck to all Rajahs and rebel Nagurs," hiccuped the O'Toole,
making a grasp at my arm to preserve his perpendicular, as I
rose to leave the tent, for the arrack punch had made considerable
impression upon him, so much so that I had some difficulty in
getting him home. As it had been a day of universal jollity,
we succeeded in reaching our lines unquestioned, though we were
not allowed long to enjoy our rest, or to remain inactive, for
about four o'clock the next evening, an order was issued by the
Commanding Officer for the re-forming of the light brigade, which
was to march the following evening ats un-down, and by ten,
p.m., we found ourselves once more on the banks of the Kishna.
What direction we were to take after crossing, was known only
to the Brigadier in command. The next morning we made out

way to the high-road that led to Neepanee; halted at that
place during the night, afterwards turning off to our right, entered
the jungle the next morning by a cart track. Now it became
known that our destination was the fortress of Ranghur, on the
Hunmunt Ghaut, and the object of this forced march was to get
there before the rebels could establish themselves at that place.
After four days' marching through a dense jungle, during which
time we had accomplished a distance of about ninety-seven
miles, found ourselves halted about sixteen miles from Ranghur,
to allow the artillery to come up. On the arrival of the
guns we again resumed our route. In consequence of the
intricacies of the way, the cavalry were sent on some time in
advance, but the brigade started at the usual hour. It was a
lovely morning when we commenced our march. The moon
shone bright and clear; the air was cool and refreshing; the
heavy floods caused by the monsoons no longer drenched the
earth; all nature teemed with luxuriant wild vegetation, bright,
green and beautiful, and although it impeded our progress to some
extent, yet it was pleasant and cheering to look upon. The
month of December is in my opinion the most delightful time
of the season of the year in India; that is in the Southern
Mahratta country. We had completed about half our distance,
when an aide-de-camp came hastily back to order the artillery
to the front at the trot, and the infantry to follow at the double.
The cavalry had been attacked, and were now engaging the
enemy. We pushed on as rapidly as possible, for a number of
their men had fallen. We soon came up with the doolies and
hospital paraphernalia of the cavalry. The medical staff surrounded by a strong guard, were busily engaged in dressing, and
binding up the wounds of those who had suffered in the skirmish. It appears that at this spot a number of the enemy had crept
up the sides of a ravine concealed by the thick brushwood, and
poured in a heavy volley from their matchlocks, as they rode by,
putting *hors-de-combat* about twenty troopers. The enemy then

fled and rejoined their main body. Near a jambool bush, knelt a fine-looking Mahommedan, a troop havildar, bending over the dead body of his only son, who had been slain by the fire of the murderous foe. He drew his sword in silence, and vowing on his Koran, swore by both, and all that he held most dear, to take bitter vengeance on the murderers of his gallant son ; then springing into his saddle quickly overtook his troop. One of the advance guard, who had lived some years in the neighbourhood, said he knew a short cut that would speedily bring them into the very heart of the rebel encampment. No sooner did this become known through the regiment, than they were clamorous and vehemently requested to be led on to them without delay. The treacherous attack had roused their blood. The officer in command acceded to their demand, and off they went at a hand gallop. We pushed after them with all speed, but did not arrive in time to take any part in the fight, for the artillery and cavalry had driven and dispersed the Mahrattas effectually without our aid. Many fled to the Fortress of Ranghur, leaving their dead, wounded, and prisoners in our hands. It was a splendid affair; I heard it described by the European sergeant-major to a number of our sergeants, who had gathered round him as he sat smoking at the foot of a shady banyan tree. Our guide turned into a narrow path ; here we dismounted, each trooper leading his horse, for there was scarcely room for one at a time to pass. In this way we advanced about one and a half miles as silently as possible. The moon had gone down, the day had not yet dawned, and all was dark around us, but the grey light of the coming day became visible as we emerged from the jungle, and entered a comparatively clear spot, where we formed to the front by troops. This space had the appearance of a small park, in front of which grew a large patch of joarree, under cover of which we made this movement, by the leading file halting, the remainder coming up into their positions. "Steady," cried our commander, and the word forward was given, and with drawn sabres we advanced a little to our front, and as the ground opened, formed into line at a trot. Our guide now crept through the corn, and soon returned with information, that the rebels in large force, with artillery and some cavalry, were pitched not more than a quarter of a mile on the other side of the grain fields. Making a detour, we saw before us by the light of the coming day the burning matches of some of the enemy, who acted as a sort of outlying picket. We then advanced without sound of trumpet, the pickets fired their matchlocks at us, and then fell back, in considerable consternation, so unexpected had been our appearance. They were prepared to meet us, but not from that point. Forward we went right at them, the blare of the trumpets ringing on the flank of each troop as we came in full view of the foe. Their infantry in line, with a few guns and cavalry on their flanks, came on to meet us; they greeted us with a heavy discharge of matchlocks, which caused many of our troopers to fall dead or wounded from their saddles. Our colonel now gave the word "prepare to charge," and the whole of the cavalry, advancing first at a canter, then rushed on at the charge. The enemy was enveloped in smoke, from which there came a discharge of grape and canister that swept through our line with frightful effect, while the surrounding hills rang with the din of battle. "Gallop, charge," thundered the Colonel, and on we dashed like an avalanche, knee to knee, and bridle to bridle, the very earth seeming to shake beneath our horses feet; everything went down before us. Their infantry being unprovided with bayonets or pikes, could not resist our terrific onslaught, and after a few more discharges of matchlocks, turned and fled in wild confusion. Our artillery opened upon them with several discharges of spherical case, mowing them down like grass. Their loss was immense, but their thorough knowledge of the country enabled many to escape through the jungle. Their cavalry, with their long steel-pointed spears, made several ineffectual attempts to arrest our progress, but finding all lost,

21

sought their own safety in a rapid flight, leaving us masters of the field.

"Do you see yonder havildar," said the sergeant-major, pointing as he spoke to a fine-looking man, who was carressing his horse while feeding; "he is the finest man in the corps, and made great havoc among the Mahrattas." He had a son killed by them, early this morning, and vowing vengeance against the whole race, fearfully did he keep his vow, for no sooner was the word given to pursue, than he sprang his charger two lengths in advance of his troop, and wheeling to the left, dashed after a number that were flying down a narrow track, hewing, hacking and cutting right and left, every one he met with the powerful strokes of his avenging sabre, and it was not until both horse and rider were nearly exhausted that the work of slaughter was stayed. He then rode slowly back to his troop, avenged. The number slain by his single arm was almost incredible. Had the infantry arrived in time they must all have fallen into our hands. As some time would elapse before either the tents would arrive, or the breakfast be ready, I strolled over to the scene of action; it was a sad spectacle. The wounded and dying were being removed for medical treatment. The bodies of the fallen on both sides had been gathered; those of the Mahommedan faith to be buried, while those of the Hindoo were conveyed to the funeral pile, the smoke and flames from which soon burst forth and curled upwards, and the odour from this burning mass was offensive and disgusting in the extreme. To European minds this ceremony conveyed a sense of complete barbarism. Riderless horses were caught, and not a few of the camp followers, those pests of the army, were making their harvest by despoiling the bodies of the slain. Weapons of all descriptions were scattered about; many were broken and useless. One of the cavalry standards, cut to ribbons by bullets, was found among a heap of dead, with its gallant bearer pierced through the heart lying lifeless beside it, his noble steed quietly standing by the side of its late rider. Nor were the ravens and kites absent from their sanguinary banquet. The theatre of this bloody drama was both wild and picturesque, with a dense jungle for a background—the open park-like table land, on the mountain tops, where the conflict had raged so furiously, with its rugged peaks and numerous cascades of bright falling waters dashing from crag to crag, in their downward course, till they reached the stream, which flowed through the valley below. From many spots a magnificent view of the Indian Ocean could be obtained, which to those whose eyes for many a month had looked upon nothing save sandy plains and thick jungles, was a charming relief, and in fact a great treat. From one of the numerous pretty promontories that jutted out above a deep ravine, to which I had the good fortune to stray, and seating myself on a piece of rock beneath the shadow of a clump of trees, I beheld the glorious orb of day, rising from its ocean bed, its bright golden rays lighting up the eastern hemisphere and smiling down upon the fair face of nature's garden stretching out for many a mile towards the sea shore, from the foot of that magnificent range of Ghauts which have been so often and so ably portrayed by writers on British India.

The country in the immediate vicinity of the Fortress of Ranghur, presenting no facilities for the development of cavalry evolutions, it was decided that they, together with a battalion of native infantry, should be left here to act as a corps of observation, while we, the remainder of the brigade, should march on that place at an early hour the following morning. We moved about daylight, and when the sun had dispelled the clouds and vapours that surrounded us, we found Ranghur to be situated on a rocky eminence of a similar height to the table land on which we were marching, and approachable on one side only by a narrow neck of land, whose steep and almost precipitous sides rendered it very difficult for artillery or

bodies of infantry to cross, provided the occupants of the fort
were disposed to dispute the passage. A small village on the
verge of the Ghaut, where the track to the fort opened, was
immediately taken possession of by us, and a strong picquet
posted there. The inhabitants, after exchanging a few shots, fled
to the fort. A little later in the day an officer, with a flag of
truce, was sent to demand a surrender of the place, but having
been fired upon, returned without having effected anything.
During the afternoon the artillery was got into position at the
village above alluded to, and in the evening some shells were
thrown into the fort to let them know that we were within
range. Early the next morning an artillery man, who, during
the previous night had taken more grog than was quite good
for him, had wandered out of the camp and lost his way
in the jungle. After roaming about for a couple of hours,
and on emerging from some bushes, he was surprised to
find himself close to the principal gate of the enemy's works.
Crouching as near as possible to the wall, so that he might
not be observed, he began to meditate what he should do
to enable him to return to camp without being discovered. He
remained in this position about a quarter of an hour, and every
thing being quiet around him, he listened attentively, but
hearing no voices, he imagined the place was empty. Taking
courage, he crept softly up to the gate, and found the wicket
to his surprise was partially open. Looking about, and observing
no one, he cautiously entered and found that the place was
deserted, the enemy having evacuated the fort during the night,
taking with them everything of value that was portable. Having
satisfied himself of this fact, he returned quickly to camp, and
meeting the brigadier, who was walking alone, reported the
circumstance to him, omitting to say, however, that in consequence of his having indulged in too much grog the night before
he wandered abroad, and while endeavoring to make his way
back, came accidentally upon the fortress. But he accounted for

the discovery in such a plausible manner, that subsequently the commander promoted him to the rank of sergeant. The place was immediately taken possession of, and we found that one of our shells had fallen among the retreating rebels, killing eleven of them as they were making off by the rear gateway. A few days afterwards, meeting the color sergeant of the company coming from the C. O. tent with the order book, I enquired if there was anything new stirring. "Yes," he replied, "the heavy brigade from Punnella are expected in the morning, and the light brigade are to march to a new position, near the Vingorla road, in order to endeavour to force our way down the Ghaut to Seevapoore, a large village in the Sawaunt Warree jungle, near the Fortresses of Monahar and Monsontosh, where the rebels appear to have concentrated their entire force, and are making a final stand ; but my dear fellow I believe that I shall soon have the pleasure of congratulating you on your promotion, for the captain has just told me that your name has been favorably mentioned in the general's dispatch to the government, and it is expected by the officers that your dashing conduct at Punnella, will be rewarded by a commission, but nothing is to be said to you about it, until the reply from government arrives." Thanking him for the information, and having heard something of the rumor before, fervently hoped that it might turn out to be correct. As "there is many a slip between the cup and the lip," I did not allow my mind to dwell long upon it, I therefore busied myself in preparing for the coming march, which had been rendered necessary by the change in our base of operations.

CHAPTER XVI.

MONAHAR and Monsontosh, are two rocky eminences rising out of the Sawaunt Warree jungle, which stretches from the foot of the Ram Ghaut to the sea shore, between the ports of Vingorla and Rutneegerry, and towering in altitude to nearly the level of the Ghauts themselves, and on which two fortifications had been constructed many years ago. The difficulty of access, and the natural defences of these forts led the Mahrattas to the belief that they were impregnable. Through the valley at their base ran a broad but shallow stream, which, after crossing the high road, and meandering through many a hollow and shady dell, found its way to the sea near the Portuguese settlement of Goa. On the bank of this stream, and immediately at the foot of the Hunmunt Ghaut, stood the large and populous village of Seevapoore, in which and the vicinity we found the remnant of the rebel host who had escaped from our cavalry at Ranghur. They had likewise conveyed large quantities of provisions and munitions of war to the two mountain fortresses, as a place of retreat and shelter, should we succeed in routing them. Here, also, were congregated hundreds of " Budmashes," thieves and vagabonds of all castes, who had an antipathy against honest labor, and a propensity for plunder. These hordes infested the public road leading from the sea-board to Belgaum, Bellary, and other large military stations, murdering or maltreating all who fell into their hands, and plundering any vehicle that passed without a sufficient escort. They pillaged the smaller pettas, when the inhabitants refused to join or aid them in their schemes against the Government. To put an end to this state of things, two small but effective brigades were organized and despatched ; one to the top of the Ram Ghaut to keep open the main road, and protect life and **property,** also to capture as many of these scoundrels as could **be pounced** upon. The other to a smaller Ghaut—the name **of which** has escaped my memory, but it was situated between the latter post and the **heavy brigade** on the Hunmunt Ghaut—in order if possible to force our way, **(for** to this brigade my regiment belonged) down some of **the** narrow ravines to the valley below, and effect a junction with a force that was to be sent from Vingorla to meet us, and separately **or** conjointly rout the enemy, and if found necessary, reduce **Seeva**-poore to ashes. After a three days' march through a dense jungle, **we arrived** at the post assigned to us. The first thing to be **done,** after taking up our position, was to pitch camp, entrench **it, and** make our quarters as comfortable as possible. Reconnoit-ering parties were next sent out to ascertain the possibility or prac-ticability of a descent. On our arrival a few fellows showed them-selves on the crest of the hill, and wasted a few shots on us, then retreated, conveying information of our whereabouts to their friends in the valley, who lost no time in stockading every possible avenue that led to the plain below. " I tell you what it is, Martin, these ruffians are trying to out-flank us," exclaimed an officer of ours, who had charge of a party, consisting of fifty of our men and about the same number of native rifles, who were acting as coverers to a working party engaged in constructing a road along a ravine, to get our light howitzers into play, should opportunity offer. The remark was made to a handsome young man, apparently about five-and-twenty, who was reclining at full length on the soft mossy grass, beneath the shade of an overhanging nym **tree,** puffing clouds of smoke from a **genuine Manilla,** consoling and amusing himself from time **to time in knocking** off the white ashes from **the end of his** cigar, with **the gloved tip of his little finger,** without moving from his recumbent position. **This** youth was an exquisite of the **first** water, and affected all the peculiarities of that class, who usually exist only in the drawing-rooms of St. James' and Pall Mall. I

have said that he was very handsome ; he dressed always with
studied elegance, and his uniform fitted him to a charm. He wore
kid gloves on all occasions, and never condescended to wear any
other than patent leather boots. The air became impregnated
with the odour of some exquisite perfume whenever he flourished
his handkerchief, which he did frequently. During the day,
while moving about, except when on parade, he assumed a very
slow measured step ; never being hurried by any one, or any
thing, and in conversation affected a lisping drawl, most amusing
to listen to, whether the subject was of importance or of the
most trifling nature. On one occasion, when on duty as orderly
officer inspecting the rations of the men, a complaint was made
to him by the mess orderlies, that the meat furnished by the
contractor was not as good as it ought to have been, and not at
all to his own satisfaction, he turned to the butcher and said,
" Oh toom slaughter man, dooseerah, wackett toom, atcha, ghos,
ney langa, um toom, ko general Sahib report carrunga, so, toom,
decko non." What he meant to convey to the native butcher
was, that the next time he failed to supply good meat, he would
report him to the general, and that he had better look to it.
There was nothing peculiar in these words themselves, it was
the haw, haw, drawling, affected tone in which they were uttered,
and the superlative wave of the hand as he motioned the contractor to fall back that was so irresistibly comic. Stern discipline
prevented our laughing outright ; but many a time since I have
enjoyed a hearty laugh whenever the incident crossed my mind.
All that he vouchsafed to do on the present occasion, was to
raise himself a little on his elbow, look through the small field-
glass that he always carried in the direction indicated. Then,
in his most drawling and affected style, replied, " My dear fellow,
they have not the ghost of an idea of such a thing," and sank
back as if the effort had been almost too much for him. He was,
to use the expression common among the men of the brigade,
" an immense swell ;" but it was also well known to us all that

when bullets were flying and swords and sabres flashing, there was no braver or better officer in the force. If the rebels had not a ghost of an idea of flanking us, they certainly had a very sound and practical notion of it ; and if we had not changed our position, by throwing back our right skirmishers and re-inforcing them, we should have been out-flanked. On this being done, a smart fusilade ensued, during which several of our men were struck. Where was the dandy now ? All puppyism had vanished with the report of the first rifle, leaving only the cool, efficient officer, whose flashing sabre was seen waving and glittering where the fire was hottest. Skirmishes of this kind became almost of daily occurrence, in which many men were killed or wounded on both sides, without any real advantage to either party. The day before Christmas we received the unpleasant intelligence that our supplies in the shape of rations had run out, and none could be issued until the arrival of the stores then expected from Belgaum.

It was Christmas morning, a balmy coolness pervaded the air, the golden rays of the sun lit up the early dawn, and fleecy vapour-like clouds floated across the blue vault of heaven ; a heavy mist hung over the waters in the valley below, shrouding from view both stream and village—a sure indication that intense heat would succeed as the day advanced. Christmas! What recollections ? what old associations were awakened within us as the drums and fifes played through the camp some snatches from old carols or Christmas ballads so well remembered in the happy days of our childhood? Who could fail to remember (even in the far distant lands of the heathen, with the sounds of deadly strife constantly ringing on the ear,) the happy homes and crowds of merry laughing children that gathered round the social board and hearth at this festive season in dear old England ? What visions of rich sirloins, fat roast turkeys, and the never to be forgotten glorious plum-pudding, filled our hungry fancies, for beef, either roast or boiled, could not be had, and certainly

22

plum pudding was not current among us that day; besides, to the
annoyance of many, not a glass of grog could be obtained for
love or money. Fortunately we had plenty of good water and
some tobacco, so we drank and smoked, and drank and smoked
again, it being our only solace. Information was brought in
during the night that a large party of the enemy had got between
us and our supplies, but that word had been sent to the heavy
brigade concerning our situation, and no doubt they would soon
dislodge the scoundrels and open the roads. About ten o'clock
heavy firing was heard in the direction of our working parties,
and shortly after a sergeant came up for a reinforcement. Accordingly four companies of native infantry under a field officer
were sent to their assistance. The firing increased, and it was
not long before an officer came back at full speed for some Europeans. His report was that the enemy had advanced cautiously,
firing with great effect, and retiring slowly; that our men
had pushed on after them, when, on turning a bend in the
ravine, they came full on a large stockade, from behind which the
rebels poured forth a murderous volley. The men were falling
fast, and being unsupported by Europeans, could not hold their
ground, and in fact, had began to fall back. A detachment of
our regiment were told off without delay for this business; eighty
rounds of ammunition per man were issued, and in ten minutes
we were descending at the double to the post. As we
descended we met doolies conveying the bodies of those who had
fallen, and some of the most severely wounded, while those
more slightly wounded were hobbling along towards camp,
occasionally resting themselves under the shade of some neighboring bush, and as best they could staunching the blood that flowed
from their wounds, until picked up by some passing dooly.
"Ah, Major!" said young Campbell, a dashing officer of ours, as
we halted for a few moments to get breath before going into
action, "so you have got your Christmas box. I am afraid you
will not have as much jaw as usual at mess this evening." This

was said with a light laugh, without the least intention to hurt
the feelings or offend the person to whom it was addressed, for he
was a particular friend and associate. The wounded man looked
up with a faint smile and a nod of acknowledgment. He had
been shot through both cheeks, the ball carrying away his lower
teeth and fracturing the jaw to some extent. Little did the light-
hearted laughing Campbell dream that his ear would never again
listen to the chit-chat and badinage of the mess table; that in a
few short fleeting moments, he that was now all life and spirit,
would be lying dead in the cleft of the rocky water-course he was
then descending. There was a hurried consultation among the
officers; the Sepoys were ordered to fall back, and with firm step
and clenched teeth we advanced to the work of death. The first
and second stockades were carried in good style, but the third
was a regular rasper, much higher than either of the other two,
with a triple row of loop-holes and mounted with several jingals. The ravine was much narrower here, and the sides more
precipitous. Our advance was met with a heavy discharge of
matchlocks and jingals from the front of the stockade. Both the
officers with the whole of the leading section went down, and
with the exception of a man named Thacker and myself all were
either killed or wounded. The second and third sections
suffered nearly as bad, for the approach to the stockade
was enfiladed by a number of the enemy, who poured a continuous discharge on us from behind some bushes of wild cactus that
grew on either side of the ravine. It was an infernal hole, and
our commander seeing the fearful odds that was against us,
humanely, though reluctantly, gave the order to fall back upon the
second stockade. Here a post was established, in rear of which
our dead and wounded were carried. So much had been gained,
but at an awful cost of human life and blood. My left hand
man, Charles Matlow, of whom I have before spoken, was a man
of great personal courage; he had been several years in London
where he worked as a stage carpenter at several of the minor

theatres, acquiring a great taste for theatrical representations, and was as an amateur, no mean performer in the parts he usually assumed—such as a brigand, the pirate, a rebel chieftain, or the villains of the melodrama. Although a kind and good-natured fellow, he had acquired a reckless habit of swearing, and his usual oath or execration, was "bloody shoot me." He was shot bloody enough ; he was fired upon from above, and the ball entering the right temple, passed through his head, coming out at the neck, separating the jugular vein. He bled profusely, and fell forward ; but turning with his face upwards, in the same manner as I had frequently seen him do on the stage, when playing his favorite characters, and with a sound, half sigh half groan, died imme-diately. Thacker and myself carried his body to the rear, and placed it in a dooly.

It was late in the afternoon when we got back to camp, tired, wearied and hungry, but had nothing wherewith to appease our appetites. After washing away the stains of blood, dust and gunpowder, and diminishing my thirst with a long draught of good water, I flung myself on my pallet and soon lost all consciousness in sleep. I had slept about a couple of hours, when I was awoke by the bugle sounding the parade call. We were to be present at the burial service which was to be said over the bodies of the European portion of the force that had fallen. The place of interment was a clear open space at the rear of the camp—a wild romantic spot among the hills, surrounded by thick jungle over which perhaps the foot of man had never before trodden. The mournful procession, if I remem-ber right, advanced as follows : The firing party, with arms reversed ; the band, with muffled drums, playing the "Dead March in Saul ;" then came the bodies, borne in doolies on the shoulders of their comrades ; next the men of different corps under their respective non-commissioned officers, bare-headed, with their side-arms only ; and lastly, the officers of the brigade with their swords reversed. There being no chaplain with us, the senior officer read the service in a clear, calm and audible voice, commencing with that beautiful **and** solemn portion of **the** Church service, "**I am** the Resurection **and the Life,** he that **believeth** on me," &c. ; it was an affecting and impressive service. As the last of the three volleys—that final tribute **of respect** always paid to the dead soldier—echoed among the neighboring hills, the last rays of the setting sun sank below the horizon, to rise again on the morrow, but not for the glorious dead ; they would never again look upon evening's sweetness or on morning's glory. Indeed the scene and occasion was one to call forth deep reflection. Death on the battle plain amid the booming of cannon and clashing of the weapons of those engaged in bloody strife ; the wild exulting shout of victory ringing on the ear, scarcely at the time heeded—for a soldier's death and a soldier's funeral are two very different scenes—but now many a tear fell and many a gallant bosom heaved at the sad spectacle. A pyramid of small stones at the foot of several trees here and there mark the spot beneath which the heroes rest in that last sleep which knows no waking until the final trumpet shall sound. This was indeed a solemn way to end our Christmas day.

" And is it there ye are, and by jabers taking it as aisy as if ye had dined with the Lord Lieutenant. The divil a soul would believe it's fasting ye have been these three days," said O'Toole, pushing aside the boughs beneath whose shade I had thrown myself to smoke or sleep away the gnawing pangs of hunger. " What is the matter, Bob," I enquired, " you seem excited." " Excited, and what is to hinder me. Haven't I been hunting for you all over camp, and isn't there lashings of ateing and drinking going on, and be St. Patrick of blessed memory, won't the grog bugle be after sounding in the twinkling of a shillalah. Excited, be the hokey, I soon will be, or I'm no O'Toole." I needed no further spur to accelerate my movements, but accompanied my chum to the rear of our tents, where a number of camp followers were vending to a group of hungry soldiers such edibles as black pudding, fried sausages, cow-heel, curry liver cut in slices and stewed with onions and green chillie, eggs and bacon, scons or pancakes and hoppers made of rice flour, and cocoa-nut milk with plenty of hot coffee. The rations had just been isued, and the cooks were preparing them, three meals in one, but few of us waited for that, nearly all had money wherewith to purchase the savory and to us tempting morsels prepared by the camp followers, and as Bob had predicted, it was not long before the grog bugle rang out far and near, which was greeted with a rousing cheer. It appeared that the general commanding had sent a couple of regiments of cavalry, who coming unawares upon the rebels from their rear, had routed them and thus opened the road for our stores to come on.

CHAPTER XVII.

OUR attempt to force a passage down the ravine was attended
with so great a loss in killed and wounded, that it was not deemed
expedient to renew it.   And it subsequently appeared that our
loss was comparatively small to what it must have been had we
continued to advance in that direction, for stockades had been
constructed in great numbers for upwards of two miles. Securely
sheltered behind these the enemy could, with little loss to themselves, shower destructive volleys as we advanced, and then retire
to their next, and so on.   A couple of days later the Brigadier,
who with the Engineer staff had been exploring the neighborhood
on our right flank, chanced upon a spot that suited the purpose they had in view. It was a large overhanging cliff, called
the Elephant Rock, from its shape and resemblance to that animal. The greater part of the rock, towards the base, was a
perpendicular scarp, at the foot of which there was a spur or
narrow ridge, sloping down to the small plain where stood the
village of Seevapoore. To this position the greater portion of the
brigade was removed.   On the verge of the cliff a large der-
rick was erected, to which was attached by short chains, a ladder
some two hundred feet in length, constructed of rope and bamboo.
This was thrown over the face of the cliff, by which means we
were to descend one by one. It was a novel idea, and one which
had by no means been anticipated by the enemy, only a small
number of them being observed in that direction. As soon as the
arrangements were complete, a few small mortars were placed
near the edge, with just a sufficient quantity of powder to force
the shells over the rock. Volunteers were called out to form the
advance party to descend the ladder. A sufficient number
sprang forward at the first call, but a controversy arose as to who

should lead the party. I claimed the honor by virtue of having led the Forlorn Hope at Punella. This was disputed by our swell friend of the Rifles. The case was referred to the Brigadier, who decided in favor of Lieutenant Martin; it being the province of an officer to lead his men into action and where danger most threatened, but in consideration of my former service, I was permitted to be the second to descend this exciting though perilous downward course. Just prior to starting a few shells were dropped below, in order to make the jungle at the foot of the cliff especially uncomfortable to such of the foe as might be prowling about in that vicinity. The command to descend was at length given, and young Martin sprang on to the ladder with his sabre swung by the sword knot to his wrist, to admit of his using both hands going down. He had likewise between his clenched teeth by the trigger guard a double barrel pistol. He had only descended about five rungs of the ladder when he was greeted by a shower of matchlock balls, or rather pieces of rod iron cut about an inch in length, two of which took slight effect in his arm and in the leg, and the third struck the barrel of the pistol, sending it flying, with three of the front teeth of the gallant lieutenant. So great was the shock that he thought half his head was off, and he was compelled to return. I now took the lead and fortunately my nautical experience enabled me to descend rapidly and with great ease, and quickly followed by the remainder of the party. We were favored with a volley, but it must have come from a greater distance, as few of the shots took effect. One carried away my left shoulder knot, but drew no blood. While forming upon the ridge, a few of our number got hit, but as we advanced the insurgents retreated to Seevapoore. On arriving at the plains, we halted until the whole force had descended and joined us. We lost no time in preparing for an attack on the devoted village. It was to be altogether an infantry engagement on our side, as it was not quite an easy matter to lower horses and artillery from the heights to the plain below. The ball was

opened by our skirmishers firing upon those of the enemy, on
the opposite bank of the stream, which was about knee-deep
where we crossed. At first they seemed determined to resist,
but the accuracy and rapidity of our fire told fearfully among
them, and after some twenty minutes of hot work, they bolted
to the cove rof the village. We posted on after them, and a
fierce contest raged upwards of two hours. The enemy were
defeated at all points; those who escaped sought safety in flight
through the jungle in the direction of Monnahar and Monsontosh. The half of Seevapoore had been burnt to the ground
before the scoundrels could be effectually routed. We now
waited for instructions from General D——, relative as to what
was to be done, concerning the fortresses of Monnahar and
Monsontosh. On the day preceding the capture of Seevapoore,
I received instructions to return to camp, on the top of the
Elephant rock, and to wait on the officer in command. This was
regarded by my friends as being very significant, and I left them
in high expectation of some coming event of importance to my
future well-being; and so it turned out, for on my arrival, I was
handed a despatch from the general commanding, announcing
my promotion, with an appointment in the Quarter-master
General's Department, with directions to report myself at the
head-quarter camp heavy brigade forthwith. This was joyous
news indeed, for I had by an act of daring which could have
been done by any one else possessing presence of mind and
having the same opportunty, cleared at a bound many of the
rungs of the ladder of promotion. My friends, comrades,
and others, congratulated me when they heard of my good
fortune, and after bidding them a hearty farewell, I left
the sphere in which I had seen so much rough-and-tumble life.
Procuring a guide, and a powerful young horse which I had
purchased at the bazaar, I soon mounted and made my way to
the Hunmunt Ghaut, where I reported myself to the Quarter-
master General, and without delay was installed in my new

23

office. The force from Vingorla having joined the light brigade, the whole of the Sawaunt Warree jungle was thoroughly scoured, and the rabble captured or dispersed, with the exception of those who had sought the shelter of Monnahar and Monsontosh. The Sappers and Miners, with the assistance of large working parties from the different corps, soon constructed roads down the ravines to the valley, by which means the artillery and heavy ordnance stores were transported to the base of the acclivity on which stood the last two strongholds of the insurgent Mahrattas. Two divisions were then formed; one consisting of Her Majesty's troops, who were to make the false attack, to be converted into a real one if opportunity offered; the other, those of the Company's service, who were to lead the real attack. The mortars having been got into position on several parts of the steep ascent, the enemy were treated to salvos of shells, with a view of making the place too hot to hold them. The signal for the combined assault was given, and the whole force moved forward, toiling and struggling up the rocky eminence, till they gained the summit, and then the fight began in earnest. In about an hour, both places were carried in grand style, and the remnant of the rebel horde, supplies, and loot, &c., were captured. The fortifications were then dismantled, and our men returned to camp beside the clear stream which ran through the valley, where we remained for some few weeks. By this time the rebellion had been entirely crushed; peace and quietness restored throughout the entire Southern Mahratta country, and the Mahratta chiefs taught a lesson they were not likely to forget in a hurry. The General in Chief received instructions to break up the force, and order them to return to their several stations. The campaign having been brought to a satisfactory close, my post on the Quarter-master General's staff was consequently abolished, and I rejoined my regiment at Belgaum. However, I did not remain long doing regimental duty, for the Government, in consideration of the services I had rendered at Punnella and elsewhere, bestowed a civil appointment on me, as chief of a division of police at the Presidency, a position which for some time I had been anxious to obtain. Shortly after my arrival in India, I began to study hard to acquire a knowledge of the native language. I now spoke Hindoostanee fluently, with a tolerable smattering of Mahratta and Goozeratee, and passed my examination in good order. Without a knowledge of the vernacular, I should not have been eligible for this position; therefore it was with unfeigned satisfaction that I proceeded to Bombay to take up the duties of my new appointment. Scinde and Afghanistan were quiet, and the Mahrattas had learnt a severe lesson during the recent campaign, consequently there was no likelihood of another outbreak taking place for some time to come. The monotonous routine of regimental duty at up-country stations, far removed from the pleasures of civil life, was to me irksome in the extreme; therefore, the change from a dull cantonment to the gay capital, was highly satisfactory to one who had for so long a period looked on the latter only from a respectful distance.

The Island of Bombay, the capital of the Presidency and the seat of government, is about eleven miles in length, and three in breadth. The fort or citadel is encompassed on three sides with walls of solid masonry, and surmounted with bristling cannon of heavy calibre; surrounded by a wide deep moat, and entered by three double gates, protected by ponderous portcullies and heavy draw-bridges. Its principal buildings are the castle, mint, barrack, custom-house, cathedral, supreme court of judicature, dock-yard, town hall, and other public offices. The island formerly belonged to the Portuguese, but on the marriage of Charles the Second of England with Catherine of Braganza, a princess of Portugal, it was ceded to the British as her dower. The original settlers did not however remove, and there are still a large number of their descendants on the island. Many turned their attention to the study of medicine, and were employed as private practitioners, while several entered the military and naval service of the Company as apothecaries and stewards to the hospitals. Others entered the secretariat and other public offices as clerks; but by far the greater number are hired as domestic servants, and are be found as such in every large station throughout the Presidency. But certainly the most energetic and enterprising race are the Parsees, who are chiefly merchants, shop keepers, and dock-yard employés; in fact the principal or master builder is a Parsee. As a community they are rich and influential, and the only caste that has had the honor of knighthood conferred upon them. The present Baronet is Corsetjee Jamsetgee, son of the late Sir Jamsetjee Jeejebhoy, better known among the natives as the Bottle Walla, from the fact of his having started in life by selling empty bottles. He subsequently amassed an immense fortune by opium and other speculations. He was widely known for his benevolence and generosity, having erected an hospital and endowed a medical college for the native population. The Mussulmen are furniture dealers, ship-brokers and boatmen. The Banians deal in grain, groceries, oil, drugs and dye-stuffs. The Borahs in dry goods, cotton and ready-made clothing, while Arabs, Moguls, and Persians trade in horses, carpets, perfumes, hookas, pipes of all descriptions, coffee and sherbet. The Memons from Cutch are gold and silver smiths and dealers in precious stones. A peculiar caste called Marrwarries are pawn-brokers and money changers. Very few Europeans live in the Fort; they chiefly reside at Girgaum, Mazagon, Byculla and Tardeo on Malabar hill. The Governor's principal residence is at Parreel, five miles from the Fort. There is a very large native town out-side the citadel and beyond the esplanade, where thousands of artizans earn their daily bread by carrying on their different avo-cations. There is little in the shape of amusement for Europeans except what they create among themselves. There is a good theatre where some excellent amateur performances occasionally take place. There is also a first-class race-course, as racing is entered into with great spirit by both European and native, and large sums of money exchange hands during the racing season. There were quite a number of balls and public breakfasts given at the Government House, which excellent example was followed by all the members of the Council, and principal merchants. The native dignitaries frequently gave grand entertainments to the European gentry. The uniform of the service and the dress coat of the civilian being a sufficient passport, there were no invitations issued; but the privilege of entry is granted by circular notification published in the newspapers. There is at Byculla an excellent institution or school for the orphans of soldiers; the boys are educated and then put to some employment; some are trained as engineers and employed as such on board the small steamers that run to Vingorla, Surat and other ports on the coast. Many find a field of labor in the dock-yard, while others are clerks in public offices, and several enter the army and navy. The girls are kept at the institution until they marry. A great many find partners in life among the young men who have been brought up at the school and are doing well in the world, but by far the greater number are married to non-commissioned officers, soldiers and sailors. As the *modus operandi* of the courtship is somewhat peculiar, I cannot refrain from attempting a description of it. The practice may have been altered since, but some years ago it was certainly as nearly as possible as follows: The soldier who wishes to become a candidate for matrimony obtains permission from his Colonel, and provided with a letter of representation as to charactér, &c., waits on the chaplain of the institution, and from him receives a note to the matron who blandly receives him, and forthwith parades some twelve or fifteen girls all in a row in order that he may select his intended. After walking down the line, and taking a good look at each, he desires the matron to call out Nos. 3, 5, 7, 12, or 1, as the case may be, and the others are sent back to their rooms. The matron then gives the aspirant for matrimonial honors the names of the five young women, and requests him to return on the following evening to take tea with herself and the girls in question, to which of course he assents. The evening having been spent together, and just as he is about to leave, he makes an offer to the one he prefers ; she is at liberty to refuse or accept ; and if her answer is negative, he then proposes to the second on the list, and so on till he is accepted. But the girls rarely refuse, being in most cases anxious to leave school for an establishment of their own. On consent being given, he is informed when the ceremony will take place ; the institution being at all expenses attending the wedding, the bride being furnished with a complete outfit for her new position in life. When the ceremony is over, the happy pair then proceed to join the regiment to which the bridegroom belongs, which at that time might have been stationed several hundred miles up the country.

Prior to the opening of the overland route, very few ladies came out to India. The long sea voyage which then occupied from five to six months, was the great stumbling block that deterred many who would otherwise have joined husbands or relations in that distant land. It was chiefly owing to the absence of the society of their fair countrywomen, that the European having been removed from all restraint of their relatives, followed the bent of their inclinations, and indulged in those sensual excesses usally practised by Orientals of all classes. It was then the rule and not the exception, for officers of rank and rich civilians, to form illicit connection with beautiful women of the native community, who were usually entertained in handsome apartments in their own bungalows. Fortunately this state of things is rapidly dying out, and I believe at present seldom resorted to, thanks to the overland route and the accession of many European ladies to the country. There is rather a good story current in India, relative to the said overland route. I do not vouch for its accuracy, but I know that it is pretty generally believed. An officer of the Company's service, who had been a considerable time in Egypt, Arabia and Aden, conceived the idea of the practicability of shortening the passage from India to Europe, *via* those countries. He communicated his impressions to a rich old nabob, who had retired from the service, and was living luxuriantly in the most delightful part of the presidency. The old gentleman who been been much in the parts mentioned by the lieutenant, agreed to furnish the capital required for carrying out this project, but wished that strict silence should be kept on the subject until they had fully embarked in the undertaking. The young officer then started overland for the purpose of taking sketches, diagrams, &c., of the proposed line of route, and afterward returned to India, but had only arrived a short time, when by the failure of one of the principal banks of the country, his patron's immense wealth was swallowed up in the general wreck. Instead of wasting time in vain regrets, he at once sent for his young friend, and explained to him what had taken place, and said, " Now is the time to test in our persons the possibility of your scheme ; can I but reach England before the news of the great smash arrives there, I may be in time to save my fortune, in which case I will place two-thirds of it at your disposal for the construction of the route." To this proposal the lieutenant gladly assented. They started, and within seven weeks these energetic men were in London. The old nabob lost no time in transferring his capital to another banking establishment, and left for India two months before the news of the great failure reached England, taking on their return the route which has since proved such a signal success. For some time after this line had been completed, there were comparatively few ladies who availed themselves of the great facility which was afforded thereby, and consequently there was still a scarcity of the fair sex throughout the country.

CHAPTER XVIII.

THE following incident will serve to shew or illustrate the truth
of the concluding paragraph of the last chapter   A few years ago,
during my sojourn at Sallampoor, in Rajahpootana—a very pretty
station, but as usual, blessed with very few of the fair sex—there
were, between military and civilians, some sixty-five gentlemen,
and only eight ladies, all married. Not a miss in her teens within
several hundred miles ; therefore, you may imagine our balls and
parties were not the most brilliant or entertaining in the world,
but there was no help for it, for the same thing had gone on for
years, and consequently we got used to it. However, one fine
morning after parade, our major who had dined at the cavalry
mess the night previous, communicated to us the welcome intelligence, that a beautiful young, accomplished unmarried lady,
was shortly expected from England. She was coming to her
uncle, the prince of good-fellows, the staff surgeon. This was
glorious news ; and immediate arrangements were made to hail
her arrival at the station, in a manner worthy of the occasion.
Amateur theatricals were got up ; a ball was inaugurated, and a
ten days' pic-nic resolved upon. All the young men curled their
hair, twisted their moustaches, and made themselves as killing
as possible, in order to fascinate the young lady, and secure her
as speedily as might be, but the odds were in favor of the
brigadier, who was very handsome, and quite the ladies' man ;
besides he was reported to be very rich, and not at all averse to
matrimony. All preparations for the lady's reception had been
completed, and every one was on the tip-toe of expectation, when
the worthy surgeon received a letter with the astounding
announcement that his niece had embarked at Southampton on
board the P. and O. Company's mail steamer *Sultan*, for the East.

That on the passage she had suffered much from sea-sickness, and was attended by the surgeon of the vessel, and it having been a regular case of love at first sight, the affair was ended in their marriage on the arrival of the ship at Alexandria. The happy couple were united at the chapel of the British Embassy, and they returned to England by the same steamer; therefore we were left lamenting—it was a decided sell.

Quite a number of young gentlemen constantly arrive in India with the most absurd notions regarding the habitats of the animal creation, arising no doubt from the many tough yarns imposed upon them during their long voyage ; consequently on landing they expect to meet boa constrictors, tigers and other wild animals at every street corner. I remember a circumstance that took place during my stay at Bombay, and which afforded considerable amusement to my friends and myself. I was sitting in the office of my friend Craig, editor of one of the daily journals, who had a pet tiger, which he kept chained on the leads outside his office window. The chain was sufficiently long to admit of his putting his paws on the sill and looking in, which occasionally he was in the habit of doing. On the day in question, a young ensign of recent importation called at the office and was standing conversing with my friend with his back towards the said window. Now, Craig was a fellow full of fun, and fond of practical jokes ; in looking up from his desk, he observed the tiger, and, deeming it an opportunity too good to be lost, without moving his position, called out to his native servant, " Luximon, be quick, hand me my rifle ; here is another of those infernal tigers." The ensign turned about and to his horror and consternation, beheld the head of the enormous brute within a few inches of him. Uttering a shriek of dismay, and with terror depicted on every lineament of his fair young face, he sprang through the door, down the staircase, and never stopped till he gained the shelter of his palanquin. During the five years in which I held my appointment, I had an opportunity of wit-

24

nessing a great deal of the under current and private doings of society both European and native. However, I am not going to inflict upon my readers the experiences of a police officer, but there was an episode which took place during my term of office, that I fancy possesses a sufficient amount of interest to warrant its introduction in these pages.

It was a glorious morning in October, the monsoons had subsided, and left all nature clad in verdant beauty. A gentle breeze played among the picturesque branches and groves of noble palms, and wafted upwards sweet odours from the numerous plants and many-hued parasites that grew in great luxuriance on the sunny slopes that stretched away towards the sea. Over the tops of the fragrant pomegranate trees could be discerned the silver waters of the bay, on whose rippling bosom glided hither and thither the gaily painted bunder boats, and those belonging to the vessels that crowded the harbor, their white sails gleaming in the golden beams of the morning sunlight. In the back ground, rose the wooded heights of Elephanta, that island so famous for the superb sculpture of its extraordinary caves. I was reclining on an ottoman in my private office, facing an open window, inhaling the rich perfume of some magnificent wild honeysuckle that hung in festoons, and interlaced the lattice work of the verandah, throwing a cool shade into the apartment, and while thus gazing on the quiet scene below, I was debating in my mind, whether to jump into my palkee and be carried to the fort, or indulge in that oriental luxury, a bath and siesta during the excessive heat of the noon-day sun, when a door that led to the entry which communicated with my tastefully fitted up bachelor quarters, suddenly opened, and Acbar Ali, my private orderly, one of the smartest detective officers in the force, entered, making his usual profound salaam. "What is it ?" I inquired, glancing in his direction. "A European Sahib wishes to see you in private," was the reply. "Do you know the gentleman," said I, without moving my position. "I have seen him before, but it is evident he does

not wish to be recognized by **any but** yourself," quietly answered
the havildar, in Hindostanee. Although master of several native
languages, he could not speak five consecutive words in English.
"Show him into the library, and say **I** will be with him in a few
minutes." He saluted and retired. **I knew** it would be useless
to conjecture as to whom **the** visitor might prove, for my position
as chief of police brought me **in** contact with all classes of socity.
I went to my dressing room, **and** having made a slight addition
to my toilet, entered the so-called library, for in fact it was my
smoking room and general sanctum sanctorum, by a small door
partially concealed by a moveable screen, where I had an opportunity of observing my visitor unseen. He was a tall, handsome
figure, and apparently about 28 years of age. His features
reflected in an opposite mirror, for he was standing with
his back towards me, were regular and finely cut; the **lower**
part of the face was concealed by a heavy beard, moustache and
whiskers of raven hue, which contrasted strangely with the few
curls of rich brown hair that escaped from beneath the folds of
the silken puggree that encircled his sola topee. His whole figure
was familiar to me, but I could **not** at **the** moment remember
when or where we had met. My orderly was right ; **he** was for
some purpose or other in disguise. "Is this visit intended for
the chief of police, or are you the bearer of any message or commission from a friend?" was my enquiry, as I stepped further
into the room. At the sound of **my** voice, he turned, advanced
two or three steps towards me, and exclaimed, "Fortescue, are we
alone?" I replied in the affirmative. He then removed his hat,
and with it the beard and whiskers alluded **to**, and disclosed the
handsome though pallid features of **my** friend **and** comrade Oscar
Pemberton! "What **my dear fellow**, where on earth did you
spring from? Why **this** disguise? But you are unwell, let me
give you some wine. **Nay** I insist," said I, filling out a tumbler
of iced sherry, and forcing him to **take** it. He swallowed **it** evidently with reluctance and more with a view of satisfying me

than from any benefit he expected to derive from it, or to remove
the depression under which he was laboring. "Fortescue," said
he as he placed the half emptied glass on the table, "tell me, but
do not tamper with me, have you seen or heard anything of
Clara?" "Of Clara!" said I in astonishment. "Why, I understood she was in Europe?" "She is in Bombay," he replied
gloomily. "Impossible, I must have seen her name among the
list of passengers," I reiterated. "Nevertheless, she is, or was
here. Listen while I explain myself more fully. About six
months ago I was prevailed upon by my family in Europe, much
against my better judgment, to allow Clara to pay a visit to England, especially as I was unable to accompany her. It was a
hard trial to me,—parting with one I so dearly loved, and who,
I had long believed, loved me with equal tenderness. I finally
consented, and she sailed for England. Four months passed. I
had letters from her frequently during her stay. At length I
received one to say that she was going up to London to spend a
few weeks with some distant relatives of her father's whom she
had met, and that she would embark for Bombay on the mail
steamer, that would arrive here on or about the third of the
month. Unable to obtain leave of absence, I wrote to Shirlock, of
the Ordnance Department, who with his family were residing on
the Esplanade, and requested him to go on board, and fetch Clara
ashore, and give her apartments in his bungalow, until I could
make arrangements to send for her. Judge of my surprise and
consternation, when I received a letter from my friend Shirlock,
to this purport, 'That he had boarded the English mail very
shortly after her arrival, but that Mrs. Pemberton was not there!'
A lady calling herself Mrs. Percival Clifford, and who answered
exactly to the description of my wife, had embarked at Southampton, and had left the vessel with one of the gentlemen passengers in the first bunder boat that had come along side; but no
one knew which of the passengers had accompanied her, nor had
he up to the time of writing, obtained any clue to her where-

abouts. I had a sad foreboding that some scoundrel had either by force or sophistry, persuaded her to leave one that loved her more than life, in order that she might minister to his licentious passions. And now, my dear fellow, I believe that you are the only one that can assist me in this sad emergency. I know that in asking you, I shall not meet with a refusal or a lukewarm assistance ?" " My dear Oscar, are you not too hasty at jumping at a conclusion ? Clara may *not* have left England, and your friend may have been misled in the description given of the lady, Mrs. Percival Clifford, that would warrant the supposition that she was your wife. However, I will leave no stone unturned to ascertain the facts of the case. This I can easily do through the agency of my secret police." He appeared to be satisfied, and thanked me warmly for taking the whole matter in hand. He had left his station without leave of absence, hence his disguise, and the necessity of his immediate return, or his absence might be discovered by his superiors, and lead to further trouble. I obtained from him his wife's portrait, the better to enable me to prosecute my search. It gave him much pain to part with it, but he saw the propriety of my request. I promised to write to him full particulars of what transpired should I succeed in tracing the lady. I was to obtain an interview, and report the result to him, and forward her address, so that he could if he wished communicate with her in writing. He then took his leave, having to call upon his friend Shirlock, prior to his departure on the evening boat for Surat. Determined to lose no time in ascertaining whether my friend's wife had in any way compromised herself, and if so, to what extent and with whom, I returned to my office, and sent my orderly to the head clerk, for a list of the passengers arrived by the last overland mail. He returned in a few minutes, and handed it to me, when I found the name of Mrs Percival Clifford. " Acbar Ali, tell the Purvo Ramchumder, to get this copied into Mahratta. Then go to the Town Major's, Adjutant General's office, and anywhere else, that

may be necessary, and find out how many of these persons have
gone up country, and how many remained in Bombay, and where
they are at present residing, and let me have your report early
to-morrow morning." The detective took the list, made his
salaam, and vanished. Thus having set matters in train, I indulged in the siesta before alluded to. The following morning
after the usual routine of my duties had been gone through, I
summoned my orderly to make his report, which he did, reading
it off as follows: "Of the passengers arrived by the steamship
China, seventeen had left the Island, and six remained, Major and
Mrs. Selby Hope, Hall Hotel, Mazagon; L. P. Sandhurst, Civil
Service, at his bungalow, Race Course Road, Byculler; Ensigns E.
Comee, J. Bemick, attached to the companies European Regiment stationed at Colaba, and Mrs Percival Clifford, residence
unknown." "Am I to find out?" said he looking up, as he
finished reading his report. "Not at present, but you may tell
the Hamalls to bring my palanquin round to the office door, and
do not leave here on any account until my return, as I then may
require you."

The first point for me to determine was, whether Mrs. Percival
Clifford and Mrs. Oscar Pemberton were one and the same person,
I prepared myself for a visit to the Hope Hall Hotel. Writing
the lady's name on a card, and placing the portrait with it in my
sabretash, I jumped into my palkee. "Is Major Shelby staying
here?" I inquired of the proprietor of that establishment, half
an hour later. "Yes, Sir, you will find him in yonder verandah"
—pointing across the spacious hall—replied that polite individual. Advancing in the direction indicated, I found the
gentleman in question. "Good morning, major, are you disen-
gaged for a few minutes?" I inquired as I approached. "I am
at your service, Sir; but you have the advantage of me," he
replied, bowing politely. I handed him my card. "Chief of
Police!" said he, looking up enquiringly? I bowed. "To what
am I indebted for this visit, or in what way can I serve you?"

" You arrived from Europe by **the steamer** *China*, I believe." He assented. " Among the **passengers, there** was a lady named Mrs. Percival Clifford, was there **not,** Sir ?" " There was indeed," he unhesitatingly replied, "**and** a most beautiful creature she was. In fact usually styled, the fascinating Clifford." " You then would have **no** difficulty in recognizing her, if you should meet ?" I inquired. " None **in** the least," he answered. I produced the likeness I had **received** from Oscar, and handed it to the major, "That is her," **he** exclaimed the moment he saw it. " But I hardly think the artist has done her justice. This looks much younger, **but I suppose** it may have been taken some five or six years **ago** ?" I assented. " Has **there** anything gone wrong ?" enquired the major. I **answered,** by a shrug of **the** shoulders. " I fancied there **was a** screw loose somewhere from the violent flirtation that was continually going on **between her** and **Mr.** Sandhurst, of the Civil Service. She is young and beautiful, and he rich and handsome ; **and** if report speaks truly a great admirer of the fair sex generally. But for that matter half the young fellows on board **were** going crazy about **her.**" While the major was running on, evidently carried away by the recollections of the fascinating Clifford, I quietly wrote down the name **of "Sand-** hurst" in my memorandum book. Then after a few comments on the weather and other matters, I took my leave, and returned to my office, and summoning Acbar Ali, I gave him the following instructions : " You will ascertain if there is any European lady residing **at** Mr. Sandhurst's bungalow. If any of the bungalows at Tardeo, Walkeshwa, Mharluximee, Byculla or Chingleparra have been occupied recently by any European lady, and find out whether Mrs. Percival Clifford, who arrived by the overland mail, is residing there, or if she **has left the** island. **Look at this and** remember the features," said **I,** showing him the **likeness of Clara.** "This is **Mrs.** Percival Clifford, should you meet her anywhere, place her under strict *surveillance.* Take any number of men you require, but the utmost secrecy must be observed." During the course of

the next day, I received from my subordinate this information—
" That Chittygong Lodge, the property of Sorabjee Pestonjee, and
situated at Shingleparra, had been sold to a Mrs. Oscar Pemberton,
and been elegantly furnished by Rantoola and Jaffa Sullimon,
furniture dealers, and the bills which were all paid, were made out
in the name of the same lady ; that Mrs. Percival Clifford, passenger
by the last overland mail, after residing for four days in the
British hotel in the fort, had moved into the said bungalow,
where she was now living with her servants only ; that Raggoo
Bappoo, No. 342, of the detective force, had been installed as
house hammall and had reported that the lady received no visitors,
except Mr. Sandhurst, of the Civil Service, who called usually
after sunset, and generally remained there until after supper,
which was usually served at eleven p. m.   That he, the havildar,
had seen the lady walking in her compound or garden, and that
she bore a striking resemblance to the portrait shown him by
the chief." This was the substance of my orderly's report ; and
from the information gained, there was no reasonable doubt but
that my friend's secret foreboding had been but too truly verified.
That his wife, young, inexperienced, and alone among strangers,
had fallen a victim to the lures and wiles of that polished man of
the world and heartless libertine, Leonard Sandhurst.   This
would be a bitter draught for poor Oscar, when he should learn the
result of my enquiries, which I was very loath to communicate.
But he had wrung from me a promise to conceal nothing from him,
and I had no other alternative than to comply ; but I deferred
doing so until after I should have had an interview with Clara.
She might be persuaded to leave her present protector, and return
to her home, and thus I should be spared the pain of a recital of
what had transpired since her arrival from Europe.   And Oscar
was too fond and forgiving to distress her by any question on
such a subject.   Oscar Pemberton and I entered the service
about the same time, and made each other's acquaintance on board
the Indiaman, during our passage out.   He was of Irish

parentage, but born and educated in England, and possessed all those dashing military qualities so characteristic of his race. He was brave and impetuous, confiding and generous, almost to a fault. On our arrival in India, we were posted to the same regiment, and remained fast friends and comrades until he and his beautiful bride left to join his staff appointment in the Northern division, procured for him through the influence of the colonel of her father's late regiment.

Captain Stanley, Clara's father, had been an officer in a light dragoon regiment, and while out tiger shooting in the Warree jungles, had made his head-quarters at Goa, a Portuguese settlement on the coast near Vingorla. Here he met and fell in love with the beautiful Isadore Braganza, who was being educated in one of the convents outside the city. She was of Portuguese descent on her father's side, her mother being an Italian. After a few stolen interviews in the convent garden, he persuaded her to elope with him to the nearest European station, where they were married. She being an orphan with no fortune wherewith to endow the church, the Portuguese ecclesiastics gave themselves little trouble concerning her marriage with a heretic. Clara was the fruit of this union, but unfortunately her mother died before she had reached her seventh year, and her father transferred that love, with which he had almost idolised his young wife, to his motherless daughter. He would not hear of her being sent to England for education, and being a man of a refined and cultivated mind, and highly educated, he devoted himself to the superintendence of her studies. Her music lessons were directed by the bandmaster of the regiment, in which she made rapid progress, astonishing and delighting her friends with her brilliant performance of Bellini's and Verdi's Operas, both vocally and instrumentally ; her voice being a superb soprano. When she was about fifteen her father managed to get into some difficulty with a superior officer, which resulted in his having either to stand a court martial or resign his commission.

25

CHAPTER XIX.

In this unpleasant dilemma, Captain Stanley chose the latter alternative, and left the service, retiring into private life. But the monotony of civil life was ill-suited to one who had been so actively employed for years; having still many friends in the country on whose influence he could rely, he entered the Company's service, and was immediately appointed a warrant officer, with the post of riding-master in a regiment of native cavalry, a position of great respectability, and one that he was well qualified to fill. Shortly after our return from the Southern Mahratta campaign, their regiment came to our station. Oscar Pemberton and I had been invited to a ball at the artillery mess, and here we first met Clara Stanley; and I remember that my impressions at the time were that she was one of the most beautiful creatures I had ever met—scarcely seventeen, above the middle height, and graceful as a young fawn, delicate and regular in feature, with a soft fair complexion, warming into a richer tint upon the cheeks and lips—with long jet black hair reaching to her waist, and large long-lashed dark eyes, with an ineffable grace in every glance and motion. She was attired in a pale Axureien satin dress, with an over-skirt of white crape, looped up with small bouquets of white convolvulus; her pretty little feet, which peeped from beneath her dress as she glided gracefully about, were encased in white satin slippers; a necklace of pearls encircled her swan-like neck, and she wore no other ornaments, save an exquisitely wrought gold cross set with rubies. A single white camelia was interwoven in the rich tresses of her luxuriant hair. I solicited and obtained her hand for a set of quadrilles, which she danced with exceeding grace, and was much charmed with her wit and gentle manners.

During the evening I was introduced to her father, who, being an Englishman, and brought up in London, had many topics of mutual interest on which to base our conversation. He seemed pleased with my manners, and gave me a *carte blanche* to visit him at his pretty little bungalow near the cavalry lines. Pemberton, who had been waltzing with Miss Stanley, now came up and led her to a seat near her father; he also was included in the same courteous invitation, very much to the satisfaction of that gentleman, for it was quite evident that he had fallen head and ears in love with the little divinity, for he had neither eyes nor thoughts for any but her the rest of the evening. I never saw a fellow so desperately in earnest, or so far gone in love on so short an acquaintance. He could think and talk of nothing else but the fascinating Miss Stanley. He declared to me, that come what might, he would never rest until she had consented to become his wife, though he had to fight every fellow in camp that might lay claim to her hand. " Well," said I, laughingly, " as I am in no hurry to become a benedict, and certainly have no inclination to be shot through the head for the love of the lady, charming though she be, you need fear no rivalry in me, but on the contrary, I shall be happy to afford you all the assistance in *my* power to further your interest in this matter." " Thank you, my dear fellow ; of course I count on your good nature to aid me in case of an emergency. I fancy there will not be any very great objection on the part of my enslaver ; but her father, who is as proud as Lucifer, doubtless expects a much higher position in the social scale for his daughter than I can at present offer her ; but you know the old saying, a faint heart never won a fair lady, and I am resolved to carry the fortress either by strategem or by a *coup de main !*" We called frequently on our new acquaintances, sometimes together, and occasionally alone, and I was not long in discovering by the heightened color and sunny smile with which she always greeted my friend, that she was not insensible to the gallant attentions

and handsome person of young Pemberton. He at length made
a formal application to her father for her hand in marriage, and
was politely but firmly refused, and it was intimated that his
presence at the bungalow hereafter would be considered as an
intrusion ! This was a sad damper to Oscar's hopes, but nothing
daunted, he determined to proceed, well knowing that he had a
powerful ally in the daughter who did not disguise her love, or
willingness to receive his attentions. Mr. Stanley was an excellent
chess-player, and always ready to meet an antagonist at that
noble game, and finding that I had acquired considerable proficiency at the game, he regularly challenged me to test his skill
for an hour or so whenever I made my appearance beneath his
hospitable roof. This I did not fail to turn to good account on
behalf of the lovers. Clara would watch the progress of the
game for a short time, making comments on the various moves,
until her father was deep in the mysteries of check and check-
mate. She would then take up a book and saunter out and on to
the verandah for the ostensible purpose of enjoying a quiet hour,
reading her favorite author, but in reality to met her lover
among the rose bushes that skirted her pretty flower garden.
The trysting place was a quiet spot, screened from the bungalow
and shaded from the heat of the sun by the over-hanging
branches of some mango and custard apple trees. He had given
her a code of signals, by which from the back of the summer-
house she could let him know when I had succeeded in
inveigling her father into some difficult problem at the chess
board, a circumstance which Oscar never failed to take advantage
of to urge his suit ; and in this way their clandestine courtship
was carried on for some weeks, when an accident happened which
entirely changed for a time the aspect of things. Mr. Stanley,
while at riding drill in the manege, received a kick from one of
the troop horses, and died within a few hours after the unfortunate occurrence took place. Clara left an orphan by this sad
event, and having neither relations nor connections in the country,

thankfully accepted the proffered hospitality of Captain and Mrs. Barrington, who having no child of their own, extended to Miss Stanley their sympathising friendship, by offering her an asylum in their comfortable home, so long as she should desire to remain with them. Six months after the death of her father, Oscar Pemberton renewed his application for her hand, and with so much ardor did he press his suit, that he overcame all the objections that she could raise, and she finally consented to become his wife. The good natured quarter-master and his amiable lady, seeing that both had set their hearts upon the match, and having no legal right to object to or postpone the wedding, did all in their power to give the greatest possible *éclat* to the celebration of the marriage ceremony. There was a wedding breakfast at noon, and a ball in the evening, which proved one of the most brilliant of the season. I occupied the position of bridesman on this auspicious occasion. The happy couple left after a few days *en route* for Ahmedabad. Oscar and I had frequently met since his marriage, as his public duties often brought him to Bombay ; but Mrs. Pemberton I had not seen since the morning I wished her farewell, prior to her departure for the Goozeratt, and I was now called upon to seek an interview which I felt would prove not only distressing to her, but embarrassing to myself. I therefore delayed it as long as possible, hoping that some circumstance might arise that would obviate the necessity for my so doing.

" I say, Fortescue, why the deuce do your people not put a stop to this abominable nuisance," called out my friend Morton, as he passed me, at a smart canter, as I entered the fine road that led from the native town across the esplanade of the fort and the Apollo bunder. The abomination alluded to was the long lines of byragges, or professional beggars, who regularly every evening took up their position on either side of the road in question, to await the arrival of the rich baronet, Sir Jamsetgee Jeejeebhoy, whose daily custom it was to ride slowly along, distributing with a bountiful hand to these miserable impostors pice (copper coin). This certainly was a nuisance, but not more so than many other customs of the rich natives. For instance, if a Banyan wished to entertain his poorer caste men with a dinner, the side of the street near his residence was swept clean, and his friends, in two lines, to the number of several thousand, would seat themselves, or most generally squat on their hunkers in double rows, each having before him a large plate or mat made of leaves sewn together. The cooks then came round and filled each man's plate again and again, until the appetite was appeased. They then rose and departed. No knife, fork or spoon were used. The fingers of the right hand sufficed. For all this, be it remembered took place in the open street in view of every passer-by, and to European ideas this disgusting exhibition was anything but agreeable. The government, no doubt, had their own reasons for allowing these things to be carried on, and I was not authorized to interfere with them.

It was a beautiful evening, the sun had lost its power, and the esplanade looked fresh and green. Hundreds of natives of all castes and occupations were passing and repassing from the fort to the several bunders or their homes in the native town. The spires of the churches and the tops of the lofty government buildings in the fortress rose above its embattled walls, and stood out in bold relief against the serene and crimson-tinted sky. On one part of the green some regiments of native infantry were going through their evolutions, to the no small amusement of some groups of seamen belonging either to the Indian Navy or Merchant Marine, who were ashore on liberty for a few hours. The splendid band of the garrison was enlivening the scene with some excellent music, for the amusement of the Europeans, who both rode and walked round and round, and chatted freely in little clusters concerning the latest news, or the last on dit. Arabs, Moguls, Persians and Hindoos, dashed past in splendid equipages. Their rich and varied oriental costumes tended much to heighten the gay and picturesque appearance of this great moving panorama. As the bright orb of day sank beneath the watery horizon, casting its golden and purple shadows on rock and tree, the devout Parsees knelt, and bent reverently their heads to the sand at the edge of the water on Back Bay beach, and paid their daily homage or worship to the glory of the setting sun, for they were disciples of Zoroaster, the fire worshipper. I had reined in my horse to listen to one of my favorite operas, when my orderly advancing gave me a piece of blank paper, which he took from the folds of his turban, and then said in a low voice, " Brown shigram ; bay horses ; just in front of your horse's head, lady from Shingle Para." I handed the paper back, saying, " No orders at present." He saluted, and then retired. I presently glanced in the direction indicated, but could only make out the outline of a lady's figure, the venetian blinds of her vehicle being so arranged as to admit of the occupant seeing as much as she wished of what was passing around without being subject to the scrutiny of those she might wish to avoid. Not wishing to be recognized by her at that time, I cantered on towards the Apollo bunder, to give some orders to the police on duty there. I had put off my interview from time to time with the lady, and was still cogitating as to when it should take place, when my revery was interrupted by some well-known voices exclaiming, " Hallo ! old fellow ! are you going with us ? Don't say, No. We will show you some capital sport, I promise you." " Where are you going ?" I inquired, as my eye fell upon some hampers, guns and fishing tackle that were being carried down the steps and placed on board of a large bunder boat. " We are going for a three days' excursion up Pen river. Will you not join us ?" " Who is that lying at full length on the cushions in the cabin ?" said I, without seeming to notice the question. " That is Sandhurst, of the Civil Service ; a first rate shot, I am told. It was he that got up the party. Will you not come ?" I politely declined their invitation, and wishing them success,

turned my horse's head homeward, for I was determined to take
advantage of the absence of Sandhurst to pay the promised visit
to Mrs. Pemberton *alias* Clifford, which I resolved to do on the
following day.

The retreat chosen, purchased and presented to Clara by
Sandhurst, as her future home, was indeed a beautiful place, and
one which under other circumstances she might have been proud
to own ; but this desirable residence, pretty as it was, cost her,
as the sequel will show, more than fifty such places were worth.
It was a large, handsome bungalow, with a deep verandah running completely round it, on which the long French window
of the drawing-room opened. The chandeliers, pictures, statues,
and other elegancies, were of the most costly description. No
expense had been spared. The grounds were beautifully laid
out, and were filled with dahlias, roses and other flowers. A
grove of stunted date trees ran along the whole of one side, and
a tall prickly-pear hedge on the front, which sheltered the house
to a considerable degree from the dust, heat and glare of the
public road. The other side of the garden was separated from
the adjoining grounds by a closely trimmed hedge of milk-bushes,
over which from the drawing-room windows there was a fine
view of Love Grove, Breach Candy, and the gilded cupolas of
the far-famed Hindoo Temples of Mahluximee, all very picturesque
and pretty. Leaving my horse in charge of my Sycee, I entered
the bungalow, passed into the drawing-room, and directed the
Puttawalla, who was dozing on the verandah, to announce to his
mistress that a gentleman wished to see her. For a few minutes
I walked up and down the spacious apartment, which, like most
others in this class of bungalow, was separated from the dining-
room by a rich silken screen set in an elaborately carved black
wood frame with moveable sides or wings. In one part of the
room stood a handsome grand piano ; in another, a harp ; a
guitar, and a roll of music were lying on one of the lounges.
While engaged in looking over some fine engravings, I heard one

of the dining-room doors open, and in another minute Mrs. Pemberton entered through the folding screen. " Oh! Fortescue," she exclaimed, " is it indeed you ?" as she advanced quickly towards me, extending as she did so both her hands; but she stopped short ere she reached me, and said, " No, no, I had forgotten you were his friend, his brother in arms !" and sank pale and agitated on the nearest ottoman. She was but a girl, scarcely eighteen when we last met; her then budding charms were now fully developed in the superbly handsome woman before me ; her foreign tour, and moving as she had done in the best European society, had imparted to her a deportment at once elegant, graceful and bewitching ; yet it was sad to think that one so young and lovely, had fallen from that position she was so well calculated to adorn ! With an effort she controlled her emotion and said, " Oh! Fortescue, do not upbraid me with my wretched infatuation ! I cannot bear it from you, who in happier years was my most valued friend." " Believe me, Mrs. Pemberton, I came on no such errand," I replied kindly. " At the urgent request of Oscar," (as I mentioned his name, she trembled violently, turned deadly pale, and gasped out hurriedly,) " Is he here ? Does he already know ?" " He is not here," I continued, " but has been, and is aware of your arrival in Bombay. He has commissioned me to say that he is willing to forget the past, and receive you to his heart again, if you will but return home. Believe me, he is too much attached to you to reproach you for anything that has transpired since you left him." She remained silent for a few minutes, and then said with a forced calmness, " It can never be, it is too late ; I can never again return to that home which I am so unworthy to enter. I know his generous and forgiving nature, but do not attempt to dissuade me from my purpose, it will be worse than useless. No ; I would sooner perish by my own hand than meet the husband whose feelings and whose honor I have so grossly outraged. No ; I have taken my fate in my own hands, the die is cast, and I must bear the burden which I

26

have brought upon myself. But tell me in what way Oscar became acquainted with the fact of my dishonor. Speak out," she said, seeing that I hesitated. " Do not spare me, I have nerved myself to hear all," and she sank back among the cushions of the ottaman, and hid her face in her hands. I then related to her Oscar's visit to my office ; his application for my service to ascertain her whereabouts ; the exertion of the police to trace her, and the surveillance she had moved under. At the word *surveillance*, she started up ; the crimson flush of anger, or offended pride suffused her brow, and her magnificent eyes flashed with some of their usual fire, as she drew herself proudly up. " Clara," said I, seeing that she was about to speak, " hear me out. Were it not for the steps that had been taken by the police at my instigation, your real position, in spite of your seclusion, would long ere this have become the talk of the whole island. It was for your own and Oscar's sake that I have taken these precautions, which will prevent the intrusion of those who would force themselves upon you, and from whose society you would turn with loathing and abhorrence. I have at least saved you from that degradation. Only a very few, those immediately concerned, are aware that the wife of Oscar Pemberton is in Bombay." " Oh, Fortescue, forgive me for my unjust suspicions of your motives ; accept the thanks of one who must have lost the esteem of so valued a friend." I felt much embarrassed, both on her as well as on my own account, especially as I had failed to accomplish the object of my visit, and shortly after I rose to depart ; but before I did so, I obtained from her a brief account of her entanglement with Sandhurst prior to her leaving England. It appears they had met at the house of a mutual acquaintance. He was struck by her exceeding loveliness and charming manners, and as they moved in the same circle, he had every opportunity of making himself agreeable to her. At the ball, the opera and route—he paid her those attentions so pleasing to one in her peculiar position ; and with such tact did he veil his real intentions, **that she** soon learned to regard him with anything **but indifference, and to look up to him** for counsel and advice.   **And** as they were to sail **for India** in the same vessel, he persuaded her to allow **him to make** all the arrangements for the passage out.   A short time prior to her departure from England, they were engaged in some private theatricals, in which she played the part of a Mrs. Percival Clifford, and he that of her former lover. This was the forerunner of her ruin—for it was owing to this circumstance that Sandhurst had conceived the idea of engaging her passage under the name of Clifford—trusting to his power of persuasion and the general influence he had over her to gain her consent to assume it.   He did not overrate his powers; but it was not until she was **on** board that she became acquainted with this circumstance. **Being** thrown constantly together during the passage, he had an opportunity in their long conversations, and during their visit to Gibraltar, Malta, and **other** places of interest on the route, to undermine or destroy the better principles of her nature, and prepare her for the part he intended her to play on their arrival at Bombay. In this he succeeded only too well; one by one her scruples vanished before his passionate appeals, and she finally consented to take that downward step which resulted so fatally for the happiness of those most concerned. On my return home I wrote to Oscar, telling him what had transpired in my unsuccessful attempts to induce Clara to rejoin him, and request him to take no rash step in consequence thereof, which would lead to a public exposure of his domestic affairs, and no real good could be effected by such a proceeding.   "What is it, Acbar Ali?" I enquired, as I observed that energetic officer coming rapidly towards me, as I was in the act of mounting my **horse** to attend a ball at Government **House** at Parrell.   "The gentleman who gave the information concerning the lady at Chittagong **Lodge** is here, and is going to visit her at nine **this evening." "Are you sure? I did** not know **he was** in Bombay," I replied.   **"I saw him enter the**

Byculla Club House, and heard him tell the hamalls, that he should require them to carry him to Shingle Para at nine o'clock, and to be sure and not be behind time," said Acbar Ali. I looked at my watch, it was half-past seven. Rash, impetuous, Oscar, should he and Sandhurst meet, there would be blood spilt between them. This, I determined, if possible, to prevent; and made arrangements to meet such an emergency should it arise. " Request Dr. DeCosta to meet me a quarter before nine, near the bungalow on the Parrell road. Tell him to bring his case of instruments with him, and have a dooly in attendance, and let the bearers go by the back way across the Byculla flats, and enter the date grove at the side of the house, and remain there until called for. Be smart, Acbar, and let no mistake or delay occur." I then re-entered my office (for I had an hour to spare) to arrange my plans. Dr. DeCosta was surgeon to the force, a gentleman of Portuguese descent, very skilful, quiet and good-natured; in fact, the very man to send, should any contingency such as I anticipated arise. At half-past eight I mounted my horse and rode towards Shingle Para. "Is that you, Dr. ?" I called out in a quiet tone, as the figure of a man moved beneath the shadow of a date tree. "It is!" was the subdued reply. I dismounted and explained to him the business on hand. I gave him a brief sketch of the whole story, and he promised hearty co-operation in my plans. I suggested that he should not enter the bungalow until he heard my signal, or the clash of weapons. As I left him he bowed approvingly, and I quietly made my way through the shrubbery, and posted myself on the verandah, close to one of the drawing room windows. The night was dark, but the room was brilliantly illuminated, revealing everything distinctly in the apartment. There were six French windows to it, all of which I could command a full view of with the exception of one near the door which was partially concealed by a silk screen. Clara had been playing, for I heard the sound of music as I approached, but it ceased as I stepped on the verandah,

and I saw Sandhurst lead her from the piano, and seat her
beside himself on a superb conversation-couch in the further end
of the room with one hand round her waist in a most loving
manner, while with the other he played with the luxuriant tresses
of her beautiful black hair that fell on her magnificent shoulders;
her face was partly turned from him as if in thought. He was
evidently urging her to accede to some request, but I could not
ascertain the purport of his words. A slight noise at one of the
front windows caused me to glance in that direction. I saw over
the top of the screen that it was being quietly opened, and in a
moment after a figure entered the room in rear of the screen.
This I was certain must be Oscar. I passed rapidly round the
angle of the verandah in the hope of being in time to prevent a
collision, but I was too late, for as I entered, I heard Oscar thunder out : "Scoundrel, take the reward of your villany," and in
another instant the report of a pistol was heard through the bungalow. At the first sound of Oscar's voice, Sandhurst sprang up,
and turned in the direction from which he came, and received the
bullet in his shoulder. With a cry of pain and rage he fell back
on the couch. Clara, terrified beyond measure at the sight of the
bleeding and prostrate form of her protector, started up and recognized the pale and livid features of her husband as he stood
beneath the glare of the chandelier, vengeance gleaming from
his flashing eyes, which were bent upon the fallen man. Uttering a wild piercing shriek, she turned and fled through the folding screen to her own apartment, the door closing behind her.
Oscar stood for a moment as if paralyzed. He allowed me to
take the pistol from his hand. I had scarcely done so, when a
dull heavy sound smote the ear, as if something had fallen in
the adjoining apartment. With one bound he cleared the inter-
vening couch, and dashed into his wife's room. I followed him,
but we were too late, for there extended at full length on the
Persian carpet in front of her toilet table lay the lifeless form of
his wife; her face was turned upwards, and in one hand was

firmly clutched in the grasp of death a small vial labeled Prussic acid, the contents of which she had swallowed, and the effect must have been instantaneous. The report of the pistol had been heard by the surgeon who now entered, and, on examination, pronounced life extinct. He assisted to place the body on the bed, and at my request he went to attend to the wounded man, who had fainted from loss of blood. I succeeded in drawing Oscar from the room before any of the servants entered. I led him through an ante-room to the back verandah, where by entreaty and persuasion I prevailed upon him to quit the place. I pointed out to him the event that must necessarily follow, if he insisted on remaining. A coroner's inquest would elicit the whole facts of the case and supply a theme for gossip to thousands ; if he would trust the matter entirely to me I would manage that his name or hers should not be made public, and the real nature of the occurrence should never be brought to light. Then, in a voice hoarse with emotion, he answered : "Fortescue, I will trust to you to see that my poor lost Clara be properly attended to, and no expense spared in the arrangements for her interment." He then sprang from the verandah, disappeared among the rose bushes, and before sunrise the next morning he had left the Island of Bombay far behind him. The surgeon having dressed the wound which Sandhurst had received, he then had him placed in the dooly that had been brought to the bungalow. Having given the necessary instructions to the servants and prevailed upon the good natured surgeon to give me the required certificate, and also a promise of assistance in carrying out the arrangements for the funeral, I left two of my men on duty at the bungalow to prevent any intrusion, I proceeded to the ball at Parrell, and then returned to my office. On the following morning I wrote two notices, which I caused to be inserted in the morning papers, as follows : "Died, of Asiatic Cholera, at her residence, Chittagong Lodge, Shingle Para, Mrs. Oscar, wife of Capt. O. Pemberton, Staff Corps, deeply regretted." "Serious accident.—Yesterday, while

Leonard Sandhurst, Esq., C. S., was engaged in cleaning his rifle, the weapon accidently exploded, and the ball passed through his shoulder, shattering the bone to a considerable extent, but it is the opinion of his medical men that the wound, although serious, is not likely to prove fatal." A copy of which I sent to Oscar and one to Sandhurst, in order to enable them to govern themselves accordingly in this matter; but my old friend and comrade, the gay and light-hearted Oscar, never recovered from the shock his feelings had sustained. He shortly after exchanged into one of the regular regiments, and during the Persian campaign, at the battle of Kooshab, fell at the head of his troop while making a dash on one of the Persian squares; nor did the unprincipled author of all this misery long survive his victims, for Judge Sandhurst died of jungle fever at Rhutnagerrie, on the coast, four months subsequent to the conclusion of the Persian war, and as none of the servants were aware of the proper name of the mistress, I believe that the Doctor and myself are the only parties who are in possession of the facts concerning the sad fate of the beautiful and unfortunate, though erring, Clara Pemberton.

CHAPTER XX.

It was about two years subsequent to the event related in our last chapter, that the tocsin of war again sounded through Scinde and Afghanistan, and on my regiment being ordered for field service, I threw up my civil appointment, and leaving my wife with her relations in Poona, (for I had married some months previously), rejoined, and during the campaign which followed, we took part more or less in the various engagements which ensued, at Mooltan, Chillianwalla, Peshawa, Ferozashah, and others of minor consequence. The brilliant exploits there achieved, hardships, difficulties and privations endured, have won for them a name on the page of history, and have been painted in more glowing colors than I can dare aspire to ; therefore, with this brief notice I pass on to scenes and incidents of a comparatively later date. At the close of this successful campaign, we returned to our own presidency, and an appointment on the staff of a native regiment having been offered me, I accepted ; and on my way to Neemuch, where the corps was stationed, while travelling through Khandiesh, we overtook Captain and Mrs. S———, like ourselves *en route* to join their regiment at Musserabad, some hundred and fifty miles beyond the head-quarters of the one I had been posted to, we travelled together the remainder of the way I had to accomplish. On arriving at the Nerbudda, one of the largest rivers in that section of the country, the following circumstance occurred. On a beautiful moonlight evening, Captain S—— who was a short distance in advance, mounted on a powerful thorough-bred charger—for I had dismounted some half-hour previous and had taken a seat in the garrie or travelling carriage, for the purpose of enjoying a social chat with Mrs. S—— and my wife ; the former had been several years in the country, and was quite accustomed to the difficulties and annoyances usually to be encountered while travelling from one station to another, and always, whenever practicable, made it a rule to accompany her husband. The approach to the river was rather steep and somewhat rocky, consequently much caution was necessary in descending. On arriving at the top of the bank Captain S—— halted, and turning round in his saddle, called out to our driver to get down and "chark bundda," or put on the drag, to prevent a too rapid descent. While speaking his horse suddenly bounded from one side of the road to the other, nearly unseating the gallant Captain by his sudden movement; and the poor animal trembled violently. The Captain, on recovering his balance, looked about to ascertain what had startled the noble creature, and to his surprise and dismay, discovered a genuine Bengal tiger quietly lapping the water at the brink of the river. He drew his revolver, and called to me for assistance, as he was sure that if the tiger made an attack, it would be either on his horse or the bullocks drawing the garrie. At the sound of our voices, the tiger looked towards us and growled fiercely, at the same time slowly moving his tail backwards and forwards as he re-entered the jungle, thus so far assuring the ladies who were naturally somewhat alarmed, that they were in no personal danger, for we considered ourselves more than a match for the four-footed foe. I slipped out as quickly as possible at the back of the vehicle, with my double barrelled rifle, and took up a position under cover of some bushes on the verge of the jungle. I had scarcely gained the spot when I observed the animal break through the brushwood that skirted the road and with glaring eyes, settle himself for a bound at my friend's horse. It was a critical moment, and it would be useless for the Captain to discharge his revolver, which would have had no effect on the tough hide of the tiger; his only chance was, that should the brute pounce upon the neck or shoulder of the horse, as is their usual custom, to thrust his weapon into the creature's mouth, and blaze away. I cocked my rifle, and as the

27

lord of the jungle was in the act of springing, discharged both
barrels simultaneously, and succeeded in lodging a brace of bullets
in his shoulder; uttering a growl of pain, he fell with great force
to the ground, mortally wounded, within a few feet of Captain
S——, who immediately dismounted, and with his revolver finished
the business by emptying a few of its chambers in the ear of the
expiring foe. It must have been half-famished, for this class of
animals seldom attack mankind unless pursued, wounded, or
ravenous for food. This little matter having been settled, we went
on our way rejoicing. In travelling through almost any part
of India, it is necessary to carry with you ham, bacon, salt,
beef, tongues, tea, sugar, coffee, brandy, beer or wine, and in
all cases your bedding, for there are no hotels or other places
of refreshment where you could be accommodated. There are
villages about every two miles along the public high road,
where the traveller may obtain milk, eggs, fowl, rice, oil
and native vegetables ; and at some of the largest ones, where
Mahomedans are living, you can sometimes obtain a young
kid or goat's meat. Dawk bungalows, or halting places for
European travellers, have been erected by the government
about every fourteen miles along the principal road ; they
are substantially built, and usually contain three rooms, each
having a cane-bottom bedstead, two chairs and a table, also a
good punka ; there is likewise a cook-house and stable attached,
with a putta walla in charge, whose duty it is to fetch from the
nearest village such supplies and articles that the traveller may
require, provided they can be obtained. Your own servants do
the cooking and all other attendance ; but no person is allowed to
occupy one of these rooms longer than three days, unless in case
of sickness, when permission must be obtained from the nearest
engineer officer in charge of the building. One rupee (two shillings sterling) is the fee charged to each person per diem. The
rank and name of the parties, with amount paid, has to be
entered by them in a book kept for that purpose, as a check

upon the putta walla in charge. Game, such as deer, pea-fowl, grouse, partridge, quail, duck and pigeon, are very plentiful in all parts of the country. I had been about fifteen months in the native regiment when Mr. Murry, British ambassador at Bushire, hauled down his flag and returned to England, the why and wherefore I never rightly knew, but it was left to the Indian army and navy to hoist again. A rather large number of troops and vessels were sent into the Persian Gulf, and a land transport corps was inaugurated to accompany the Persian expeditionary field force. Having some interest at head-quarters, I obtained an appointment in that corps, and at once proceeded to Bombay, *en route* for Persia. No ladies being permitted to accompany the expedition, I sent Mrs. Fortescue to Poona, one of the most healthy and pleasant stations in the presidency, there to remain until my return ; and having received my instructions from the chief director, I embarked on board the Honorable Company's war steamer *Punjab.* The naval squadron, comprising many of the largest steam-frigates and fastest sailing vessels, had been despatched by Admiral Sir Henry Leeke, the superintendent of the Indian navy, and placed under the command of Commodore Ethersay, I. N., for service in the Persian Gulf. Upwards of two hundred vessels of the merchant marine were employed as transports for the conveyance of troops, cattle, stores, ammunition and baggage. The field force was under the command of Major General Stalker, C. B., of the Company's service. We had a very pleasant passage up the gulf, touching at Muscat, and going ashore at Bassadore, a coaling depot and sanitary station for the crews of the vessels cruising in the gulf. The crews were dis-embarked at Reshier, without much difficulty, although a large number of the enemy were in the immediate vicinity. The affair commenced by one of Her Majesty's regiments acting as light infantry, and driving before them the Persian skirmishers. A desultory sort of firing was kept up by them as they retreated, but the Enfields of our men thinned the ranks of the followers of

the Prophet. During the skirmish an unfortunate occurrence
took place, resulting in the loss of a valuable life, and at the
time disclosing the treachery and ingratitude of the Persian
character. One of the men of the regiment engaged had fallen
to the rear for some purpose or other, when he noticed among
the killed one of the foe, apparently only slightly wounded ; he
was just about to thrust his bayonet through him, when his
colonel seeing his intentions shouted to him to desist and join
his company ; the man obeyed, and the Persian was saved ; but
the humane colonel, who was riding in rear, had scarcely passed
him, when the wretch raised himself on his elbow, and drawing
a long-barreled pistol from his waistband, took deliberate aim,
and shot the gallant officer through the head—he who but a few
seconds before had saved him from immediate death. The capture
of the port and city of Bushire, by the combined efforts of the
army and navy, soon followed with comparatively little loss on
our side ; but decidedly the most brilliant affair of the campaign
was the battle of Kooshab, in which we suffered considerably.
The gallant conduct of Lieutenant Moore, of the Bombay native
cavalry, in breaking one of the Persian squares, followed by an
officer of the Scinde horse, won the admiration of the whole force.
In this engagement the Persians were so completely routed and
scattered that they abandoned that part of the country for many
miles around Bushire, which was made the base of our future
operations. The island of Karrack was taken possession of, and
a large expeditionary force was sent up the river Euphrates, the
enemy having concentrated under the Prince of Persia, son of
the reigning Shah, at Mahmorah, situated at the junction of the
rivers Croone and Euphrates. After a few hours' bombardment
of the town, the troops were landed under cover of the fire from
the fleet, and with such rapidity did we advance, that the son of
the Shah had a very narrow escape from his large octagon tent.
The amusing feature of the case was, that at the time of our landing, a few moments previous to his flight, he was engaged in

writing a letter to the Shah, stating that he had driven the whole of our force into the Euphrates, and utterly destroyed the invaders. This unfinished letter, with the ink not yet dry, was found on a table by some of our men who entered the tent in hopes of catching the prince himself, who commanded the Persian army. The last stand made by the Shah's zadda, and the remnant of his army was at the battle of Awaz, at which point they were completely routed, and became so demoralized as to be unable to make any further opposition to our advance against the principal cities of the empire. Sir James Outram had joined us, and assumed the command of the entire land force. A remarkably strange circumstance or train of circumstances transpired about the time Sir James took command of the army. On being relieved from command, General Stalker shot himself; this was followed by the officer commanding the naval squadron putting an end to his existence by cutting his throat; and the political agent, a civilian, sought to terminate his career in life by poison. Many were the reasons assigned as to the cause for these catastrophes; dame rumor with her thousand tongues was rife with conjectures. Some affirmed that the unfortunate General had destroyed himself because he had been superseded by Sir James Outram, but in what way could the advent on the scene of action of his superior officer interfere with the duties of either Commodore Ethersay or Mr. Jones of the Civil Service, we were at a loss to conjecture. There were many other causes assigned, and among them one that gained more credence than the rest, but in all probability just as incorrect as the others. It was stated that a Persian had waited on the three gentlemen in question with a proposal to the following effect, that if they would secure him against any legal proceedings hereafter, he would disclose the secret where a large amount of treasure was concealed, which he was willing to divide equally between them, himself of course receiving one-fourth. This proposal, it was affirmed, was acquiesced in by the parties,

and a division of the spoil made accordingly. Scarcely had this
been done when Sir James arrived to take charge. The story
went on to show that no sooner did the Persian become acquainted
with this fact than he waited on the new Commander and related
the whole affair, suggesting that he should take a share which
would be one-fifth. To this General Outram would not listen, and
threatened to bring to a court martial all the parties concerned.
Whether there was any truth in this I cannot say, but it was generally believed to be the true version, although I am not aware
that the Government took any action in the matter. A treaty
of peace having been signed between England and Persia, the
troops prepared to return to their several presidencies, and it was
fortunate for the supremacy of British rule in India that the
war came to so speedy a close, for very shortly after this the
bloody and much to be lamented Sepoy mutiny broke out, to
check which required the whole energies of the Government and
every available man. The Persian war having terminated, the
troops were hurried back to India with all possible despatch, to
take part in the fearful struggle that was raging throughout the
country. After getting the stores, baggage, &c., of the army on
board the vessels appointed to receive them, the transport corps
returned to Bombay; but I and a few others were directed
to proceed to Margell and Bagdad to take charge of a number of
mules that had been purchased by the Government for service in
India. This was pleasant enough, and enabled me to see much
more of the country than I otherwise should have seen. I visited
the Turkish port of Bassora and the city of Bagdad, both of
which places were associated in my memory from the numerous
stories I had read in my boyhood concerning them in the " Arabian
Nights Entertainments." On my return I obtained a tolerable view of the spot where once stood the ancient city of Babylon. A few days subsequently, the captain of the vessel informed
us that we were opposite Koorna, where the Tigris falls into
the Euphrates and Shatal Arab, at the same time pointing out a

spot declared by the Arabs and others to be the identical locality
of the once garden of Eden, and offered to drop anchor for a few
hours if we felt inclined to go on shore.   To this we gladly
assented, and in a short time we were strolling beneath the welcome shade of the date, pomegranate, apple trees and grape vines,
or lounging on the short soft grass enjoying our biscuits, sardines,
pale ale and cigars with a gusto that would have astonished either
the original proprietor of the grounds or his amiable lady of
fig-leaf notoriety, could they but have dropped in upon us.   For
five or six hours we did thus enjoy ourselves, not that there was
anything more to be seen than in many other parts I had visited,
but in the first place it was a relief from the close atmosphere of
our small cabin on shipboard ; then it was something in after life
to state that we had ruralized in the pleasure grounds of our first
parents, and ate of that fruit which proved such a stumbling
block both to them and their descendants.   On the return of the
transport corps to the capital of the Presidency, it was broken
up ; but the cattle, carriage and all that appertained thereto were
transferred to the Commissariat Department.   Such of the
officers as so desired were allowed to retain their appointments
in the new organization, which was designated the cattle branch
of the department.   It suited my views to remain in it, and I
was directed to repair to Falkland Bunder to superintend the
landing of the mules and stores ; then to move on to Poona,
which was to be the head-quarters.   Subsequently we were told
off into divisions, and despatched to the different large military
stations.   Any force, brigade, regiment or detachment requiring
carriage sent their requisitions to the nearest of these stations,
which were immediately complied with.   If a large force was on
the move, a European officer from our department accompanied it
in charge of the government cattle ; if a smaller one, a native
inspector or muccadum was sent in charge.   For upwards of two
years, during the most stirring time of the mutiny, I was continually on the move with the troops, marching from one part of the

country to another, wherever their presence was most required ; and while so doing I became acquainted with the details of acts of so horrible and revolting a nature perpetrated on our helpless country women and children by the bloodthirsty native soldiery, the mere relating of which would curdle the blood of any European ; but there occurred others of a less terrible character which came under my own immediate notice, or were witnessed by those on whose veracity I could rely, which I believe I may relate without harrowing to any great extent the feelings of my readers; for it must be borne in mind that this was not a general uprising of the native population against British rule, but a regular concerted mutiny by those who for years had received the pay and support of the government whose service they had voluntary entered and had sworn to uphold. Nor were they misled or ignorant of the penalty attached to the offence, as the Articles of War and provisions of the Mutiny Act had been regularly read and explained to each regiment once every month ; and they were well aware that the punishment for the crime of mutiny was death ; but apparently this was not enough to restrain them, as the following incidents may tend to shew. The native regiment to which, previous to the outbreak of the Persian war, I had for some time belonged, had been transferred from the north-west provinces to Kurrachee, in Scinde ; it was chiefly composed of high caste men, but still there were quite a number of inferior castes in its ranks. Things were progressing very quietly when the news of the mutiny at Neemuch and other places reached them ; they appeared to be little affected by the intelligence, yet the seed of rebellion was germinating within them, which only required a little fanning to burst forth into open mutiny. On the day previous to the sailing of the mail steamer for Bombay, a native officer of the regiment requested a private interview with the Brigadier, and there and then made disclosures to the effect that on the night of the day following it had been agreed that the regiment should quietly leave their lines, murder all the Europeans they fell in with, and after looting the treasury and bazaars, make off for the nearest town or city in possession of the mutineers, and cast in their lot with them. All he asked in return for his valuable information was a furlough to Bombay by the **packet** that was to leave the harbor the next morning, and the leave of absence to be dated some days back, so that he might not be suspected of having betrayed the secret. His request was immediately complied with, and he sailed for his native place, somewhere on the coast near Malwan. The Brigadier sent for the officers commanding corps without delay, and held a consultation, at which it was arranged that no intimation of the approaching event should be made known to any of the other officers or men for fear it should leak out and reach the ears of the natives, and so put them on their guard. On the night in question, the instructions were that about eleven o'clock the European troups were to be made acquainted with the circumstances. They were to load in barracks, and move as quietly as possible; the words of command to be passed in whispers, and the wheels of the artillery muffled. As the clock or gurry at the quarter guard of the native regiment struck twelve, a slight bustle was heard on the private parade ground of the native regiment who turned out rapidly and formed up without noise; having loaded, they were then told off into different divisions : one to proceed to the European General Hospital and murder all the patients, others to fire the officers' bungalows, slay the inmates, men, women and children, while a large party were suddenly to attack the treasury, overpower the guard, and carry off whatever money they might find. All these directions, although given in a low tone, were distinctly heard by those stationed close by for that purpose. **The** signal for the moving of the different parties **to** perform their work of slaughter was to be a rocket sent up from the guard **house** before mentioned. Exactly at half-past twelve this light went up; but imagine the horror and dismay of the miscreants, when at the same instant, fifty

28

blue lights shot high in the air, illuminating all around for a considerable distance, disclosing to the terrified natives, our artillery drawn up immediately in their rear, and the European infantry in line on both flanks, ready to pour in volley after volley. They were ordered to throw down their arms and surrender; some did so, but the greater portion broke and fled across the open plain in their front. Two or three rounds of canister was sent among them, and our infantry started in pursuit. Many fell from the fire of our guns, and of those who were captured, after trial by court martial, some suffered death ; and a very large number were transported to one of the Andaman Islands, situated in the Bay of Bengal, where it was thought there was no probability of their escaping on account of their isolated position. A comparatively small guard was deemed sufficient; but they had not been there long before they managed to overpower this little force, and in large parties proceeded further into the island. This was only jumping out of the frying-pan into the fire, for the islanders were not only savages but cannibals of the most ferocious kind, and Jack Sepoy soon fell into their clutches, serving as a gorgeous banquet to the captors, who ate them as soon as caught. Thus, a terrible retribution overtook them for their fiendish designs.

CHAPTER XXI.

THE Asiatics, even among themselves, are both relentless and cruel, whenever chance or circumstances **throws** one into the power of the other, as what I am about to relate will, **I** think, amply testify. On one occasion, while making a forced march through Khandiesh with the Lancers, Royal Artillery and other troops, and having ascertained from a reliable source that there was no signs of the enemy within at least thirty miles **of us,** I mentioned to the officer commanding the force **that it** was the intention of the officer in charge of the provision branch and myself to ride on to the next large native town, distant about twenty **miles,** for the purpose of procuring rations and forage, that there **might** be no delay on the following morning, as he wished to make **a** rapid advance. " You will run considerable personal risk **in so** doing; I will send a score of Lancers with you as **a guard,"** replied Colonel Benson. To this we objected for reasons **of** our own, and started early in the evening, but in consequence of the bad state of the roads we did not reach the place **until** after night-fall, when we found the gate closed—for all **towns and** villages in that part **of** the country **are** walled in **as a** protection against the band**s** of roving plunderers and numerous wild beasts that infest the north-west provinces. **Knowing** that it would be useless to attempt to gain admittance after the gates had been once closed, we picketed our horses under a large tree, near the principal gate, and using **our saddles** for pillows, refreshed ourselves with a draught from our flasks, then filling **our** pipes we smoked, and soon afterwards **fell** fast asleep. " Rouse up, Fortescue," **said my companion,** yawning as he spoke. " The day is breaking ; **let** us get out of this ; **there is** a fearful smell, strong enough to choke a dead black." I was up in **an** instant, and a

most villainous odour affected my olfactories. "I suppose the
enemy have left some of their dead cattle in our neighborhood," I
said, taking a good draught from my flask and then handed it to
my friend. Standing erect, and giving myself a stretch accompanied with a yawn, but casting my eyes upwards, I beheld the
cause of the vile stench, for high above us, dangling from the
branches like jack fruit, hung the bodies of seven natives in a
state of semi-decomposition. On entering the town we learnt
that Tantia Topee had visited this place five days previous, and
on their demurring to furnish him with supplies, he looted the
town, and hanged seven of the principal men, leaving instructions that they were to be left there until the fowls of the air
picked out their eyes, and the heat of the sun shrivelled their
bodies into mummies; in short, if his orders were not obeyed he
would return, and serve the remainder in a similar manner. The
cause of their refusal to comply with the rebel chief's demand
was, that they had private intelligence of our approach and were
hourly expecting us. During the few hours we remained here
the tree at the main gate was relieved of its unnatural fruit; the
effluvia arising from which being decidedly more powerful than
pleasant. The force moved forward with all possible dispatch,
in hopes of coming up with the rascally perpetrators of this villainous outrage. As we were looking out for our camping ground
a few mornings afterwards, we came quite unexpectedly on a
large number of Tantia Topee's men—Goolundauz, Sowars and
Sepoys. In such cases as the present, being a non-combatant,
my place was in rear with the cattle and baggage, but like the
Irishman at Donnybrook Fair, there never was a fight that I did
not manage, either by hook or by crook, to be present at, if it
was only to see what was going on. On this occasion I rode on
the flank of the supernumaries of the cavalry, and was handling
my sabre with the best of them, when by a rapid wheel of the
Lancers, I found myself alone, but only for a moment, for I was
instantly attacked ; one fellow fired, missed me but killed my

horse. I had scarcely gained my feet when a Sowar in passing made a cut at my head, but he was a little too far off, so that his sword's point only reached me, inflicting a slight cut about two inches long on the upper part of my forehead above the left eye, causing the blood to flow freely. I took my revolver and in an instant shot the rascal in the small of the back and I had the satisfaction of seeing him fall from his horse. The fellow who had killed my nag clubbed his matchlock and made a rush at me, beating down my guard and breaking my sabre at the feeble, also smashing my collar-bone on the left side. Flinging away the useless sword, and before he could recover himself, I **changed the** pistol into my right hand and shot him through the head. Another Sowar made a point at me with his spear, but his horse stumbled over the body of the man I had just sent to glory ; he missed **his** mark and only succeeded in making a slight wound in my right side just above the hip-joint. He would doubtless have finished my career, as at this time from pain and loss of blood I was **in a** weak and almost fainting condition, when one of our Lancers noticing the predicament I was in, rode up and with his lance transfixed my opponent by thrusting his weapon through the man's body. I was carried to my tent, and a little sticking plaster sufficed for my head and side, but I had to be carried in a dooly for nearly six weeks. Fortunately the fracture being on my left side, and only requiring rest, I was enabled to carry on the duties of my office with my right hand, without much difficulty ; however, it was upwards of two months before **I** could mount my horse or use my left arm to any extent. As usual, after a short but obstinate struggle, the mutineers fled. It was their tactics to fight in three lines ; on **the** first being beaten, they retreated through the second, who generally managed to hold their ground until the third and first with their chief and **his** principal officers were **in** full retreat ; they then broke **and** scattered through the jungle, their perfect knowledge of which enabled them to join their main body with little difficulty. A

few weeks later, Tantia Topee, the fighting general of the
cowardly Nana Sahib, Rajah of Bittoor, was captured at a place
called Sepree, where he was tried and sentenced to be hanged, which
was carried into effect without any unnecessary delay. After his
death the rebel soldiery left that part of the country altogether.
Shortly after this event the brigade to which I was attached was
transferred to the Bengal Presidency, and I was directed to return
to Poona, the head-quarters of our department. Although there
was a large number of Sepoys stationed here, and the greater part
of the European force were absent, actively employed in crushing out the mutiny, no sign of disaffection or disloyalty had as
yet manifested itself among them. There were many reports
circulating daily through the bazaars of a general rising of the
native population, but this was regarded as emanating from native
dealers in order in some way or other to affect the markets. Yet
there was no knowing at what hour, during the day or night, the
native force in conjunction with the Budmashes, and doubtless a
large portion of the evil-disposed inhabitants of the city of Poona,
might rise in rebellion and murder such of the Europeans as lived
at some distance from the barracks of our troops, and as there were
many ladies living alone in the station, whose husbands were on
service up country, it was arranged that immediately on the
appearance of a red flag displayed at a given point during the
day, or the report of three guns fired in succession after sunset and
before sunrise, that the sick and those not doing duty, and especially ladies, should fly at once to the spot where a large supply of
provisions were stored, strongly guarded, and every arrangement
made for the security of those seeking shelter. Although in hourly
peril, things went on in the usual routine. A ball was given at
the Artillery mess, at which among others, my wife and myself
were present. Dancing and hilarity appeared to have totally banished from the minds of all present the thoughts of
an outbreak among the natives, when just at twelve o'clock the
report of a gun was heard, then another, quickly followed by

a third. For an instant all stood aghast. "It is the fatal signal," gasped out some anxious mothers, terrified at the thought of the danger of their children who had been left in charge of native servants at their bungalows. Immediately there was a general rush to the doors ; ladies half fainting with fear and anguish were hurriedly helped into their garries by their partners, who did their best to tranquilize them. Seizing my wife round the waist, and snatching my pistol and sabre which I had left in the ante-room, we were about to start for the place of rendezvous, when it occurred to one of the party that it was the first night of the new moon, and it was well known to all present that it was customary with the Hindoo priests of the Temple of Parbattee, at no great distance, to fire three guns on the first appearance of the new moon. This partially re-assured us, and we listened intently for some moments, but heard no further sound or tumult breaking the stillness of the night. Confidence being restored, the waltz, polka and quadrille were resumed with increased animation, together with the agreeable chit-chat usually indulged in on such occasions. Of the twenty-nine regiments of native infantry belonging to the Bombay Presidency, there were but two that threw off their allegiance and joined the standard of revolt The outbreak, capture and ultimate fate of one of these corps I have already brought to the reader's notice, the other instance I am about to relate came more immediately, though only partially, under my own observation. I was with the Dragoon Guards and Royal Artillery, who were marching through the Mahratta country to Belgaum. We halted at Koolapoore, near to the scene of my early military exploits, to witness the carrying into effect the sentence of several courts martial. The native regiment which had been stationed at this place had mutinied, and after murdering several of their European officers, and committing other atrocious acts, endeavoured to join another body of mutineers. However in this they were disappointed, and quite a number of them were captured and brought back to the

station. They in most cases were to suffer death. Those of the
lower caste were hanged or shot by musketry; the officers who
were of higher caste were to be blown from the cannon's mouth.
The execution of the lower castes excited but little attention,
but the peculiar mode of enforcing the death penalty on the
native officers, who, although of different creeds, were all of the
highest caste, drew an immense concourse of spectators to the
spot, and I believe that it was anticipated that a rescue would be
attempted, we were therefore delayed in order to swell the parade
and overawe the populace. The artillery and infantry received
orders to load on their private parade ground and proceed to the
place of execution, prepared for immediate action. The dragoons
kept a sharp eye on the native cavalry and irregular horse.
Three sides of a square was formed by the troops, and in the
open front were drawn up the guns to be used on this terrible
occasion. The prisoners were then brought into the square,
marched up to the guns, which were loaded with blank cartridge,
and a slight degree of elevation given to them. The unhappy
wretches were then bound singly with the lower region of the
back against the muzzle of each gun; they were placed alter-
nately, Hindoo and Mussulman. As soon as this was effected,
the proceedings of the general court martial and the sentence
were read aloud to them. The artillery officer then slowly
advanced and gave the word of command, " Number one, ready,
fire;" and instantly the whole chest and loins of the first of these
wretched criminals was blown into fragments, the head going
straight up into the air twenty or thirty feet. Again the fatal
word was given, and particles of human flesh were scattered far
and near, the head ascending as before, and so on until the last
man had paid the penalty of his crimes. When the smoke
cleared away, nothing was to be seen of those who but a few
moments before were living and breathing creatures, but their
lower extremities which still remained lashed to the guns. The
bungays or camp sweepers then swept up the pieces of flesh and

bones of both castes that were lying about and consigned them to one common grave. It was a sickening scene, and I never wish to witness such another. The reason why this particular mode of punishment was resorted to was I believe at the time but little understood out of India, and has been caviled at and censured by many as being an act unbecoming the dignity of an enlightened and civilized nation like England. But it should be remembered that the mutiny arose from a fanatical spirit which had been aroused within the native soldiery, fostered and fanned into a flame by the Mahomedan priests and Hindoo Brahmins, who impressed upon the minds of their followers that it was the intention of the British government to crush out and eradicate by a *coup-de-main* the religion of their forefathers, and pointed to the great influx of Christian missionaries who were permitted to disseminate tenets of their creed throughout the native army by means of tracts and personal expoundings. The greased cartridge for the Enfield rifle just introduced was denounced by the priesthood of both creeds ; those of the Mahomedan declaring that the fat of the pig, their utter abomination, was used in its construction, while the Brahmins insisted that the fat of the sacred cow was the principal lubricating ingredient used, the biting or tasting of which would defile and break the caste of either. The result was that thousands flocked to defend their faith against the common foe, and were assured by their religious advisers that to lose their life in such a cause was a sure passport to the celestial regions. While this idea lasted the natives waged this struggle for supremacy with all the ardour that hatred and religious fanaticism is capable of. And brutal enormities and acts of unparalleled atrocities, unfit to be related in these pages, were almost daily committed by the now frenzied and remorseless natives. To such an extent did their cause gain ground that, **owing** to the paucity of European troops, we were scarcely able **to cope** with them. At this juncture it was determined to enforce a punishment which would at once

strike terror to the hearts of the native community of all castes.
According to their religious creed, they lose all hope of heaven
and are eternally damned should their remains mix after death
with those of any other caste; hence the fact that Mussulmen bury
while Hindoos burn their dead, to prevent the possibility of any
such contamination. The mode of punishment above described,
was then carried into effect in such parts of the country as was
deemed necessary. As soon as this became generally known, it
had such an effect upon the mutineers, that they considered themselves God forgotten, and that the whole thing must be displeas-
ing to the Deities, and so disconcerted and dismayed did they
become that they eventually deserted the cause. British supremacy being again in the ascendancy, quiet, law and order was
once more restored, and rebellion had to hide its dark and super-
stitious barbarism from the face of stern retributive justice. I
had been appointed to take charge of a branch of our department
in the southern division, but after a few months my health began
to give way; the great strain that my nervous system had sustained during the past three or four years proved too much for
me, and I began to sink under it, I was therefore advised to
present myself before the Medical Board at the capital, at whose
recommendation I was granted leave of absence to Europe for
two years on medical certificate. My early chum, rollicking,
roystering, devil-may-care O'Toole I occasionally met, though our
spheres of action were very different in character. Shortly after
I left the regiment, thinking to make some noise in the world,
he joined the buglers, and rose to the rank of Bugle Major. For
three or four years he strutted about in the gorgeous plumage of
that important leading character, but finally his predilection for
spirituous liquors swamped him, and he sank to the foot of the
ladder to rise no more; yet the good humored, witty, though
incorrigible Bob was still a great favorite with the men of his
regiment. I met him a few days previous to my embarkation;
he seemed somewhat crestfallen, and after some hesitation

admitted he was in difficulties and debt. I told him to meet me
in the evening and take a parting glass to the memory of old
times, and not to trouble himself about his liabilities, as I would
see to that matter. He was evidently much relieved and went on
his way whistling with great glee the air, "Widow Machree."
I proceeded at once to his barrack, sought out the pay
sergeant, paid his debt, bought him an entire new kit, and
left a handful of rupees in the color sergeant's hands, with
instructions that it be paid to him by small instalments daily.
This would keep him flush for a considerable time. I knew that
giving the whole to him at once, would be about the worst
favor I could do for my old comrade, for in all probability the
use he would make of it would be to purchase a court martial
with its attending consequences. In a comfortable easy chair on
my back verandah, which commanded a view of the moonlit sea,
sat mine ancient comrade, the witty and good natured O'Toole,
a decanter of his favorite weakness at his elbow, and near by an
allowance of the weed he usually indulged in. At a convenient
distance, I lay at full length on a Persian carpet, with my
head supported by several cushions, the amber mouth-piece of
my hookah between my teeth, and a large goblet containing a
concoction of sherry, sugar candy, lemon and ice, the beverage
I most delighted in, at hand. I had made myself thus comfortable in order to listen to the out-pourings of poor Bob, for this
was in all probability the last time we should meet. For a time
he seemed less communicative than usual, but after two or three
smacks from the decanter, the contents of which became smaller
by degrees and beautifully less, he soon brightened up, and old
recollections of dangers and difficulties were freely discussed, and
thus we passed our time commenting on the relative positions
occupied by each. "And its going back to the ould country
that ye's are, Ned avic ; on sick lave overland too, free gratis and
for nothing, at the expence of government ; be the powers, it's a
mighty pretty thing to be on the staff, so it is ; it's yourself that

has the luck ; but bad cess to me for a gommerill, sure you
desarve it all, and its a full colonel ye's ought to be this blessed
night, and a divil a less." And with this somewhat confused
oration he drained his tumbler of its contents with great satisfaction, which I judged from the hearty smack he gave his lips.
During the evening I endeavored to explain to the O'Toole that
although promotion from the ranks to the higher grades of the
service was a thing of very rare occurrence, yet numbers of the
rank and file had it in their power by general good conduct and
sobriety to obtain the non-commissioned or warrant rank, and
leave the service in the prime of life, with a pension varying
from two to four shillings per day ; however, by this time
Bob was beyond all care for the present or future. Liquor
might have spoiled his promotion, he said, but not his
health; he was only thirty-eight, had but eighteen months to
serve, and was strong and hearty enough to do a good day's
work on his return to old Ireland, and his pension would procure
all the whisky and tobacco he should require, and what more
than that did he want. I admired my friend's philosophy, and
was meditating whether in his robust health he was not in a better position to fight out the battle of life than the shattered state
of my constitution led me to anticipate for myself, when a prolonged note from O'Toole's nasal organ aroused me to the fact
that brandy and tobacco had done its work, for Bob had glided
gradually from his chair to the carpet and was soundly sleeping.
I had taken the precaution to procure him a pass until morning,
and so left him to enjoy his slumbers for the remainder of the
night. An hour after sunrise I drove him to his barrack. I allowed him to take a long pull at my spirit flask ;
shook him heartly by the hand, wished him good luck and then
drove off. Such was the last interview between myself and
O'Toole.

Although I had obtained a two years' furlough, it was not my
intention to remain in Europe more than one-third of that time,

if my health was sufficiently recruited to enable me to return to duty; therefore I paid but a flying visit to such of my friends as resided at the capital. I disposed only of such of my property as might otherwise become damaged or destroyed during our absence, and contented myself with taking home a few of the Indian curiosities as *souvenirs* of my sojourn, intending to amass a considerable collection previous to retiring from the service. A few days after my name had appeared in General Orders for leave of absence, I engaged a passage on board the mail steamer *China*, and embarked on the afternoon of the twenty-third of July, and sailed within an hour after. As the island, its surroundings and the well remembered features of the Malabar coast faded from our view, the bell rang announcing dinner; we descended to the saloon to take our places at the table. This is a matter of some moment, and should not be done without due consideration, for the seat you occupy at your first meal you retain during the voyage—this rule, like the laws of the Medes and Persians altereth not. During the first four or five days we had heavy rains and boisterous weather ; on the sixth, however, we had passed beyond the influence of the south-west monsoons, and found ourselves in a beautiful mild latitude, which continued to become warmer as we approached Arabia Felix. On the ninth we dropped anchor off Steamer Point, Aden, that Gibraltar of the East, at the entrance of the Red Sea. As the vessel was to remain some twelve hours to take in coal, many of the passengers went on shore. Having some friends in Aden, which is about five or six miles from the landing, we mounted two strong donkeys and ascended the road leading to the main pass, the only access to the town, which is built in the crater of an extinct volcano. You may imagine the delights of this place—not a blade of grass grew on the dry and arid soil—not a bird fluttered its glossy wings or carroled its sweet note in this heated atmosphere. There were no fresh springs or running waters to cool the tongue of the thirsty traveller or refresh the wearied inhabitants ;

sea-water condensed by steam-power was the only resource
for the thirsty. No wonder there is so great a demand for pale
ale and French brandy among the Europeans. Aden is frightfully hot. There is an opinion prevalent among old inhabitants
to the effect that there is but a sheet of paper between this place
and the regions of his Satanic majesty. By eight p.m. we were
again on board, and for five days steamed up the Red Sea, the
weather being exceedingly hot. On reaching Suez we found the
train waiting for us ; very little delay ensued, and we were soon
whirling across the desert, stopping occasionally at the different
places along the line to obtain refreshments and wash the sand
out of our eyes and parched throats. The railway *employées*
are chiefly Frenchmen, though dressed in the oriental costume.
This is done by order of the Pasha of Egypt, at least so I was
informed by an official. At Grand Cairo we halted for a few
hours and dined, after which we visited the far-famed Pyramids
of Egypt, and several ruins of ancient date. Some distance after
crossing the Nile, we stopped again and had supper, and arrived
at Alexandria at two a.m. the next day. As the steamer did
not sail until mid-day, we embraced the opportunity of examining
the catacombs or receptacles for the embalmed dead. On the
fourth day we reached Malta, where we obtained a guide, and we
rambled about the place for several hours, seeing much that was
new and interesting. Having purchased some Maltese lace and
other fancy articles as mementoes of our visit, we returned to the
vessel. We had a delightful voyage down the Mediterranean, and
the atmosphere clear, soft and balmy, until we reached the far-
famed rock of Gibraltar, which being a coaling station, most of
the passèngers went on shore. It happened to be Sunday, and
the inhabitants were in their gayest attire. Bright eyed senoras
and swarthy Spanish cavaliers were on their way to or from mass.
The variety of costumes to be met with in Gibraltar is truly
astonishing. Hiring an open carriage and pair we drove to the
Spanish lines, and on our return passed the 100th Royal Cana-

dian Regiment, who had an encampment on what is called the
neutral ground outside the fortifications. We were fortunate
regarding the weather while crossing the Bay of Biscay, and
experienced nothing unpleasant in that usually turbulent water.
On nearing the English coast it rained very heavily, and the
night being intensily dark, the speed of the vessel was greatly
reduced. Previous to retiring for the night, it was understood
that we should land at eight o'clock the following morning, thus
doing the entire distance from Bombay to England in thirty-one
days, stoppages included. At day-light in the morning we found
ourselves running along the pleasant coast of the Isle of Wight,
and could clearly distinguish Osborne House, the residence of
Her Most Gracious Majesty. Before breakfast bell rang, we had
entered the P. and O. Company's dock at Southampton. All was
now hurry and bustle; passengers hunting for their luggage;
custom house officers examining the same; cabin stewards rushing
here and there in anticipation of their usual fee; hasty adieus
between friends and fellow travellers; and finally a rush for the
express train, and, presto, we are all off in various directions. It
was four o'clock in the afternoon when we entered the modern
Babylon. Yes, it was London, the same London, which as a
boy I had left to seek the " bubble reputation at the cannon's
mouth." I now returned in ill health and shattered constitution;
yet hoping that my native air and a quiet retirement for a season
or two, would suffice to restore my nervous system to a healthy
condition. We remained long enough in the gay metropolis to
enable my wife, who had left England when a mere child, to see
the wonders and gorgeous spectacles she had often heard me rave
about. After acquainting the authorities at the India Office of
my whereabouts, I established myself at a snug little cottage at
Pinnar, near to the old fashioned manor house where twenty-five
years previous I had received the first rudiments of my education.
Should I sufficiently recover, I shall doubtless on the expiration
of my furlough return to India, to complete the remainder of my

service; but if otherwise, I must retire on half-pay, and endeavor, metaphorically of course, to smoke the calumet of peace beneath the shade of my own fig tree.

And now having brought back the hero of our story after an absence of a quarter of a century to the pretty little village where we first met, we will leave him to enjoy his *otium cum dignitate ;* and the author will feel satisfied if he has succeeded in enabling the reader to wile away a few hours pleasantly by the perusal of the many incidents in the eventful career of Ned Fortescue while roughing it through life.